UPFRONT WITH CHELSEA

Upfront
with Chelsea

The Inside Story of the Forward Line
From Cooke to Osgood, Nevin to Zola

Chris Westcott

MAINSTREAM
PUBLISHING

EDINBURGH AND LONDON

First published in Great Britain in 2001 by
MAINSTREAM PUBLISHING COMPANY (EDINBURGH) LTD
7 Albany Street
Edinburgh EH1 3UG

ISBN 1 84018 450 7

A catalogue record for this book is available from the British Library

Typeset in Futurist & Joanna
Printed and bound in Great Britain by Butler & Tanner Ltd, Frome and London

ACKNOWLEDGEMENTS

It takes more than a gift for striking the ball to be a sporting hero. To qualify you need many qualities including skill, bravery and sportsmanship. Barry Bridges, who embraced all these attributes, was my childhood hero and remains modest about his achievements. This tribute to Chelsea forwards was inspired by Barry and would not have been possible without his invaluable assistance. I am hugely grateful for the support of the other subjects, who generously gave up their time to an unknown in the footballing world. I am also indebted to Terry Venables for kindly penning the foreword. Locally my research has been aided by the support of Roger Barnes, Andy Gordon and Eric Stone senior. As ever my wife Linda has borne the brunt of my 'sabbatical' whilst researching and writing. Finally the book is dedicated to my two sons Nick and Mark, whose passion of football is such that cricket hardly gets a mention in the household. *Quel dommage!*

CONTENTS

FOREWORD

I am delighted to add my name to this tribute to Chelsea forwards, as I loved my time there so much I wanted to stay all my career. I am particularly pleased that it also includes the influence of one of my own personal heroes, Dick Foss, the manager of the youth team and a wonderful man. With his side parting, slicked down, he was very smart, very stern, but had a good sense of humour. I liked Dickie a lot and he was very successful with the kids. He masterminded the first Chelsea Youth Cup victory in 1960, which I skippered, and I rated him very highly as a big influence on my career. I was introduced to the club by Jimmy Thompson, an outrageous character completely different from anyone else you'd ever meet. He had a bowler hat with his hair slicked down, a bit like Ted Drake. He was always chewing and his big false teeth kept dropping down. Even if he was serious you got the impression he was still laughing because his teeth were so big! But Jimmy had an infectious humour and had you in fits, even though he told the same jokes over and over again: 'He can't hit the goal, he's knocked the linesman's hat off.'

The nucleus of the youth side blossomed into one of the strongest teams in the First Division and it was a great privilege for me to be captain. We had a good blend with an excellent goalkeeper in Peter Bonetti, and overlapping full-backs Ken Shellito and Eddie McCreadie, a quality defence. They would attack, play it to me and I'd put long balls through to Bobby Tambling and Barry Bridges. After winning the League Cup in 1965 we got very close to further honours and had some memorable European encounters. I remember the Roma game at Stamford Bridge for the fondest of reasons. I scored a hat trick, a rarity in itself, and some say it was my finest game for Chelsea. For one of the goals George Graham passed to me and I hit it on the volley. Another was a cheeky free kick. I paced out the wall, turned to come back to the ball, and then went back again; it was played alongside me by Joe Fascione and I hit it in the net. But after we were beaten in two FA Cup semi-finals Tommy Docherty lost his patience and wanted to break up the team. When he came into the dressing-room before my last game against Barcelona and introduced Charlie Cooke, I knew my days at the Bridge were numbered. I'd always wanted to play for Chelsea and didn't want to go. We felt we could have actually been one of the best sides in the land and it was frustrating not knowing how far we would have gone in the 1960s. Chelsea continued to do well, but in a different style, with more individual players.

We grew up together and talked about football and tactics in the café on Fulham Broadway for hours – it didn't surprise me that so many went into football management. I've always taken football seriously, but I've not always taken myself quite so seriously. We had a great camaraderie and I loved to mimic people like Max Wall and Tommy Cooper and tell jokes and sing a few songs – it was all innocent fun and helped foster a great team spirit. I am pleased to see good friends like Bobby Tambling, Barry Bridges and Bert Murray included in the book. They deserve the recognition and I thoroughly enjoyed my time with them during an exciting era for the club. I wish Chris every success with his labour of love.

Terry Venables

PREFACE

Few clubs can lay greater claim to such a distinguished line of forwards, whose mere mention sends a tingle down the spine of those immersed in Chelsea's tradition and history. It cannot always be quantified in terms of success, we can recall periods of underachievement, but it is always there in spirit. That indebtedness to the past, to the people who built the traditions that the current players have inherited, should be the fundamental core for all sports, the sustaining root from which nourishment derives. Football careers today are not geared towards loyalty and, sadly, too many players do not stay long enough to know or care about their club's history.

That charge can hardly be levelled at the supporter and, whilst the odd flat cap may be missing nowadays, the loyalty of Chelsea fans, young and old, remains unquestioned. We are mostly fashioned by what we learn in our youth and inevitably our footballing eyes focus on the glamour boys, the heroes who create or convert chances to win our hearts and minds. The book is a tribute to these players, some high profile, others who plied their trade in a supportive, but no less influential manner.

For an appetising hors d'oeuvre we look back to the wingers, sadly marginalised by the development of wing-backs. But what entertainment they provided, what artistic value they left as a legacy of their halcyon days. In the old days of the attacking 'W' formation, with two inside-forwards and two wingers in addition to the centre-forward, Chelsea were blessed with abundant talent out wide. We examine the contrast between the Scottish imports, who graced their talents with classical dribbling skills, to the blistering pace and more direct style of their English counterparts. And one cannot ignore the debt they played in fashioning opportunities for centre-forwards over the years.

We linger over a crucial phase in the club's history, when Ted Drake developed the youth policy conceived by his predecessor Billy Birrell. Ted enjoyed particular success with talented young forwards and a number of his Ducklings became the cornerstone of subsequent teams. Others, notably Jimmy Greaves, achieved greater heights elsewhere.

Upfront then to the strikers, the crowd-pullers who found the back of the net in imperious fashion. We focus on the development and expansion of some of the principal alliances. How the style of a Chelsea centre-forward was copied by the great Hungarian playmaker Nando Hidegkuti and mirrored a decade later by the King of Stamford Bridge. How a diminutive Scottish forward from the 1930s bore comparison for contrasting reasons with two of his successors. How opinion is polarised when it comes to talking about some of the club managers.

Experiences are shared as the individuals narrate career highlights and their time at the Bridge. Having enjoyed such a high profile, discover how the stars adapted to life after football. Compare the footballers of today with the pensionless decades and limited range of options for retiring players. There aren't many cosy closets for footballers once they've binned their boots. Quite a few stayed in the game; others bought sports shops, or guest houses or newsagents. One or two would run a pub – a few sadly sat in it. Some tales are therefore poignant, but the majority are expressed with due humility.

Those selected are an individual choice and not an exhaustive list – no doubt debate will ensue as to why some have or have not been included. The abiding intention is to share in a conversational stroll through history, to take us into the dressing-room, and share the nostalgia. The anecdotal support has been provided through extensive interviews and my text is deliberately unfussy, merely a thread to maintain continuity. If the reader derives half as much enjoyment as the writer in compiling the book, then the exercise will not have been wasted.

WINGERS

BOBBY McNEIL – *307 appearances*

Bobby McNeil was the first in a line of distinguished wingers to display similar traits. At five feet seven inches he was very fast, a fine dribbler and more a creator of chances than a natural finisher. Nonetheless he had a powerful and accurate shot, and was capable of testing the keeper from some distance. His astute footballing brain made him one of Chelsea's most popular players. But for the intervention of the First World War, his appearances would have been appreciably more.

Born at Gowkthrapple, Glasgow, in 1890, Bobby was spotted playing for Glasgow Juniors on the left-wing, a position he held for the remainder of his career. He signed for Hamilton Academicals in 1910, where he was known as the 'Dabber'. Bobby was chosen to play for the Scottish League against the Irish League in both 1912 and 1913. His consistency was rewarded with a move to Chelsea in April 1914 and within days Bobby was selected to play in a North v South match in England. Fellow Scot and Chelsea manager David Calderhead never concealed his penchant for the intricate ball skills associated with Scottish artists, and several other players were successfully imported from north of the border.

Bobby scored in his League debut on the opening day of the 1914/15 season, a 1–1 draw at Spurs. There was initially a shaky honeymoon period, as the fans didn't warm to Bobby's style of football overnight. They felt his dribbling was over-elaborate and slowed down the pace of attacking movements. Bobby won over their hearts and minds once he became attuned to the pace of English football. It was an extraordinary season for the Scot, playing in Chelsea's first FA Cup final against Sheffield United at Old Trafford in April 1915. Against the backdrop of wartime Britain, the Blues underperformed and lost 0–3 in a one-sided contest. Chelsea also suffered the indignity of relegation, only to be reprieved after the war when the First Division was expanded by two additional clubs.

During wartime Bobby returned to Scotland, signing for Bathgate in August 1915. In 1916 he once again joined the Accies and in October 1918 was released to play for Celtic in the Glasgow Cup final. By this time he played sometimes as a wing-half and also guested for Motherwell in 1919. With the war over, he returned to Stamford Bridge and was a regular in the side for seven seasons. Bobby finally lost his place to George Pearson after playing three of the opening four fixtures of the 1926/27 season. He retired at the end of that season, aged 36, the last survivor of the 1915 'Khaki' Cup final team.

Bobby became Hamilton Academicals' trainer in 1931, where he was a strict disciplinarian. It was said that Accies were one of the fittest teams in the Scottish League thanks to his methods. During the Second World War he was a member of the Hamilton Burgh Police War Reserve. Bobby returned to Accies after the war but died prematurely in the late 1940s. His son Willie followed in his father's footsteps, also as a winger for Hamilton in the 1930s, and only passed away in 2001 at the age of 87.

As recently as the late 1970s Bobby's qualities were highlighted in the Sunday Telegraph by older supporters of the club. Subsequent to an article on Chelsea wingers, there were a number of dissenting scribes questioning why the greatest of them all had not been mentioned.

JACKIE CRAWFORD – *308 appearances*

Another Calderhead signing, Jackie Crawford was a lightweight who became one of Chelsea's most versatile wingers, operating on either wing with equal effect. He was a winger in the old-fashioned sense of the word, in that he didn't stray too often into his own half of the field. His job was to use all his energy and skill in confusing the opposition, which he did in style. Jackie was virtually the complete player, with a deftness of control and change of pace that confused and demoralised the opposition, and a sublime crosser of the ball.

Born at Jarrow in 1896, Jackie began at his South Shields school as a full-back. He was fed a mountain of porridge to try and build him up: 'I measured five feet three when I really stretched myself!' He played for Jarrow Grange in the Durham District League, where it was felt Jackie's tiny frame would hinder his progress, so he was moved to the wing. Jackie joined Second Division Hull City in December 1919 and, while he made his debut in March 1920 on the left-wing, was subsequently switched to the right flank with immediate success. Jackie starred in a 3–0 defeat of Championship winners Burnley in the FA Cup and such talent was bound to draw attention. After 134 games (11 goals) for the Tigers a fee of £3,000 secured Jackie's transfer in May 1923; the only surprise was that his move to Chelsea did not come earlier. He had to wait patiently for his debut, which came in a 2–0 defeat in November 1923 at Middlesbrough.

For a decade Jackie was a permanent fixture at outside-right, initially dovetailing with Bobby McNeil. He was unfortunate in playing during the 1920s when the Blues were unable to find the back of the net with any sort of regularity. Countless chances created by Jackie's dazzling runs were spurned by a variety of centre-forwards, and the club suffered inconsistencies as a result. Undeterred, one of Jackie's principal characteristics was a cheerful optimism, expecting to win every match. His flexibility was also evident when Scottish legend Alex Jackson was signed. After being dropped to accommodate Jackson at the start of the 1930/31 season, Jackie merely reverted to left-wing and performed to such good effect that he won an international cap against Scotland at Hampden Park in 1931. The all-international Chelsea forward line of Jackson, Wilson, Gallacher, Cheyne and Crawford looked formidable, but frustrated the fans with their unpredictable performances.

Jackie finally lost his first-team place after a 0–1 home defeat to Huddersfield in January 1932. Calderhead departed at the end of the season and Jackie did not figure in the plans of incoming manager Leslie Knighton. In May 1934 he was transferred to QPR, then in Division Three South. After a previously barren time finding the back of the net, in his first season he finished second-top scorer on nine goals from 28 appearances. New manager Billy Birrell, later to make a name for himself at Chelsea, was appointed at the beginning of the 1935/36 season and Jackie was one of the few players to be retained. However, his appearances became infrequent and, after just three games at the start of the following season, Jackie retired from football. A likeable and popular individual, he stayed in the game by accepting a coaching position at Queens Park Rangers until the outbreak of the war and later at Malden Town. Jackie died at Epsom in July 1975 at the age of 78.

DICK SPENCE – *246 appearances*

A recurring theme of wide players is, of course, their pace: Dick Spence was a master craftsman of his era. His speed exposed many defenders, who in that era were often less mobile and heavier built. He could operate down either flank, although he preferred the right. Dick had a wiry, lightweight frame which maximised a fleetness of foot, and his blistering acceleration created many goalscoring opportunities for both himself and his team-mates.

Born at Platt's Common near Barnsley in 1908, Dick was brought up in the heart of one of the great coal-mining areas. His ability as a footballer shone at school and he received rave notices playing for Thorpe Colliery, where he worked as a coaltrimmer, and Platt's Common YMCA, albeit not as a winger.

> I went down the mine when I left school at 14 and waited until I was 20 before signing as a professional with Barnsley. I wanted to be reasonably certain of making a living in the game, because we were a big family, my dad was off work and if I didn't make a go of it once I'd packed up the pit, I'd be pushed to find a job. It was like that in those days. I was an inside-left when I joined Barnsley. The day I signed the manager Brough Fletcher said, 'From now on, you're an outside-right.' And that was that. I was on £3 5s. a week when I was in the first team and £2 10s. when I wasn't. But I was glad of anything to get away from the pit.

Dick scored 20 goals when Barnsley won the Third Division North Championship in 1934. Chelsea manager Leslie Knighton was seeking a goalscoring winger and Dick fitted the bill perfectly. He was one of Knighton's most imaginative acquisitions at £5,000 in October 1934. Dick's response was telling: his 19 goals for the season remain a record for a Chelsea winger, all the more remarkable as he didn't make his debut until nine matches into the campaign. An early highlight was scoring all four goals in a 4–1 win against Liverpool at the Bridge in December 1934.

> I jumped at the chance of coming to a big club and it turned out to be the best thing I could have done. When I came £8 a week in the winter and £6 a week in the summer was the top rate anywhere – less at many clubs – and at the end of the season even the stars were anxious in case they didn't get signed on again. I was five feet five and a quarter inches and eight stone nine pounds when I left Barnsley. Up there they

wanted to put me on a pint of Guinness a day to build me up, but I
didn't like the stuff. By the end of my first season at Chelsea I was up to
nine stone six pounds.

Before the war Dick was a contemporary of Stanley Matthews among others,
but still played twice for England in 1936, against Austria and Belgium, taking
over from Sammy Crooks. He packed a surprisingly powerful shot for such a
small man, particularly with his favoured right foot.

I suppose I had a bit of a shot for my size and could use both feet, but I
think what drove me hardest and made me so enthusiastic was the
knowledge that I'd be back on the floor if I didn't make the grade.

He was an automatic choice for the right-wing position in the five seasons
leading to the outbreak of the war, during which time he served in the
Metropolitan Police Reserve. During wartime football he made 170
appearances, scoring 50 times, demonstrating what additional records could
have gone his way but for the hostilities. Dick retained his fitness and, once he
resumed his familiar beat in 1946, was the sole survivor of the pre-war team
to regain a first-team place. During Tommy Lawton's brief tenancy he revelled
in being the principal supply line of crosses.

When making his final first-team appearance in September 1947 at 39
years 57 days, Dick was the oldest player to appear for Chelsea in a League
fixture. Shortly after, he broke his right leg playing in a London Challenge
Cup-tie against Spurs, ending his career. A year later Billy Birrell offered him a
post on the training side, where his speedy incursions onto the pitch as trainer
often raised the biggest cheer of the match. After several seasons with the 'A'
team he switched to Dick Foss's youth side.

A loyal servant of Chelsea, Dick became part of the furniture for over 40
years. He was a buoyant, chirpy character, invariably smiling, and enjoyed a
joint testimonial with Harry Medhurst in 1976. He was a great family man
with three sons: Eric, Richard and Geoffrey. Popular and recognised to the
end, Dick never left the London area and was a regular visitor to the Bridge
almost to the time of his death in March 1983.

Dick enjoyed all sports: he played cricket into his fifties, was a frequent
visitor to the White City athletics meetings and loved a day at the races, where
no doubt he would have a modest flutter. He was not one for the high life,
never forgetting his working-class roots: 'Give me a couple of winners, a plate
of jellied eels and a drink of tea and you can have all the bright lights.'

ERIC PARSONS – *176 appearances*

To enjoy a nickname of 'The Rabbit' demands little explanation, as Eric Parsons was another lightning player who ignited the enthusiasm of the Stamford Bridge faithful during the early 1950s. Born at Worthing in 1923, Eric was destined to become a winger from his schooldays, where he excelled as a natural athlete.

> I did a lot of sprinting and was the 220-yard champion of Sussex and a member of Worthing Harriers. I loved running, but I always wanted to play football. I was an attacking centre-half at school as I was virtually the biggest lad in my year. I could also score goals from that position as I had a good shot on me.

Unknown to Eric, the key that altered his life was an English Schools' Shield tie for Worthing Boys at Upton Park in 1937, when West Ham manager Charlie Paynter noted the kid's undoubted potential. On leaving school, Eric went into a poster and ticket design office, having won an art scholarship, but didn't pursue a career outside football.

> As I had a good game against West Ham Boys they wanted me to sign amateur forms. When I said they had better see my teacher, they told me they already had! The West Ham chairman Mr Pratt came down to Worthing to talk to my mother and father. Even though I had won an art scholarship it was not a difficult decision and I was all for it. I was also selected for The South v The North in an England Schoolboys trial at Shrewsbury in 1937. Although still a centre-half I played wing-half, but found myself running between the inside-right and outside-right trying to cover them and didn't have a good game. As a schoolboy of 15 I remember W.J. Cearns, a well-known East End builder who was the chairman of West Ham, put me in a local league side – I played on Hackney Marshes and scored five goals!

In October 1943 Eric signed professional forms for Second Division West Ham, who gave him a wartime debut against Southampton at the age of 20. During his army service Eric came into prominence, initially at inside-right, playing in the British Army of the Rhine team.

> I was converted to a winger in the forces, playing with Eddie Baily and

Les Compton amongst others. We had a good side and played in the
Berlin Stadium and all round Europe just after the war in 1946,
entertaining the troops. Once I had returned from the forces I
remember an evening game against Spurs. I got a ball from 25 yards
out and whacked it past Ted Ditchburn. I think there were one or two
England selectors watching which led to me going on the
Scandinavian tour in 1949. I was in the company of the likes of Billy
Wright and Tom Finney and made my debut for the England 'B' side
against Finland in Helsinki. We won 4–0 and I was awarded a statuette
as best player. We then played Holland in Amsterdam, again won 4–0
with Roy Bentley in the side and I scored a goal. I thought I had a good
chance to break into the England side, but for the next international
Tom Finney was switched to right-wing, Jimmy Mullen to outside-
left and that was that.

Eric spent four years at Upton Park and, after 152 appearances and 35 goals,
was transferred to Chelsea in November 1950, negotiations having gone on
for some weeks. He had interested Chelsea for several seasons and a dispute
about his £750 benefit proved a turning point.

I felt I was entitled to a benefit, but they said the two years I was in
Germany didn't count towards the five years needed. Chelsea came in
for me and paid about £20,000, which was a big fee at the time,
although it never preyed on my mind. After I signed for Chelsea the
West Ham directors decided to pay me my benefit in full.

Eric was not an instant success, restricted by an injury he picked up towards the
end of his West Ham days and he even had a spell in the reserves. However, after
a cartilage operation he became virtually an ever-present and was one of Ted
Drake's key figures, as he shaped a side capable of challenging for honours.

I hurt my right knee playing at Ewood Park against Blackburn for West
Ham and had a cartilage removed not long after I went to Chelsea. That
put me out of contention for an England place, which was a pity as
they were looking for fast, direct wingers at the time. I thought Ted
was a good manager, he had faith in me and I knew exactly what he
wanted. He said, 'Eric, I want you to get down the wing – if you don't
I'll get someone who will,' so I always played that way.

Eric was ever present in the 1954/55 Championship-winning side, scoring many vital goals, as well as creating countless opportunities for his team-mates, particularly Roy Bentley. He was at the peak of his form, with an uncomplicated but effective style, relying on pace and excellent ball control to beat his marker. His brilliant play again impressed the selectors in 1954, but Stanley Matthews was enjoying a great run of form. The dénouement of that historic season was fittingly played out at the Bridge in April 1955:

> For the last home game against Sheffield Wednesday we wanted to win to clinch the Championship at the Bridge. All the team were motivated and I was very pleased to score two goals. My most memorable goal for Chelsea was the header in that game. I used to lose my marker when jostling for position and when Frankie Blunstone put the corner in, there was no one near me. I headed the ball over the left-back Curtis and it dropped into the far corner. The other goal I hit with my left foot, my swinger.

There were memorable post-match scenes as Chelsea comfortably beat Wednesday 3–0. The crowd swarmed across the pitch and the players paraded at the front of the directors' box for the speeches to follow. The proceedings ended on a note of humour with the crowd repeatedly chanting, 'We want the Rabbit.' But Eric, in tracksuit top and towel round his neck, was lost for words, overcome with emotion:

> There were great celebrations after the game and we had champagne in the directors' room. I was interviewed by Eamonn Andrews on the radio, but I can't recall being lost for words at the front of the stand. I just sat there on the ledge and let the fans shout my name. There hadn't been a lot of talk about us being in with a chance of winning the Championship, as six weeks before the end of the season there was a paper strike (caused by the electricians), which was called off just in time for the Wednesday game.

The two fixtures during the season against Wolves were crucial. Eric recalled the away match in December 1954, when Wolves were leading the table, with Chelsea in a modest 11th position:

> I especially remember the Molineux game when we were right up against it, but the determination of the side showed through. Les Stubbs and I both had good goals disallowed in the first half and we finally clinched it with two goals in the last few minutes.

Eric modestly underplayed his 50-yard dash along the right touchline, ending in a perfect cross for Les Stubbs to force the ball into the net from close range and equalise at 3–3. Almost immediately afterwards Roy Bentley was given a free run on goal from the halfway line to score a sensational winner. Ted Drake was fulsome in his praise of Eric at the time: 'I know the other lads will not only forgive me but join me in saying a special word for Eric. It was simply wonderful to see him ploughing through the mud and leaving his opponents at a standstill.'

> We had a good side and didn't know when we were beaten. Apart from Roy there were no real stars – Stan Willemse, Stan Wicks and Ken Armstrong collectively played well as a team. Maybe Ted based our style of play on the old Arsenal, as Les Stubbs was a bustler, a bit like Ted. I made a few goals for Roy, who had a bit more finesse, was good in the air but also a strong challenger. Johnny McNichol was a very good ball-player who linked up well with myself and Roy.

In November 1955 Eric completed five years as a Chelsea player and qualified for another benefit. Chelsea's application for permission to pay him the maximum £750 was approved by the FA. 'The Rabbit' had become a firm favourite with the crowd and there was a buzz of expectation when Eric embarked on one of his thrilling runs. He had the beating of the best defenders of his day, but remembered a handful who gave him a hard time:

> Running like a rabbit was my style and the nickname originated at West Ham when somebody in the crowd called me it. I moved pretty quickly and my nickname came with me when I went to Chelsea. I think the public like that style of play and what makes Manchester United so attractive today is the way Ryan Giggs runs past people. I never had a good game against Bill Eckersley of Blackburn or Willie Cunningham of Preston because of their style – they were just as fast and small as me. I also had a battle with Len Millard, the West Brom captain and left-back – I always knew I'd been in a game against him.

The sense of a Chelsea side nearing its sell-by date was growing and Eric's tenure came to an end in November 1956, when he was released to Brentford on a free transfer. He had been a regular in the side for four seasons, scoring 42 goals.

> I was playing quite well in 1955/56 when I was dropped towards the

end of the season and Peter Brabrook came in. I still felt I was playing well in the reserves when that happened. I was eventually transferred and was disappointed, as we still had a good side, but Ted wanted to bring in some fresh blood. Bill Dodgin senior signed me for Brentford, who were in the old Third Division and I stayed there four years. I was happy to go as long as I could continue to travel up, as I loved Worthing. I caught the eight o'clock train every day and enjoyed my time there. I stayed fit and I think in the first two seasons we just missed out on promotion.

Eric played for the Bees until 1960, scoring 18 times in 119 games. He appeared in nearly 500 senior games despite losing several seasons through the Second World War and sustaining a broken leg whilst at Griffin Park, but his love of the game remained undiluted. He carried on in non-league football with his customary enthusiasm and had also prudently prepared for life beyond football.

I had a couple of years with Dover in the Kent League, which we won one season. I was paid £20 plus expenses, which was as much as I was paid at Brentford. However instead of having to travel and train every day, all I had to do at Dover was turn up for the matches, and I trained by running along the prom. I turned out on Sunday afternoons for Ham Sports until I was 43, I loved it!

Once I retired from football I knew I had to do something, and when I was at Brentford went into the grocery business in Worthing, which I kept for about three years. Then Roy Woodford, who I knew as a boy and had a pub in Worthing, approached me. He was losing cigarettes at his pub and I offered to install a cigarette machine for £400. I restocked and maintained it, subject to receiving a percentage, and the business expanded round the county and flourished over a period of over fifteen years. Then I lost my boy David, who was a marvellous son and big help to me, sold out to the Imperial Tobacco Company and retired.

I have been married to Joan for 52 years and we have a daughter Susan and two grandchildren Joanne and Andrew. I still play bowls, which I started during the close season when I was playing football. I have played for the county and beaten international players in the past. I am also proud of winning the county singles and pairs when I was playing a lot in the seventies. I surprised myself in 2000 when I won the club singles down at Beach House Park.

I love the reunions held at Stamford Bridge for the Championship-winning side. Tony Banks, whose father took him to watch us as a lad, goes out of his way to look after us. I've had a wonderful time and enjoyed every minute of it – they're marvellous days to look back on.

FRANK BLUNSTONE – *346 appearances*

According to Jimmy Greaves, he had a heart the size of a cabbage, a testament to Frank Blunstone's bravery and spirit. His close-dribbling skills mesmerised defenders and his penetrating runs created numerous opportunities for a variety of target men for more than a decade. Born at Crewe in 1934, Frank came from a background of modest means.

I come from a large family, eight brothers and five sisters and, with 14 children, you couldn't expect my mum to buy football boots. I have always been very left-footed, and when I played at Bedford Street School in Crewe, a very good mate of mine who was also in the team lent me his left boot and he had the right. So I played football in one shoe and a borrowed boot! We were well looked after, but every penny was vital.

The Blunstones represented Crewe Schoolboys for five years, and I played for two from when I was 14. When we played at Ellesmere Port in the Cheshire Shield I was so small they thought I was the mascot! My brother Ernie was outside-left and I was inside-left. Ernie became a referee – he was due to run the line in a League game at Anfield one year, but the Football League took him off, as I was playing. He was very upset as, of course, he wouldn't have given me anything.

I played for Cheshire Schoolboys and was reserve for England Schoolboys behind Johnny Haynes, who got the inside-left position. That year Crewe, a small town, also produced Ronnie Cope, a centre-half who played for Manchester United post-Munich.

I had six clubs after me including Wolves and my dad, a railwayman, was marvellous and let me make my mind up who to join. It was always Crewe for me and when I joined at 15, I was their first-ever groundstaff boy. There were no youth sides, I played against men from day one. There was a time I was playing for Crewe Schools on Saturday mornings, and Alexandra's 'A' team in the afternoon, and I had fish and chips in between!

Arthur Turner, who was my first manager, was very keen on cricket and played in the North Staffordshire League. On Fridays after training he would set some stumps up and get me to bowl at half a crown on the 'wicket' – if I hit it I kept it. Later on I played cricket for Crewe in the North Staffordshire League and also had one game for Cheshire against Shropshire. I think the only reason was I could get off during the week.

Harry Catterick, who helped me tremendously, took over and we had Johnny King, an 18-year-old who was also an inside-left. So Harry put me at outside-left for my debut against Barrow [October 1951]. I was still an amateur, we won 2–1 and I scored. On the Friday morning I went to the secretary's office to collect my wages of £4, and the pros were trying to get me to ask for a £2 win bonus. No way was I going to do that! At 16 years 10 months I was Crewe's youngest player until Steve Walters about five years ago – he was two weeks younger than me. Johnny and I were both very left-sided and, in Harry's wisdom, he would have us back in the afternoon, chipping balls onto our right side and make us play them with the right foot. It was the first time I was ever coached, but after a couple of weeks when we couldn't control the ball to save our lives, he gave up and we remained left-sided.

In February 1953 Ted Drake secured the services of Frank, for whom offers had been tendered by eight other First Division teams. At £7,000 he was one of Chelsea's best-ever bargain buys.

Just before I joined Chelsea, Stoke offered £15,000 for Johnny and me. We had an old Stoke player with us, Billy Mould, who was coming towards the end of his career. He said, 'If I were you, they're OK but not a big club.' I was only 18 and took his advice and Johnny, who was a good player, went for £7,500. The next thing I knew Chelsea came in for me – it was sound advice.

Sorrow and joy immediately walked hand in hand with Frank. One Monday the following month he learned a brother had been killed in a motorcycle accident and later in the week he was offered his first-team debut.

During training Albert Tennant said Ted wanted to see me – I thought I was in trouble! Ted asked me to sit down and his secretary brought me a cup of tea. He said my brother John had died, he was just 21 and it still upsets me. He sent me home straight away and made sure Len Kell, who came from Durham and was in digs with me, went back with me. We had the funeral on Thursday and Ted rang me up that evening and said, 'I've picked you to play on Saturday, but if you don't want to, I understand. Let me know tomorrow.' My mum said John would have wanted me to play.

In March 1953 Frank stepped out for his debut at Tottenham to give a brilliant display of football beyond his tender years, scoring the winner in a 3–2 win. He immediately made the outside-left berth his own and was a member of the Championship team from November 1954, when he regained his place from Jim Lewis after injury.

Many times that championship season we went a goal down, I don't know why, then we'd win 3/4–1. We went to West Brom for a midweek afternoon game and were struggling. Les Stubbs, who was a great worker, went into Jim Sanders, their goalie, who cleared the ball and promptly kicked Les. They gave a penalty which turned the game for us and we went on to win 4–2. I also remember the home match against Wolves when, in a tight first half, Seamus O'Connell fired in a shot which was going into the corner, when this fist went up. We knew Billy Wright had punched it over, but the referee gave a corner. He must have been the only person in the ground who hadn't seen it, but fortunately for us the linesman had spotted it. Peter Sillett, one of the finest strikers of a deadball I ever saw, went back about 25 yards, ran up and blasted it. It hit the back of the net before Bert Williams dived. We beat them 1–0 and that game probably won us the Championship.

What was also special was that we had played at Molineux the year before and lost 8–1. We lost two players, Ronnie Greenwood and Bobby Smith, and Stan Cullis was still urging them on to score more. Ted got very upset with Cullis and they nearly came to blows on the line.

England recognition was swift and Private Blunstone won the first of his five caps against Wales in November 1954 – he had just turned 20.

I was in the Army Medics down at Crookham, just outside Aldershot, doing my two years' National Service. My best mate was Tosh Chamberlain, who played outside-left for Fulham. We both worked in the Sergeants' mess and I was there on the Monday morning when

Tosh said the Colonel wanted to see me. I thought he was pulling my leg but the Colonel called me in and said, 'Ah, Blunstone, you're playing for England on Wednesday at Wembley. Go and change and get a pass. Get back here by Thursday, 8 a.m.' I trained with the side on the Tuesday morning but by the evening I had got the flu. Although I was ill I wasn't going to miss that match and played.

My outstanding international memory was when we beat Scotland 7–2 in 1955 at Wembley. Ken Armstrong won his only cap and Chelsea beat Tottenham 4–2 on the same day, so they obviously didn't miss us! I had the pleasure of playing in front of the great Duncan Edwards. I played against Willie Cunningham at right-back and Tommy Docherty was at right-half – I never let him forget it! Stanley Matthews took poor Harry Haddock to the cleaners, who in fairness never resorted to dirty tactics. Dennis Wilshaw scored four times, three with his head, he only had to nod them in. I'm sure I would have won more caps but for my broken leg.

Frank suffered a break in the fourth round of the FA Cup at Spurs in January 1957. He incurred the same fate the following August in a pre-season friendly, six days before the start of the 1957/58 season, and did not play another competitive game until November 1958.

I broke my left leg just before half-time when it was goalless and we lost 4–0. Tottenham, who were one of the few clubs who had an X-ray machine, X-rayed my leg but said nothing was broken. I couldn't walk though and on the Monday told Jack Oxberry I was in so much pain. They sent a car to take me to hospital for another X-ray, but they couldn't find anything. It got to Thursday and I let Jack know I was in agony, and they sent me to hospital for another X-ray. I was in the room when they again said there was nothing broken, but a nurse identified a hairline fracture on the X-ray. I had been trying to walk around for four days with a broken leg. I trained pre-season and went over to Holland for a friendly against Ajax. In the first really hard tackle it broke again. The specialist said it wasn't a bad thing, as a hairline crack was always likely to happen.

When we played north all my brothers wanted to watch Chelsea, but we were only allowed two complimentary tickets each. We played Everton at Goodison Park once when I was injured and, as we got out of the coach, Peter Sillett, who was in charge of the tickets, asked one of my brothers how many he wanted. When he asked for 12 Peter said,

'You must be joking!' To his credit he got all the lads to give up their complimentaries.

Frank bravely overcame injury to fulfil a most distinguished career and proved to be one of the finest players in Chelsea history. In November 1963 he became the first Chelsea player with ten years' service to be awarded a testimonial.

> It was a great honour and a wonderful night, as Tom Finney, Ronnie Clayton, Ian Ure, Jimmy Armfield and Tony Waiters played in an All Stars' XI for me, and 20,000 turned up.

Frank played 34 games in the 1962/63 Second Division promotion team, but an injury prior to the Caribbean tour in the summer of 1964 finally forced his premature retirement.

> We were training at Hendon when I went past Barry Bridges and felt this pain in the ankle. I turned round and threatened 'Bridgo', as I thought he kicked me – he said he never touched me. It came up like a balloon and I had an X-ray with the usual result – nothing wrong. We went on tour to the West Indies for three weeks and it got worse. I was sitting on the side of the swimming pool one day when Tommy Docherty pushed me in. I wasn't expecting it and the pain was excruciating. I nearly fainted but wasn't going to let him see it hurt. It was actually a hard tour, we played Wolves five times and were struggling for fit players. Eddie McCreadie, who was also injured, and I had a fitness test one morning, and when I went to sprint I collapsed on the floor. I saw a specialist out there, who thought I had a sprained ankle and gave me a tetanus injection in my backside! I went to see the specialist back home and he immediately saw a gap in the Achilles and operated next morning. I got myself fit and was coaching schoolboys at Spencer House School when it went again. He tried to stitch a muscle in the gap in the back of my leg but it failed and I never played again – I was only 29. Although I lost a yard of pace when I ruptured my Achilles tendon, which as a winger you couldn't afford to do, I think with an older head I was playing the best football of my career, better than when I played for England.
>
> Fortunately Tommy Doc gave me a job with the youth team from 1964 to 1968 following Dick Foss, who left after a while. To follow Dickie was hard, as he produced many great players, but I had Alan

Hudson and Butch Wilkins at 12, and it was lovely to see them coming through.

I then managed Brentford for four years – I had a wonderful time but it was very difficult. When I went there they were in Division Four and financially in dire straits, £69,000 in the red. We had no trainers or scouts and I had to cut down to one team with 16 pros – I did everything. But the second year we were promoted with an average gate of 11,800. Ron Greenwood did me a great favour and let me have Roger Cross, a target man and smashing player, from West Ham for £10,000. I also watched a six feet four inches Wimbledon centre-forward in a cup game. He was very raw but I saw something there, watched him for about six weeks and bought him for £800. I taught him the game and, although he was a fiery type and was suspended for five weeks, John O'Mara scored 24 goals that year and helped get us promotion. When O'Mara was suspended I was down to 12 players and our sub was Gordon Phillips, our second goalkeeper. Dave Sexton offered me Stewart Houston on loan – he was, of course, a full-back, but Dave said to stick him upfront. He did ever so well for us and at the end of the season Dave offered him to me for £15,000, with 10 per cent of any future transfer fee over £15,000. When I told the chairman his wages at Chelsea were £45 per week, he said to offer Stewart £40. I said he had to be joking, he wouldn't leave a First Division club to go to Brentford for less wages. Fortunately another director put his hand in his pocket to give Stewart £250, so I got him.

Ken Furphy bought O'Mara for Blackburn for £30,000, where he never scored a goal and Bill Dodgin at Fulham bought Cross for £30,000. We never had any money and were a selling club, and the next year we went back down. Although we reduced the debt to £29,000 the chairman lacked ambition. After we lost a home game he said to me, 'Frank, why don't we get better players?' I said, 'Mr Chairman, if you paid the fees clubs want for these better players and you paid them wages, I'd go and get them Monday morning,' and walked out. I was very upset and resigned a week later.

Tommy Docherty had previously asked me to join him at Manchester United, but I wanted to have a go at managing. So I met Tommy and agreed terms with him, but on my way back from Manchester to London I had a bad car-crash on the M6. My seat belt locked and the car caught fire. Fortunately a lorry-driver got a jemmy out of his lorry, smashed the window and pulled me out. I broke both legs, fractured five ribs, crushed my jaw and was in hospital for three months, but United were fantastic and kept my job open. Tommy asked me if I had any decent players at Brentford and I mentioned Stewart Houston. Tommy bought him for £60,000 and, of course, he went on to play for Scotland. I started as youth team manager, but it wasn't easy to get the kids through to the first team, as Tommy was buying players. Arthur Albiston and Jimmy Nichol came through successfully and, when they sacked Paddy Crerand, I took over as assistant manager for two years until 1978.

I then had 18 months with Tommy at Derby – I always got on well with him, maybe because I was the opposite of him. But when Tommy got the sack in 1969, Ron Atkinson brought Colin Addison in as his assistant, so I was sacked. I then got a job in Greece for a year. The President at Ethnikos offered me a £10,000 signing-on fee and tax-free wages for nine months. However, I got the sack after nine months, then had three months at Aris Salonika.

Back in England I met John Harris, Sheffield Wednesday's chief scout at a match. He said Jack Charlton was looking for a coach and I had a very enjoyable three years there. Then Howard Wilkinson came in – he was a schoolteacher and organised staff meetings, where you had to take notes, which I had never done before. He got promoted playing with a back five marshalled by Mike Lyons. When the back players got it they had to whack the ball up to the part of the park between the 18-yard line and the touchline. Gary Bannister and Imre Varadi were playing upfront – one forward chased the defender, the other stopped the backpass to the goalkeeper, so it forced the defender to give away a throw-in or a corner. Then he sent the three big central defenders up for the resulting set-piece. Gary Megson, who played in midfield, went mad – he never got a kick as it missed the midfield out. The lads would spend long periods on these set-pieces in training and got fed up with it – even though the defence could have stayed out there all day stopping it, they let the forwards score so they could move onto something else. I couldn't handle that style of play and resigned after three months.

I went back to Brentford as assistant manager for six months with Fred Callaghan, until he got the sack. Frank McLintock came in and brought with him John Docherty, so I finished.

My best Chelsea goal was against Leeds at the Bridge [April 1963]. They used to say to the full-back, 'Send him inside, he can't use his right foot.' I came inside Paul Reaney and let fly with my right foot, it flew right into the top corner! Mind you, that's the only time I came inside and really caught it perfectly.

The most difficult full-back I faced was the South African, Eddie Stuart of Wolves. He was not technically a great full-back, but was the hardest one to go by. He wasn't dirty, but when he hit you, you knew it. I loved playing Don Howe, one of the first overlapping full-backs, who used to like to get it down and play. But when I ran at him he turned with his back to me, so it helped me go either side of him.

We always struggled against Bolton – Nat Lofthouse used to say, 'I don't know why you bother about coming, just send the shirts!' When Peter Bonetti got injured one year at Burnden Park and didn't look as though he could carry on, Ron Tindall and Jimmy Greaves were almost fighting to get the shirt off his back. They were both good keepers and definitely preferred playing there than upfront at Bolton. The only time in my life I went over the top was against Roy Hartle – he was carried off and I wasn't proud of it, but it had to be done. He'd been kicking me to pieces for years. He came back with his leg heavily bandaged and I thought he would be after me, but he never came anywhere near me. He said later I was the only player who really hurt him.

My wife Doreen and I have had a newsagent's shop in Wandsworth, a sports shop in Lavender Hill, a wine bar at Ashbourne, two pubs, and finally a bed-and-breakfast business at Putney, before retiring in 1991 and returning to Crewe. We have one daughter, Carina, and two grandchildren, Charlie and Gemma. Golf is my passion now – I play off a handicap of 16. I also like tending my rose garden.

PETER BRABROOK – *270 appearances*

Nearly a decade later than anticipated, West Ham United finally got their man. Born at Greenwich in 1937, Peter Brabrook's outstanding ability in the Napier School team at East Ham earned him selection in representative football for East Ham, Essex and London Boys. Nonetheless he slipped through the Hammers' scouting net to join the Chelsea groundstaff at Easter 1953.

When I was 14 I played inside-forward for London Schoolboys

against West Germany at Highbury in front of a big crowd. We won 2–1 and I got both the goals, they were decent ones too, one was a semi-volley from about 30 yards and the other a diving header. There were quite a few scouts there and Wally St Pier, the chief scout at West Ham, wanted me to go training, but they didn't have a place for me on the groundstaff when I left school, which was what I wanted. I hadn't even got home from the game when Jimmy Thompson was outside our door. The following Monday morning my aunt took me to Stamford Bridge by train, which seemed like the other side of the world from the East End!

Ted Drake also visited Peter's parents to confirm Chelsea's interest and convinced them within 15 minutes. Less than an hour later Peter was on the field at the Bridge, playing in a trial match alongside Roy Bentley. As if that wasn't enough for a 15-year-old, after the game he was taken to lunch by the Chelsea skipper, a characteristic gesture on Roy's part. As a natural ball-player, Peter soon showed that he was ideally suited in the Chelsea Junior side to the inside-forward berth, and in the 1954/55 season gained England Youth caps, initially against Wales and then Scotland. He signed professional forms in March 1955, playing three games that season for the Championship-winning side. Peter made his League debut in place of the injured Seamus O'Connell at home to Sunderland in March 1955 and 'scored' in the 11th minute.

Before I made my first-team debut, the youth team were doing really well and we had some good runs in the Youth Cup. Ted Drake came to watch us a couple of times and I played on the strength of those performances. I didn't know I was playing until the Friday lunchtime after training, when I got a call from the office that Ted wanted to see me. He said, 'Seamus isn't fit, you'll be playing tomorrow at inside-left. I've got full confidence in you.' Ted was good like that. It was a big game, we were top of the table and they had a decent side with the likes of Charlie Fleming and Len Shackleton. I scored the first goal – I just run on to it and struck it. It hit somebody and went in but I claimed it. I felt like I had a half-decent game and everything went quite well. We won 2–1 and it kept us in the running for the Championship. In my two other games we won and drew. It was a good introduction to play in a Championship side at 17.

Quite early in my career [1955/56 season] Eric Parsons got injured and Ted put me wide and said, 'With your pace I think you could do all right out there.' I found it a lot easier than in midfield where people were whacking you. I seemed to get a bit more room and caused a few problems with my pace. It's strange that when Seamus was injured I got my chance in the first team, then when Eric was injured another chance came my way and I never looked back.

One of my best Chelsea games was against Burnley at home [September 1959]. We won 4–1 and I had that good a game I couldn't believe it. Everything came off and I was scintillating. I made three goals by beating not just one player, but three or four and scored the other. It was one of those days everything went right and I slaughtered the left-back Doug Winton.

I didn't score that many spectacular goals and wouldn't say I was a prolific goalscorer, but I made 90 per cent of the goals Jimmy Greaves scored. My most memorable Chelsea goals were probably two headers in one game at Highbury [April 1960 in a 4–1 win]. I wasn't the best header but they were decent goals, both at the back post.

With his intricate footwork Peter developed as a fast and skilful winger with a direct approach. He was a regular fixture at outside-right for seven years until the end of the 1961/62 season, when Chelsea were relegated. With a goal tally of 57, his departure to West Ham in October 1962 coincided with Tommy Docherty's first full season in charge.

As soon as he came I knew that was the end of Drake's Ducklings and we all started to drift out. Docherty wanted to bring his own boys in and didn't fancy me from day one. Whether it was because I was one of Ted's boys or he didn't like my style, I don't know. West Ham kept on putting an offer in, but Docherty didn't want me to go there and kept refusing it. It must have gone on for nearly six months, but there was no way he was going to let me stay in London.

Everton also fancied me, as every time I played them I had a good game. One Saturday morning I went on the Pulman from King's Cross to Liverpool on my own, and when I got out of the train there must have been 500 people there with banners, 'Brabrook must sign' and 'Peter Brabrook for Everton'. I couldn't get out of the main entrance and there was a car at the side waiting for me. I was still only young and couldn't believe the passion. I met Harry Catterick and had a look round Goodison and even looked at a lovely house in Southport. Harry, who came across as a very decent man, really wanted me to sign. The most difficult opponent I ever faced was Ray Wilson, their left-back. He was technically good, wiry, tenacious and quick, but I always had a good game against him, which was why they were willing to pay £40,000 for me, a lot of money. I was impressed with the set-up and asked for the weekend to make a decision. I was waiting to get married and, to be truthful, was hoping the West Ham deal would come through, as I only lived ten minutes from the ground. Everton was a long way away and not many players moved to the North in those days. In the end West Ham, who could have had me for nothing, paid £35,000, which was a record for a winger at the time along with Cliff Jones, when he went to Tottenham. Everton ended up paying £40,000 for Alex Scott from Rangers.

The move reaped dividends when Peter was part of the Hammers team that defeated Preston 3–2 in the 1964 FA Cup final.

The Cup final was something else and a great honour for me. There are so many players who played for England but never in a Cup Final, so I couldn't believe my luck when I was playing within two years of signing. When we beat Manchester United in the semi-final at Hillsborough all the big names were in their side, but we raised our game and won 3–1. The final was excellent and I conquered my nerves and mustered enough strength to put a decent cross in for the winning goal that Ronnie Boyce headed home in the last few minutes. It was heavy and my legs were dying a death out there.

Injury denied Peter a place in the side that won the European Cup-Winners' cup against Munich 1860 at Wembley the following season.

I got a bad pull in the quarter-final, which we won 2–1 in Zaragoza. To miss the final was my biggest disappointment in football other than getting too old! We were decent in one-off Cup games, as good as any team in the country. We got to the League Cup final the following season, but lost to West Brom, then another year we made the semi-final. With three World Cup players it's little wonder the fans think it was one of the best-ever West Ham sides.

Peter's early promise with England Youth was followed by nine Under-23 caps and three full international caps. His England debut couldn't have been more daunting – the 1958 World Cup play-off with the USSR in Gothenburg, alongside such luminaries as Wright, Clayton and Haynes.

I was the first Chelsea Youth player to play for England, which was another honour I am very proud of. I was selected for the Possibles v Probables trial game, which was actually played at the Bridge. The left-back for the Probables was Jimmy Langley and the only time he saw me was after the game! Jimmy was a lovely man but never saw my face in that game, he only saw my back! After that they picked the 1958 World Cup squad for Sweden and I was selected on that basis. I had a good game against USSR, probably the best out of the three. We were very unfortunate that we lost. I had a goal disallowed and hit the post a couple of times. I didn't do particularly well in the other two games. I played against Spain in Madrid, we were beaten 2–0 and I never got a kick. Then I did OK in Ireland, steady, nothing spectacular and we drew 0–0. My League form fluctuated and I probably wasn't consistent enough to be a regular player. West Ham were an average side in the League and I had my brilliant games and my poor ones. There was decent competition at the time like Bryan Douglas, who was playing in a good side at Blackburn. He fulfilled his promise and kept the England number one slot after the World Cup.

Peter left the Hammers in July 1968 after over 200 games and 43 goals for a three-year spell at Orient, where he made 72 League appearances and was an influential member of the side which won the Third Division Championship in 1970. All told, Peter played nearly 500 times in the League for his three London clubs. After 16 years as a pro, he turned to non-League football in the early 1970s, passing on the benefit of his knowledge and experience.

When I knew I was coming towards the end of my career my old pal Jimmy Bloomfield, who played at West Ham for a while, asked me to join him at Leyton Orient. I had quite a successful time, despite badly doing my Achilles tendon in my first year, when I only played half a dozen games. I came back just before the end of the season, played two or three games and it was fine. We had Terry Mancini, Mark Lazarus, Terry Dyson and Dennis Rofe, and to win the Third Division was a great achievement and a nice way to finish. I moved on to Romford in the Southern League and also had a couple of games at Harlow. Then I coached at Woodford Town and managed at Basildon, Ford United, Tilbury and Billericay.

Peter's love affair with football continues to this day, as he enthusiastically dons his boots daily at West Ham's training ground.

When I finished pro football I ran a young boys' side from Under-8s to Under-16s. My son was playing and went on to sign schoolboy terms with Charlton. Tommy Taylor asked me to help him out with the coaching at Cambridge, but there wasn't a lot of interest in the Youth Development at the time. Then in 1995 Harry Redknapp asked me to come back to West Ham, which I jumped at the chance of. I get involved from the last year at school with the 16-year-olds, through to the 19s. We run an Under-17 side, which I take, and Tony Carr, the Academy director takes an Under-19 side. As a full-time coach here over the last five years, to have seen Cole, Carrick and Lampard come through is an achievement in itself. It's fantastic what we have done and have in the pipeline. What we have produced is second to none so we must be doing something right!

I married my wife Doreen in 1962. We have two children, Donna and Wayne, one grandson Peter James, who they call PJ, and my son has a little girl, Daisy.

Bolton's Tommy Banks was the toughest defender I faced. You only saw the grass rustle when he used to kick, so you'd pray it wasn't windy. I remember Greavsie and I were out on the pitch before the game at Burnden Park in the 1958/59 season. We were both still youngsters at the time and Tommy Banks came out – he was massive, built like a brick ****house. He came over and Peter Sillett said, 'Do you know Peter Brabrook, good player, quick?' Tommy said, 'Yes, but he can't run with no legs!' When you were looking to push it by him and run I thought, 'Oh my God.' Instead of playing right-wing I ended up playing right-back – I didn't go over the halfway line! Greavsie said to me, 'Don't go over there, he'll kick us,' so we both ended up sticking in our own half and lost 6–0!

For me Jimmy Greaves was the greatest goalscorer of them all, and always will be. From the moment he came into the side, I found him easy to play with. So many of the crosses and passes to him finished in the net, and that made your afternoon because it looked like you'd had a good game too.

BERT MURRAY – *183 appearances*

For those fortunate to have witnessed football in the 1960s and 1970s, there was a song in the heart, a game was still a game and characters were in plentiful supply.

'Ruby' Murray was a case in point and, as a flying winger, quickly endeared himself to the Stamford Bridge faithful. Born at Shoreditch in 1942, Bert was soon honing his skills on the streets of the East End.

> As a kid I was always out of the house kicking a ball until tea was ready, if there was any on the table! Living in Hackney there was nothing else to do but play football. I was playing for my school team, Queensbridge Road Secondary, when I was picked for the District side with Allan Harris, who was at another school in Hackney. We played together for London and Middlesex Schoolboys and were picked for an England trial, where we met up with Terry Venables in 1958. Jimmy Thompson persuaded Allan and Terry, together with Terry More, to join Chelsea. I think I was the last to agree and went there as I already knew them. Jimmy was a lovable rogue and would tell us not to ride a bike, as we were using the wrong muscles, and if you had an injury he would give you a massage. I was fortunate to play at Wembley for the only time with England Schoolboys when we beat Scotland 3–1 and Billy Bremner played for them. I scored two at centre-forward and when I went to Chelsea started off in that position. Dickie Foss said he would give me six months but didn't think I would make it. But he gave me a chance on the wing and I started scoring again.

Bert was a member of the team which won the FA Youth Cup in 1960 against Preston, scoring in the first leg. He was promoted to the Combination team in September 1960, but was still eligible to play in the Youth Cup the following season. Bert scored a magnificent hat trick in the first leg of the final, as the youth side repeated the cup-winning feat against Everton. He signed professional forms in May 1961 and made his first-team debut five months later against Birmingham City – that season he scored four goals in 18 appearances. He was very agile and brave, and became a capable emergency goalkeeper, playing a whole game in goal once on tour.

> I loved throwing myself about and Jimmy Greaves enjoyed practising in goal as well. In March 1962 I went in goal at Arsenal when Peter

Bonetti dislocated his elbow. We lost 2–3 and one of their goals was a penalty from John Barnwell. He remembered it when we were together later at Peterborough, and said I stood one side of the goal and that's where he put it – he whacked it in the roof of the net. I played in goal twice in a week, as the week before John Dunn was injured in a Combination game against Aldershot.

Bert had six games for England Under-23s, the highlight being a headed goal he scored at Coventry when Bert got onto the end of an Alan Ball free kick. He became a firm favourite with the supporters and his flying speed down the right was ideal for the style that Chelsea played in the 1960s. He created a bagful of goals with his crosses, even if his pace and enthusiasm as he tore towards the goal-line occasionally led him to run the ball out of play.

The crowd, then the players, nicknamed me 'Ruby' from Ruby Murray, a singer in those days – I think I used to tackle like her sometimes! There was also a fella called 'Sach' in a group called The Barrow Boys and the players nicknamed me that as I looked like him, especially my nose! There was a great atmosphere at Chelsea with a wonderful bunch of lads, which I didn't really appreciate until years later. In the early days Tommy Docherty looked after us. We were young, didn't know anything else and would run through a brick wall for him. They keep telling me my crosses would go awry sometimes. I got my head down like all wingers and by the time I got past the defender and looked up, occasionally it was too late. Mind you some of the wide players in the Premiership nowadays are not very good crossers of the ball.

In January 1964 21-year-old Bert starred in two epic third-round FA Cup ties against Tottenham. The first ended 1–1 at White Hart Lane in front of 49,382, when Terry Dyson put Tottenham ahead but Bert equalised. In the replay 70,123 spectators witnessed a 2–0 win, an attendance Chelsea have not enjoyed at the Bridge since. Bert scored again and Bobby Tambling notched the other.

I do find it difficult to remember the matches I played in. When I was 12 months old I had meningitis, which everyone was dying of in the 1940s, and it may have affected my memory slightly. I do recall playing in those cup ties and scored a headed goal when we drew at Tottenham. Barry Bridges crossed it from the left, I got up and headed it back across the goal. John Hollowbread, who was in goal, came across to cover the near post and turned round to see it come up from the ground into the net – he couldn't believe it. Then we beat them back at Stamford Bridge and I got another headed goal from about the 18-yard line. I went up and powered it into the roof of the net – it was the best goal I scored for Chelsea. Spurs had a wonderful side, although we used to do well against them.

Bert scored freely for an orthodox wide man. He was light of build, nimble-footed, and 17 League goals in the 1964/65 season was the highest return for a Chelsea winger since Dick Spence. He made an impressive start that year in an away match at Sheffield Wednesday and the climax was, of course, success in the League Cup.

One of the best goals I scored was at Hillsborough, when we beat them 3–2. I scored two and one of them beat Ron Springett from just inside their half – it screamed into the roof of the net. The League Cup final in 1965 were very hard games. I remember Eddie McCreadie slogging through tackle after tackle to score the winning goal at the Bridge. Leicester had a good side, but we went to Filbert Street for the second leg and drew 0–0.

A chirpy Cockney, Bert's versatility and prodigious workrate were put to good effect, although he was unable to force his way into the full England team. His peak years coincided with Alf Ramsey's doubts about the validity of wingers. Later in his career he was converted into a midfield operator or full-back.

We pioneered the overlapping full-back with Dave Sexton, and used to spend a lot of time on the training pitch working these moves out. I could run as fast as anybody and worked for 90 minutes. Ken Shellito our full-back always said that if it wasn't for me he wouldn't have won his England caps, as I used to cover for him. As a winger I came back and then inside, and during the game became a midfielder. I scored 39 League goals for Chelsea, including a lot of headers, as I could jump high. Tommy Docherty said to me a few years ago I was ahead of my time and would be worth £10 million as a wing-back. I also played at full-back with my three other clubs and used to make breaks down the wing from that position.

Bert played in the defeat against Liverpool in the semi-final of the FA Cup in

March 1965. The side were also in the running for the League Championship, but suffered a 2–0 reverse at Liverpool in April. The following fixture was at Burnley, so the party stayed at Blackpool for the week. With lacerating self-confidence Tommy Docherty made one of the most controversial decisions of his colourful managerial career when he sent home eight players, including Bert, from their northern base.

> The Blackpool incident happened when the players went out after we had lost at Liverpool on the Monday. On the Tuesday night Docherty let us out until about one o'clock, bearing in mind we didn't have another game until the Saturday. Then on the Wednesday night he sat in the hotel talking with Tom Finney. He said he wanted us back by 11 o'clock, which we couldn't understand. We came back in the early hours, so he sent us home. The annoying thing was that Docherty used to come along with us and buy us drinks. To send us home for what we had always done was bad management on his part and I'm sure he later realised he was wrong. We were only kids, just enjoying ourselves as a team – it was a chance to let our hair down, which we never had the opportunity to at home.

Docherty fielded virtually a reserve team for the Burnley game, when Billy Sinclair and Jim Smart made their only first-team appearances. A 6–2 defeat put paid to any lingering hopes of securing the League. Bert had already smelt a whiff of insecurity at the Bridge – he now sensed his career was about to take a new turn.

> When Docherty bought Johnny Boyle and started playing him on the right-wing I knew it wouldn't be long before I was on my way. He wanted someone with a bit more bite and played him in the same way as I did, but I don't think he scored as many goals. At least fans will remember me for something as, when they were allowed on the opening day of the 1965/66 season, I was Chelsea's first substitute. George Graham was photographed with the number 12 shirt on in the London papers on the Friday night, then Docherty changed his mind.

Bert joined Birmingham City in August 1966 for £25,000:

> The move came through Barry Bridges, who was already there. Docherty said Southampton were interested in me and I saw Ted Bates,

who offered me a £750 signing-on fee. Then I went to see Stan Cullis at Birmingham and they offered me £4,000 over a four-year contract. I really enjoyed my time at Birmingham and I met some lovely people there, including Ron Wylie the captain. I remember playing against Hull City one night and scored a goal, the likes of which they had never seen before. I hit it about ten yards inside my own half and it just flew as if it was never going to stop. The next day they said it was the hardest shot they had ever seen, harder than Stan Lynn, who did have a hard shot on him.

Bert again suffered the highs and lows of professional football during his spell in the Midlands. The FA Cup semi-final defeat in 1968 again demonstrated the capricious nature of cup competitions.

The FA Cup final was every player's dream in those days, more so than the League. A big disappointment was losing in the semi-final against Liverpool in 1965. We were playing well at the time and I think Liverpool were in a hard European game a few days before. We thought they would be tired, but they weren't. When we played Sheffield Wednesday the following year I was on the bench. Then when I went to Birmingham we lost to West Brom when the players, supporters and directors were really up for it.

After a loan spell at Brighton, in March 1971 Bert signed for a fee of £10,000. A substantial percentage was raised by manager Pat Saward's 'Buy-a-Player' fund, and Bert was tagged the 'People's Player'. At the time Brighton were bottom of the Third Division. Bert's infectious dressing-room manner immediately lifted others, and in his second game he scored a brace in a crucial 3–1 home defeat of Gillingham. With his top-class pedigree Bert added confidence to the team, which rose from 23rd to 14th, thanks to seven wins out of the last 13 games. His talents were also exercised at full-back, and the following year Bert was appointed captain, and voted Player of the Season.

I thoroughly enjoyed my time at Brighton where Pat Saward got a good little team together. Willie Irvine came down from Preston, he was a lovely man and could knock the goals in. I scored some goals as well before they moved me to full-back. Our son Jamie was born there and we had a lovely house in Saltdean. In my second season when I was made captain we were promoted to Division Two in front of big crowds at the Goldstone.

Bert's final League move to Peterborough again followed a loan period, although he was mystified as to why he was released. Brighton received £5,000 and under Noel Cantwell he helped Posh win the Fourth Division title in the 1973/74 season.

> Noel was getting a team together at Peterborough and needed a right-sided player. Pat decided to let me go in 1973, why I don't know. I didn't really want to leave, but was offered another £4,000 signing-on fee. I played more in midfield with Peterborough and we won promotion and had a good season the following year. Then in 1976 I moved into non-League with Spalding.
>
> I loved the game and played sweeper in local football for Deeping Rangers until I was about 54. They had never had a lot of success and got to the Junior Cup final, which we won for the first time. I played football until it got cold and windy and I had to pay three quid to get my kit changed, so thought that was the time to finish.
>
> When I left Posh I took over a night-club from a good friend of Noel Cantwell. I didn't enjoy the late nights and the trouble etc. and after four months the chairman of Spalding offered me the opportunity to take over a pub, which I did in 1976. I've had four pubs now within a 15-mile radius of Stamford and it's a lovely area. I've been running The Bull in Market Deeping for the last nine years, which has been very hard work, but enjoyable. Jamie has now taken a more active role in the business. I married my wife Eileen in 1962 and we have three children, Bertie, Suzanne and Jamie, and two granddaughters. I play a lot of golf at Burghley Park and my handicap is 19 but coming down.

CHARLIE COOKE – *373 appearances*

If sport is about escapism and fantasy, it was surely fulfilled when watching Charlie Cooke in full flow. One of the greatest entertainers and finest ball-players in the world at the time, Charlie had few peers in the game. He was blessed with superb balance and supreme dribbling, and on his day lifted the game with sublime individual skills. Born in 1942 at St Monance, Fife, Charlie, with his family, moved to Greenock as a youngster, where he attended the local High School.

My father Charlie Senior used to take my older brother Ian and me to Cappielow Park on Saturdays to see Greenock Morton. We'd laugh at the shipyard workers' jokes and banter on the crowded special buses going to the game and in the queues at the turnstiles. Then we'd check the day's scores in the evening 'green' and eat fish and chips on the way home. We had seats at Cappielow in the small stand at the front of the main stand. I believe Morton's dressing room was behind us with frosted windows, and wire mesh protecting them. Every game was big for us, but the excitement of Rangers or Celtic coming to town was fantastic, an occasion for all the religious rivalries, songs and jokes, much bigger crowds than usual, and lots of booze and drunks. Our anticipation was almost as high for big-name players like Willie Fernie, Billy Steel, Eddie Turnbull, Willie Thornton, Sammy Cox and Neil Mochan, a *Who's Who* of Scottish football.

We had our own Morton heroes too. Jimmy Cowan, our Scottish International keeper, Willie Walters on the right wing, Billy Campbell a sweet moving wing-half and local fan favourite Jimmy White, another half-back who could sort it out with the best of them.

Probably the biggest thrill of those years was going to Hampden to see Real Madrid against Eintracht Frankfurt in the European Cup final. What a night with 120,000 fans delirious with pleasure, transfixed by soccer we'd never dreamed about. I remember being amazed at how happy everyone seemed to be after the game, even after watching two foreign teams. Puskas and Di Stefano scored all seven goals between them and Real won the European Cup for a record six times. It was awesome and Eintracht were no patsies either.

I was booted off our Greenock High School team at 15 as I couldn't play for Rovers at the same time. I don't believe there was a school rule to that effect, just our gym teacher's. About a year later I was signed by Renfrew Juniors, 15 miles up the River Clyde near Glasgow. They were a semi-pro club with a reputation for making money by blooding youngsters alongside old pros, then moving the youngsters on to pro clubs. I picked up 2/6d a week riding the bus an hour there and an hour back, two nights a week for training and Saturdays for games alongside Renfrew's regular old pros.

I was spotted by Aberdeen and after Bobby Harper, the Aberdeen chief scout, visited me at my parents' in Greenock early in 1959, I agreed to join them later that summer straight from school at 16½ years old. A week later the chief scout of Rangers was introduced to me in the Renfrew dressing-room and asked if I would like to visit Rangers' manager Bill Struth at Ibrox that following week. Here I was a 16-year-old schoolboy with a chance of a lifetime, flattered and flabbergasted that the Rangers' chief scout should be talking to me, but embarrased that I had no one to consult with, as my old man didn't go to the games at Renfrew. My older team-mates were getting showered and dressed and all I could think of saying was that I had promised to go to Aberdeen. It was the truth, of course, but I was caught unawares and it sounds crazy now. Passing up the dream of every kid in Scotland in the bat of an eye. I played well in the pre-season exhibition game at Pittodrie and went straight into the first team at the start of the season, still a starry-eyed schoolboy alongside pros like Billy Little, George Mulhall, Jimmy Hogg and George Kinnell.

Charlie played 125 games for Aberdeen, scoring 27 times. In the last of his four years he won the Player of the Year award and was transferred a few days later (December 1964) to Dundee for a Scottish record fee as something of a replacement for Alan Gilzean, who had just been transferred to Spurs. He was only at Dundee for one full season, playing 44 times with 11 goals, and won the Player of the Year award there, too. The very evening (April 1966) Charlie was presented with the trophy it was announced that he was leaving for Chelsea. Despite being at the club for such a short period, his enduring popularity is such that a lounge at Dens Park has been named after him. Charlie was selected for his country four times at Under-23 level and made his full international debut against Wales at Hampden Park in the 1965/66 season, collecting three more caps that year, including a World Cup tie in Naples against Italy.

> Looking back I would have preferred to come to England sooner but there wasn't a player movement between the countries then as there has been since, and it didn't feel like a hardship to have stayed up north so long.

Charlie was purchased for a Chelsea record fee of £72,000 and made his debut in the Fairs Cup semi-final second leg at home to Barcelona in May 1966. He had to wait until the start of the following season for his League debut, which he marked with the winning goal in a 2–1 victory at West Ham.

> The introduction to my Chelsea team-mates was a cracker. I arrived at Heathrow with Tommy Docherty to join the team on the way to Barcelona. It should have been an exciting moment but as soon as I

arrived in the gate area it was clear there was an atmosphere. The team was split in two factions that I would come to recognise quite quickly. There was the in-crowd with Ossie, Ron Harris, John Boyle, Marvin Hinton and co, and the out-group disenchanted with Tommy Doc, presumably led by Terry Venables, George Graham and Barry Bridges. It's all water under the bridge now of course, no pun intended, but it was indicative of the wild times ahead that were to become some of the best years in Chelsea's history.

My League debut was on a beautiful hot day, and the grass was green and plush and lovely to play on. I remember getting the ball around the halfway line and dribbling with it towards their goal. I beat someone on the edge of the box and hit a low left-foot shot from outside the box that beat Jim Standen at full stretch.

Bought to replace Terry Venables, Charlie's natural ability to carry the ball never quite freed him to be at his best in midfield, but he thrived when pushed wide. A deftness of touch and blur of intricate deception left the audience admiringly out of breath, and within two years Charlie was recognised as Player of the Year.

I played as a midfielder or a winger, whatever Chelsea needed at the time, which wasn't unusual as England had just won the 1966 World Cup with Sir Alf Ramsey's wingless wonders, and wingers went out of favour quickly in the next few years. I had some terrific seasons at Stamford Bridge. The first time I was awarded Chelsea's Player of the Year trophy [1968] I think was my best season. I was fit, strong and confident with a terrific team to play in – those surely were the days. I don't remember many details of the games, it all seemed to happen in such a rush which I regret now. We'd travel to Europe on Monday or Tuesday, then fly back Thursday, train or travel on Friday for an away game, then do it all over again. It seemed there was never time to sit down calmly and take it all in. You always remember your goals though. I recall especially a 25-yard first-time volley from the corner of the box against Fulham at Craven Cottage in December 1967, because of how clean the contact with the ball felt. It was a cracking good goal and gave the keeper no chance and helped us draw 2–2, my buddy Tommy Baldwin getting the other.

They say there are days in a sportsman's life when he can hear the mermaids sing. Cue the magical moment during the Old Trafford Cup final replay in

1970, where Leeds, in deep water, were torn apart by Charlie's gorgeous chip to Ossie.

> I was running with the ball in the middle of the Leeds half when I saw Ossie out of the corner of my eye towards the left of the Leeds box. I figured if I could float it across towards the six-yard line the big fella might have a chance at it. I chipped it as delicately as I could knowing it would have to float to give Ossie time to get there and it worked. Ossie launched himself beautifully for a great headed goal at full stretch.

Twelve months later Charlie redeemed a pedestrian Blues' performance in the Cup Winners' Cup final against Real Madrid. He started the move for Ossie's goal and took the game by the scruff of his neck, controlling play in midfield with his probing and pressing. In the replay Charlie was again in superb form in a narrow 2–1 victory.

His Chelsea career was in two parts, with a 16-month spell at Crystal Palace, where he was surprisingly sold in September 1972 for £85,000. On his return he found the club fortunes in decline, but a mature silkiness decorated his football.

> When I was transferred to Palace, Chelsea were undergoing a transitional period on and off the pitch. The new East Stand was under construction, leaving one side and end of the field without fans or atmosphere. We had lost the 1971 League Cup final at Wembley and Dave Sexton's relations with some of the more headstrong players, like Ossie and Alan Hudson had come to a head. Winds of change were definitely blowing, so it was no surprise that when Bert Head the manager at Crystal Palace came in for Paddy Mulligan and me, Chelsea accepted. Palace were a hard-working team with good guys like Tony Taylor and John Jackson and some promising youngsters, but little experience of the players at Chelsea and nothing seemed to go right that year. Games that should have been won were lost and goals given up that should never have been conceded. I remember one typical home game against Arsenal where we played well and went in front early yet still found a way to lose – it was a season of heartbreaks. When I returned Chelsea was a totally different club to the one I left. There was a drive towards youth and I suppose I was looked upon as the old head to steady the ship. It was certainly a role someone needed to play as the team was full of youngsters, some very good, some with reputations beyond their abilities and I think in some small way I helped fill the bill.

At the end of a turbulent 1974/75 season when the Blues were relegated, Charlie's form was a redeeming feature and he was again nominated Player of the Year, the fourth such accolade in his career. Thereafter his appearances became increasingly spasmodic and in 1976 he had a spell in America with Los Angeles Aztecs. An illustrious career in Britain drew to a close when Charlie finally left Chelsea at the beginning of 1978. He continued to play in the North American Soccer League.

> I came with my wife Diane and our son Chas to live in Los Angeles and play for the Aztecs where I played the previous summer on loan. Diane was from LA and we had always liked the idea of living there, although it almost felt like home with ex-Londoners Terry Mancini and Phil Beal and later George Best and John Craven among other ex-pats as team-mates. Over the next three years I also played for Eddie McCreadie at Memphis in the old NASL and ended my playing career with California Surf, coached by ex-Liverpool defender Peter Wall in Anaheim in 1983.
>
> Looking back the best defenders always seemed to play with the most successful sides. Leeds, for example, were a superb team – they moved the ball around beautifully, frustrating and tiring you. Paul Reaney sticks out as an excellent no-nonsense defender who never tried more than he was capable of. Terry Cooper on the opposite flank was more adventurous and a threat coming forward. Tommy Smith, for all his hard-man bluster which was real, was a terrific technician and an inspirational player – Liverpool at Anfield were always so tough. Our own Chopper Harris was true to his reputation, hard as nails, and quicker and tougher to get past than most gave him credit for. And Eddie McCreadie was as good a full-back as there was in the country, fast, skilful and tough.

Charlie was recalled to the Scotland team during the 1967/68 season. He was Man of the Match against England at Hampden Park and won 16 Scottish international caps in total, a meagre return in the context of his immense talent.

> My biggest regret is not winning more caps for the national team. After moving to England I felt Anglos were selected on sufferance behind the Rangers or Celtic or north of the border contenders. I think my attitude at the time reflected that and lots of youthful stupidity resulting in a couple of indiscretions on Scotland trips abroad that

made the headlines. I think that explains my chequered national team appearances that flourished early and late, but disappeared somewhere in the middle of my career.

Today we live in Cincinnati and I am director of Coerver Coaching USA, a worldwide youth soccer coaching programme. A cornerstone of the Coerver philosophy is that team systems and tactics are only as good as the individual players in it, and I am very proud of the contribution Coerver makes to youth coaching worldwide. The business of the game in Britain and worldwide has obviously changed with the huge increases in TV revenues and player salaries, but the influx of foreign stars was something the British game needed. For sure it has been an eye-opener for the coaching establishment about technical play and physical preparation and a good education for young British players on how others approach the game.

One highlight worth mentioning was playing for the World XI in Madrid against Spain at the Bernabeu in 1967. Ossie was due to play but was injured and I went with Peter Bonetti and Ian Ure of Arsenal. It was a testimonial for the Scottish international goalkeeper Zamora and there was some terrific talent on view including Burgnich, Corso and Rivera from Italy, Eusebio and Coluna from Portugal, and Hamrin from Sweden. The World XI manager was the defensive legend Helenio Herrera. I remember we joined the team for the pre-match meal and how different it was to the meal we were used to at Chelsea, where everyone had their own favourites from steak and chips to cornflakes or scrambled eggs. The world team sitting at one big table with Herrera at one end with a couple of slices of cold meat on each plate, some fruit in bowls and a very low-key atmosphere. The pre-match in the locker room was just as surprising. Herrera had everyone hopping and skipping in unison which we never did at Chelsea. Can you imagine all those big-name internationals who hardly knew each other's language or names, windmilling like a class of schoolgirls? The game itself was a cracker. Language was never a problem when we won 3–0 with a terrific team performance. I did pretty good too as I recall, although I could be biased!

CLIVE WALKER – 224 *appearances*

The weather on 7 May 1983 matched the sombre mood of Chelsea Football Club as the players journeyed to Burnden Park, Bolton. Clive Walker merits a place in the history of the club for his goal in this match alone, redeeming the Blues' embarrassment of succumbing to the Third Division for the first time. Born at Oxford in 1957, Clive joined Chelsea in 1972 and signed professional in April 1975.

> Oxford Schoolboys had a very strong side and at 15 years of age we got to the final of the English Schools trophy. Prior to that I trained with the England Schoolboys squad and played for them three times. There were a lot of scouts around and I had a number of invitations to go for trials. It came down to QPR or Chelsea, and I plumped for Chelsea, as they had done well in cup competitions, and Dario Gradi was the other main reason. He gave me a fantastic grounding and as a coach was second to none. He has done some wonderful things in his career and gave me ideas and principles that I stand by today.

Clive was soon creating waves alongside Tommy Langley, as the two accumulated 35 goals in the reserve side that won the Football Combination in the 1976/77 season. His full debut for the first team was at left-wing in October 1977, a 1–0 reverse at Newcastle.

> Tommy and I struck it off well – he played centre-forward and was as game as anything. I used to get behind defenders and put the ball in, which was ironic, as Tommy would readily admit he couldn't head it to save his life! To make your debut at Newcastle was quite an experience and I remember mainly fear! I have played there for Sunderland in a derby match since then, and the passion and noise level is incredible.

A gift for scoring dramatic goals became Clive's trademark, as his pace either through the middle or down the wing allowed him into advantageous positions. In his second full game Clive scored a brace against Wolves in a 3–1 win, then repeated that feat in the televised 4–2 drubbing of Liverpool in the third round of the FA Cup in January 1978.

> My second game sticks out, as to score twice was special. I remember

the goals vividly, one was a cross from Kenny Swain which I managed to get on the end of at the far post and swept it into the back of the net. The second one I picked the ball up deep and dribbled round Geoff Palmer, who I gave a torrid time, before rifling it into the bottom corner from the edge of the box. When we played Liverpool we were struggling in the First Division and on paper had no chance – it was like beating the team of the decade. To score twice again was special but also the fact the cameras were there, which didn't happen very often in those days. At the time the older players moved on as the club was in dire straits financially and had no choice but to go with youth. They were still trying to recover from the problems associated with the new stand. We had played together in the youth team and reserves, and were grateful for the opportunity to get a chance inside a year. Steve Wicks, Tommy Langley, Ian Britton and Ray Wilkins were good young lads coming in to try and fill a void. Looking back we struggled so it was nice to have a cup run.

As confidence ebbed away during the 1978/79 campaign, the youngsters struggled to find any consistency, and relegation to the Second Division became inevitable. However, Clive was able to escape the turmoil at the end of the season.

I went to Fort Lauderdale in the summer with Garry Stanley. They wanted a winger and a midfielder and towards the end of the season their general manager came over and a loan period was agreed. We played at Old Trafford on the Wednesday, I flew to Fort Lauderdale on the Friday and played on the Sunday. George Best and Gerd Muller played for us, which was fantastic and the standard of football was quite good. I scored a couple of hat tricks out there and had a fabulous time.

A rejuvenated Clive returned to the Bridge full of optimism for an early return to the First Division. The reality was that the side were not good enough, despite Clive enjoying two seasons where his pace was used to great effect through the middle. Thirteen League goals earned him the Player of the Year award in 1980, but when further managerial changes brought John Neal to the club in 1981, Clive's fortunes slowly worsened.

We wanted to win the Second Division in 1979/80, as we genuinely thought with another year's experience we could bounce straight back. We had a great young Chelsea side, but we didn't have a strong manager to steer us through those times. When Geoff Hurst was in charge I played in the middle for two years with Colin Lee. By Christmas in the first year we were top of the Second Division, and the second season Colin scored 15 and I scored 11. I loved it and when I look back now should have played more in that position.

John Neal had a way about him which I didn't understand, and he was the beginning of my downfall at Chelsea. Being involved with a London club all my career, for a Geordie to come down with his canny ways, as he called them, didn't quite fit in with me. Likewise Ian McNeill was a Scot with his own ideas and I clashed with him on many occasions.

Clive maintained an impressive strike rate from a wide position, with a further 16 League goals in the 1981/82 season. Despite frequently playing with two wingers, competition for places intensified with an abundance of wide players and Clive felt increasingly marginalised.

After many years at the club I had a problem with the way I was being treated. From being Player of the Year, two years later I was an outcast and it hurt, as I felt Chelsea was my club. I was behind Paul Canoville, Peter Rhoades-Brown and Phil Driver, and wasn't even getting a game, which I resented.

A reminder of his value came at the end of the 1982/83 season, with the club in serious relegation trouble. In the taut end-of-season match at Bolton highlighted earlier, a determined Chelsea performance was typified by captain Micky Droy. As the rain arrowed down, the ball was released in the 71st minute by Paul Canoville to Clive on the left. From 25 yards out, he unleashed a shot which swerved wickedly into the top corner to secure arguably the most important win in the club's history. The joy of supporters and players alike was unconfined. A week later a goalless draw at home to Middlesbrough enabled the Blues to escape by two points.

Just before the game John Neal asked Micky Droy what he felt he should do. I hadn't been playing regularly, but Micky said play me and bring back Paul Canoville – the rest is history. Some people still talk about that occasion and it is close to me because of what it meant for the club. But it was more important to those 3,500 fans in the pouring rain that the club weren't allowed to get relegated. It's nice to be remembered for that goal in my Chelsea career. Whilst it was the most significant one I scored for the club, the most memorable goal for me personally was the second one against Wolves. I would like to think it was a trademark goal in that I scored many similar ones over the years.

Ironically, Clive was enjoying some of the most consistent form of his career when injury forced him to drop out of the first team after six League games of the 1983/84 season. With the arrival of Pat Nevin, Clive was unable to regain his place and he was transferred to Sunderland for £75,000 in July 1984 at the end of the promotion-winning season. Clive had scored a highly commendable 65 goals but departed with more than a twinge of sadness.

I didn't personally think John Neal did as much for the club as others felt. We were in the Second Division and nearly got relegated, which would have been disastrous, then John Hollins came [as coach] and we won the League. The players were already there, but Hollins got them together. The last year I played I signed a one-year contract purely and simply because I loved Chelsea Football Club. We had been through so many managers, the team were still not doing well but I wanted to stick it out another year, for the people and fans. In a cynical way, I also thought perhaps Neal would be sacked and someone else might come in who would want me to stay. I only got a game at the start of the season as other players were absent. I played for the reserves in a pre-season friendly behind closed doors the week before. Usually you knew by then if you were going to start in the first team and I had a blinder. People were saying to me that I'd be in the first team, but I knew I wouldn't. Then Peter Rhoades-Brown was injured and I knew I had to play well to stay in the team, otherwise I would have been dropped. I played really well but got injured, which was rare for me.

Sunderland had good value out of Clive, who enjoyed prime form during his first season. He was their 1985 Milk Cup hero, scoring vital goals against Tottenham and Watford, to set up a semi-final clash against his old side. A clinical two-goal performance in the second leg gave Sunderland victory 5–2 on aggregate.

I had mixed emotions in the semi-final, it was really strange playing Chelsea in such a big game a year after being transferred. We'd won the first leg 2–0 at Sunderland, and there was a lot of feeling and hype in the build-up for the second leg. I didn't go out thinking I had a point to prove, as I had been there for 11 years. I looked at it foremost as a professional doing a job. It was nice for me personally, although scoring at the Shed end without them saying a word was very different! It was very scary when the lunatic side of football came on the pitch to blame me [for Chelsea's defeat]. I think they should have vented their anger on the board and manager for letting me go.

What should have been a highlight proved a massive anti-climax for Clive when on the losing side at Wembley in a 1–0 defeat against Norwich. There were several reasons for a below-par performance.

I was very disappointed to be let down by the Sunderland directors, who treated the players badly prior to the final. The training facilities were abysmal and we were thrown off the training pitch the day before the final. The board organised everything poorly and the ticket allocation was a joke, as was the way they looked after the wives. They took the tickets the players would normally have had behind the Royal Box and it all affected the morale of the players. It was a flat game and I felt sorry for the supporters, who didn't know what was going on. I missed a penalty, which was the biggest disappointment for me, but when I look back now the board got what they deserved. The Sunderland people remember me as the man who missed the penalty, which I understand, but I would also like to be remembered as having scored in every round up to the final – I think I did my bit to get there.

Clive did fulfil one of his ambitions when he scored a hat trick at Roker Park against Manchester United, which he supported as a boy, in November 1984. He moved to QPR a year later, but struggled to break into the first team and was soon isolated at Loftus Road. Fulham manager and former Chelsea colleague Ray Lewington rescued his career in October 1987 and Clive repaid his faith when top-scoring with 15 goals in the 1989/90 season.

My biggest mistake in football was going to QPR. Having played on the plastic pitch I knew it didn't suit my game, so it was my own fault. It was not a winger's pitch, but I thought perhaps I could change my game. Being a Chelsea boy it was also difficult to win over the fans, which I never did and it affected the mental side of my game. My other problem was with the chairman Jim Gregory, who stuck me in the reserves, left me to rot and didn't let me go. I was there for two years and he never spoke to me. I actually left when he was on holiday and

Jim Smith, the manager, was away scouting in Spain. The deal was done in five days with Peter Shreeves, the assistant and the vice-chairman, so I got out quick!

It poured down with rain on my Fulham debut against York, but I scored two goals, which made it easier to win the fans over. I was scoring from wide positions and obtained that edge of confidence again, which is especially important for a wide player. The supporters were great and I enjoyed it back on grass. People have highlighted the inconsistencies in my career, but in my position a lot of inconsistencies came from not getting the ball. People say that's your fault, but a winger is one of the hardest positions to be consistent in and confidence plays such a big part. It's not easy attacking defenders, especially when you think they're going to chop you in half, which was their aim every time you tangled with them.

Clive moved on to Brighton in August 1990 for £20,000. He defied advancing years by returning to Wembley in his first season, this time for the Second Division play-off final in June 1991 against Notts County.

I was aware of Barry Lloyd's interest at Brighton and Alan Dicks the Fulham manager wanted me to go. I initially said no, but Barry came back and I spoke to a couple of players there, including Gary Chivers. It was a nice move and also a step up, as Brighton were in the Second Division and I enjoyed my time there. At 33 I was offered a two-year contract, for which I was grateful, and ended up getting a one-year extension, but unfortunately I didn't get the goals I scored elsewhere. We played Manchester United and Liverpool in the Cup and I remember playing Millwall in the play-offs when Keith Stevens sent me into the advertising hoardings and I thought I had broken my arm. It put me out for the second leg but we won at Millwall and played at Wembley. I hit the post with a header in the first half and was Man of the Match, but we disappointingly lost 3–1.

After over 500 senior appearances, scoring in excess of 100 goals, Clive joined non-League Woking at the start of the 1993/94 season and found further success, albeit in a modified role.

As a pro I learnt how to play wide, but I scored 108 goals over four years at Woking and learnt how to play upfront. If I'd done that at Chelsea and scored half that number I would have been happy. We won the FA Trophy three times under Geoff Chapple, whose record was second to none. In my last season, although we won the Trophy final we finished fifth in the League, which was a failure for Woking. When Geoff left the new manager John McGovern didn't want me, possibly because I had been there a long time and he was frightened of me. I was offered a one-year contract, but with less money, so turned it down. I felt I had done a lot for the club and wasn't getting the recognition I deserved. I could still play at Conference level, but Woking pushed me out of the door.

Clive was soon given the scope to taste football management. He accepted a post as assistant to Eddie May at Brentford in August 1987, but both were sacked after just three months.

I'd done my coaching badges and had the opportunity to become assistant manager at Brentford, or so I thought! It was a great opening for me, but once I got there I realised I'd made a mistake, as David Webb gave myself and Eddie a really hard time. He'd sold the best players a few months previously and there was no money whatsoever. We had nothing to work with and the good thing was that it was only three months of hell. It came to an end sooner rather than later and I hoped it wouldn't damage my managerial prospects too much.

At an age when last orders are called on the field of play, the boots were out again, as the ever-green Clive added Cheltenham of the Conference League to his list of clubs.

I had seen their manager Steve Cotterill, who played on loan at Brighton, at a Brentford reserve game and actually told him I was going to get the sack. When it happened he was on the phone the next day, along with about four other clubs wanting me. Cheltenham had just got into the Conference and there was a buzz of expectancy about the place. I signed in November 1997 and had to get match fit again, but I came on as sub in my first game, a Cup tie and scored the winner with two minutes to go. It was great and we went on to win the FA Trophy. I played until the end of the 1998/99 season, when we got promoted to the Football League, and decided at 42 it was time to retire.

When I left Cheltenham I played a few friendlies in the summer, including a game for Chelsea Veterans at Molesey. Their chairman asked me to play for them in Division Two of the Ryman League, but I was having trouble with both my Achilles and said I was only interested in coaching or managing. He came to see me again and I watched them – they were a young side and I agreed to go as player-coach. I had nine months rest, which did me good and the Achilles seemed to be OK. Eventually the manager left and on New Year's Day 2001 I took over as player-manager. I might make myself sub next year on a few occasions, but don't intend playing regularly!

A crowd favourite, Clive maintained his fitness long after many fellow pros called it a day, despite the best efforts of the exhaustive list of full-backs he faced, and also one of his club colleagues.

The hardest defender I played against was Ron Harris in training. He'd kick us as hard as he did in a proper match, but that was just the way he was. You always picked him in your five-a-side team! Technically Steve Perryman was a difficult defender to play against – he was bright and wouldn't dive in. Kenny Sansom was another great defender, very quick and stood up. I have been very fortunate with injuries, I got hacked to pieces but didn't suffer any long-term damage, which is where experience comes into it. Enthusiasm and adrenaline keep me going and I stay fit just by playing games. I love playing in the Masters tournament for Chelsea and I've also played for a European team in the Sevens for the last couple of years in Hong Kong.

Since I left Brighton I've scratched around doing various jobs. I was an auctioneer for three years, which I loved tremendously, and did corporate hospitality for a year. Now I'm involved with Paul Walsh in a new TV channel, The Footballers' Football Channel, which went on the air in August on the Sky digital platform. It is totally football orientated, which is a really exciting concept. I have also moved into commentating on Brazilian football, which we send to the American and Middle/Far East market – the Brazilian names are a bit of a test!

PAT NEVIN – 242 *appearances*

Probably the most cerebral player in the history of the club, Pat Nevin was always going to be his own man from the day he arrived at Chelsea, nodding to his Walkman and clutching a novel by Albert Camus. An immensely talented and skilful individual, Pat took the Bridge by storm with his traditional Scottish ball-playing skills. He followed Charlie Cooke in the entertainment stakes and was a constant reminder of why we got so excited about the game in the first place. Born in Glasgow in 1963, Pat showed an apparent affinity with the Blues at eight years old.

My first football kit was a blue one, a Chelsea one – I remember the nylony feel of it! My father bought it for me when I was only a wee kid, I really liked it and used to go out all the time wearing it. It was really surreal as I was a Celtic fan and I can't really tell you why he bought it – it might have been going cheap! Chelsea were trendy at the time, but I never subsequently said I was always a Chelsea fan.

I didn't really have idols as a kid – I don't think you should idolise people, but I quite liked the way Jimmy Johnstone played. My dad gave me one of his coaching books with this method of dribbling round cones – the technique is very similar to what is practised today by Will Coerver. When I supported Celtic it was really the end of Jimmy's time, but the start of Kenny Dalglish, who was a world-class player. David Hay was one of my favourite players, and I also rated Danny McGrain highly.

I was always a centre-forward, although I was put on the wing a couple of times for a Glasgow skills select team, as Maurice Johnston was the centre-forward and scored slightly more goals than me. I was at Celtic on schoolboy forms for four years, but they turned me down as they told me I wasn't good enough. There was no bitterness, I have never been bitter about anything, but I did stop playing for a little. My first reaction was OK, I'll go and support the team all over the country, but after a while I drifted back into playing again.

Completely unfazed by this setback, Pat's football career was sidelined for a while until his destiny was shaped when he embarrassed several defenders in a seemingly meaningless match in 1981.

I started playing at Gartcosh for David Skinner, who had seen me play for Celtic Boys – he actually brought John Millar down to Chelsea. One day we played Clyde and I had a bet with a mate I could dribble the ball more than he could and score. I went round five and scored – Craig Brown was their manager and the rest . . . ruined my life! I said to Craig I didn't want to move into football at that point, I didn't think I was good enough and was a year into my degree. He offered me £30 a week and I felt relaxed and comfortable, so did it purely for fun, nothing else. It really brought it home to me that it didn't matter if I failed, and maybe that helped when I went to Chelsea. It's not that I didn't care, I always worried that I was giving value for money. It was my education that made it possible for me to have a career in football. I had this as a safety net.

I was the Divisional Player of the Year at 17, which I never expected. It was a nightmare, as I had to go down to the PFA awards dinner. At the same time I'd sneaked off some exams to play in Finland with the Scottish Under-18s in the European Championships. I didn't realise at the time how big the tournament was and told my teacher I wasn't well. I hadn't told the girl I was with at the time I played football and said I was busy studying. I scored two in the final which we won and was Player of the Tournament. I didn't know I was banner headlines all over the papers in Scotland, and when I came back my girlfriend said, 'Have you been studying well?' I said, 'Yeah, yeah!' and felt a right twat! There was a deeper reason why I didn't want her to know I was a footballer. I wanted to get away from people liking me because I was a footballer and that's always been a part of me. I've always been wary of not knowing who your real friends are, it takes a long time for me to develop true friendships.

As Chelsea sought to escape the wilderness that had enveloped them, the relatively unknown Pat signed for the team in May 1983, after badgering from assistant manager Ian McNeill, who not only staked £95,000 on the 19-year-old but also his reputation.

I only became a winger in my second year at Clyde and was really happy, it was a breeze. We won the League, which was the highlight and I was having a lovely time when Ian McNeill came up. I've got this habit of saying no all the time and, as my personal happiness was more important to me, I said I didn't want to go to Chelsea. I never had any big aims in professional football, but six months later he came back. I had played in the World Under-19 Championships in Mexico [1983], which meant I had missed my final exams. I looked at it as a two-year sabbatical at Chelsea, which was a seriously logical thing to do. If I failed my exams I had a job for two years. If I passed I could always tell Chelsea to get lost but, of course, it went really well right from the start. Ian will tell you he put his job on the line for me. Ken Bates said, 'You want me to put money on that small, skinny lad?' Ian had watched me a lot, but I wouldn't have risked it if I'd been in his shoes! It was a big chance to take and I learnt a lot from Ian, but even more from John Neal.

Pat was unable to join his new team-mates immediately, as on the eve of the new season he took re-sits of his business studies degree in Glasgow. Instead he travelled south to play for the reserves.

As it happened I passed my re-sits and played my first Chelsea game at Luton. It was the day Derby were beaten 5–0 [September 1983] and in the dressing-room everyone told us what a great game that was. Tony McAndrew and I went, 'Yes' when we heard the result and everyone else went, 'S**t!' From that moment I knew the one person I would get on with in that dressing-room was Tony, as he had exactly the same attitude I had. His heart and soul were in it and I admired him from then on. I made my first-team debut soon after and scored my first goal at Fulham [October 1983]. I don't remember goals unless they are on tape, but a Colin Lee shot fell to me from the keeper. Two defenders came towards me and I dummied past one and put it into the back of the net. Kerry scored a couple and it was a brilliant day.

In an age of systems and organisation, the idea that players have a moral duty to entertain fell into disrepute years ago. Pat felt uneasy about compromising success on the pitch, so he invariably managed both! The 4–0 demolition of Newcastle in November 1983 was a typical example. The fans had already warmed to his dribbling and, with Chelsea 3–0 up, Pat felt it time to indulge in a spot of 'showboating' – the spontaneous cries of wonderment were a tribute to the magic in his boots.

It's difficult for me to answer, but I felt my main responsibility on the pitch was to give pleasure and enjoyment. I never went out to take the p**s out of players, but when I showboated, if it got a good reaction, I'd do it again. On occasions I went out deliberately to do it, like at Newcastle I said to Johnny Bumstead at the start of the second half if we scored early I was going to have a laugh. When we scored in the first minute of the second half, I just went out to enjoy myself. My dad used to say, 'Try one of your mad, mazy runs in every single game.' Much later Ernie Walley could not hack that concept at all.

Chelsea fans will need no reminding how good a vintage the 1983/84 team became. The Second Division Championship was won in style at Grimsby. Pat's support to the front two was key.

Scottish wingers have always been known as dribblers, maybe because of the build. They didn't have the build to be pacy – Jimmy Johnstone was not quick, people from the West Central Scotland are generally quite light because of their diet, health etc. When Scottish players come to England they have to adapt their game. For the first two years I rarely shot, as I thought I should take people on, then give it to somebody. I thought as a winger all I wanted to do was create goals. I was a natural centre-forward myself, so I had to adapt to playing this wider role. When the chances came I had a good percentage, but specifically thought my job was to create and win the games. If I look back at the stats and find I created 30 goals for Kerry and 20 for Speedo, then I was happy with that. I got far more pleasure making the goal for Kerry in the last game at Grimsby than any goals I scored [Pat couldn't recall his two against Barnsley in the game before – 'blank'.] The occasion was fantastic, although I missed a penalty as well – we were a good young side and just wanted to win.

I was just loving it, then going away and forgetting about it. I walked home or got the bus or tube after a game and tried to keep myself as normal as possible, going to gigs etc. I was very dedicated but not part of the establishment. I did long-distance running all the time and loved it. I thought nothing of going for 15-mile runs along the Embankment during the week. It was very unusual at the time but John Millar, then Graeme Le Saux later, came back in the afternoons to practise free kicks or dribbling skills. You need someone to work with and I was out on the wing, and it just so happened the two people I got on with were left-backs. I hope it benefited them, it certainly helped me.

The ease with which the Blues adapted to life in the top tier came as no surprise to Pat, who was helped by John Neal's willingness to allow him to express himself.

It was a natural assumption we would do well in the First Division, as I had played 18 months with Clyde and we won the League, I played with Scotland Youth team and we won the European Championships, and with Chelsea we won the Second Division. I was a terrible loser in those days and would be fed up for the rest of the weekend. The sad thing about it was when we won, I wasn't deliriously happy for the whole weekend. It was a stupid situation as I was only happy for about an hour and should have allowed myself to be a bit happier!

I would sit in the dressing-room listening to music with my headphones on until five minutes before kick-off. Colin Pates will tell you in my second season, it got to that time just before kick-off and when I asked him who we were playing he said, 'Man United!' I really hadn't bothered much about the opposition – it felt as if I didn't care, but I did. John Neal had just one coaching method for me – he used to do his team talk then say, 'And then give the ball to Pat.' How did he know I wasn't going to crumble under that [responsibility] as I was pretty quiet in the dressing-room? He just seemed to know my response would be, 'That's excellent.'

A regular member of the Under-21s in 1984/85, Pat made his full Scottish debut in 1986 as substitute against Romania. He won five more caps with Chelsea and further domestic success came in the 1986 Full Members' Cup final.

The cameras were at Wembley, so I remember making a couple of goals for Speedo, one in particular was at the back post for him, which I was delighted at. But I do remember experiencing very little personal joy at that time, it was more for my friends and the fans, who had waited a long time for a day at Wembley. I had a lovely day, but to put it into perspective, it was the Full Members' Cup.

Pat's lasting popularity was demonstrated by his winning the Player of the Year award in 1984 and 1987. His final Chelsea goal was a 20-yarder in the first leg of the 2–0 semi-final play-off win at Blackburn in May 1988.

The Chelsea fans were behind the goal and it came to my feet. I gave it 'the eyes' going one way and curled it the other. That was one of my better ones, a longer-range effort. I played against one of my best pals John Millar and felt sorry for him, as it meant so much to him and he was desperate that day.

Pat's last game for the Blues was less pleasant – the frantic and tearful denouement of the second-leg play-off final a fortnight later at home to Middlesbrough. Both John Hollins and Bobby Campbell were said to have stifled his natural game.

> The hardest time for me was when we got relegated. The Middlesbrough play-off was my second worst moment in football, especially as I knew before the game I was leaving Chelsea. I don't want to go into detail but I knew I was going, not that I wanted to, there's a big difference. Various newspapers said I was deserting a sinking ship, but that wasn't the case. It was an unfair season as, if we hadn't have lost Eddie Niedzwiecki early on, we would not have got relegated. He was an integral part of our team, I thought he was becoming world-class and we never fully recovered from that. The fans were ridiculously, stupidly nice, brilliant to me at Chelsea for a long time, unfairly so, I didn't deserve it. When I left I had no bitterness but I would have loved to have stayed – I was delighted to have been there five years.
>
> When people ask me what was the highlight of my career, it was when I was walking back to my home at Earls Court after a Chelsea game and I was accosted by an old guy. He said he hadn't seen football for 20 or 30 years and he admired my style and the kind of football I was playing and the entertainment value. He said how much he enjoyed it and it made me feel good. It's as simple as that – the feeling that you have given someone so much pleasure, and he actually made the effort to talk to me. He walked away and I never heard from him again, but it made a deep impression on me, one I'll never forget.
>
> My best goal was the equaliser against Arsenal at the Bridge in September 1985. I picked the ball up in midfield, played it out wide and scored with a diving header from the cross. We won 2–1 and I was brought down for the winning penalty. I've never been known to dive, so it was a definite foul. I don't remember all that many good goals for Chelsea, strangely enough most of my better goals seemed to be for Tranmere or Kilmarnock. I scored 19 in a season for Tranmere, including a lot of lobs and scoops etc.

Pat's signature was sealed on a move to Everton for a fee of £925,000 in July 1988. Although he was in the side that was defeated by Liverpool in the final of the FA Cup in his first season, the Wembley event was overshadowed by Hillsborough, which devastated the deep-thinking Scot.

When I left Chelsea I had the option of either Everton or Paris St Germain, and everyone thought I would have picked Paris. I got on with Colin Harvey at Everton, but not so with Howard Kendall. There was a more rigid style of play and I couldn't showboat there, whatever the score. The worst football moment in my life was an hour after I scored the goal to get Everton into the 1989 Cup final, the news came through about the Hillsborough disaster.

Pat was loaned to Tranmere Rovers towards the end of the 1991/92 season. He played eight games and signed permanently in the 1992/93 close season for a then record fee of £300,000. Over the next five years, Pat appeared in a further 231 games for Rovers. In his first full season Pat's international career was revived, becoming the first-ever Tranmere player to represent Scotland at full international level.

I first went on loan to Tranmere, than had a choice between Galatasaray and Rovers. I went over to 'Gala' and it was a tough decision, because I would like to have had a go abroad at some point, but it would have been difficult coming back to a higher standard. The first few years at Tranmere were brilliant, I scored all my Scotland goals [five] while I was there, and had a great run for my country. Of my 28 games I won 12 caps there, so I was delighted with that. It was very strange, however, that when I scored one and made three against the Faroe Islands, it proved to be my last international, as the Scottish media didn't like me. I scored a lot of goals for Tranmere [39] but made a lot more for John Aldridge, he was amazing. He was real world-class and at Liverpool, as Kenny Dalglish adapted, Aldo also adapted his game. When Aldo was appointed manager he wanted to change things, so I left.

Pat returned to Scotland with Kilmarnock in 1997, before being installed as player/chief executive at Motherwell in September 1998. He demonstrably proved there was no conflict between the two roles, especially since he was involved in appointing manager Billy Davies, who did not renew Pat's playing contract at the end of the 1999/2000 season. Fittingly for a Celtic fan, Pat's last senior game was a cameo appearance as substitute in Motherwell's 2–0 win over Rangers at Fir Park.

The two happiest years of my career were my first year at Chelsea and the one at 'Killie'. I was playing some of the best football of my career, still as winger but in a modified role. What helped was that there were people around me that I liked. My move to Motherwell came about because of a disagreement over a broken promise. I always honoured my contracts and had a three-year contract at Killie. I am a principled person and never told my story. The only time I've ever been booed was when I went back there, but they didn't know the whole story. There was no conflict of interest between myself and Billy Davies when I became chief executive. Anyway he didn't renew my contract, so it's obvious I don't completely control him. It's important at Motherwell we try to do something different to attract the fans and the chairman introduced the cut-price admission scheme. Kids can watch us for two quid and I'm sure the Chelsea public would be impressed that they can watch the likes of John Spencer for that.

The most difficult defender I faced was a tiny, quick 18-year-old reserve full-back at Bradford. He had a lower gravity than myself, which I usually used to my advantage. The easiest defender to pass in my life was Andreas Brehme, the German full-back. I'm not saying he was a bad player, but some players suited you. The only person who can beat you is yourself – if you are on form on the day, you can beat anyone. I admired Doug Rougvie, who I felt was quite harshly treated on a number of occasions. I lived with him and his wife for a while at the end of one season, when he was getting a bit of stick, which affected his family. I realised it was serious, being quite a carefree guy and thought if ever I had a family, I would make sure it didn't happen, not that it did. My wife and kids are very cool about it all.

I am married to Annabel and we have two children, Simon, ten, and Lucy, six. I don't have time to read as much as I used to and am in to talking books nowadays in the car. I still write for the odd newspaper but less now, because my job takes up most of my time. I love the football analyst role, which I have done mostly on Radio Five, but I've also done some TV work for Channel Five. If I could do any job full-time it would be this one. I must be getting lazy and old!

DRAKE'S DUCKLINGS

The Chelsea Youth Scheme, founded in 1947 under the name 'Tudor Rose', was the inspiration of Billy Birrell. Other clubs were recognising the value of investing in youth, albeit some employed unorthodox techniques. Wolves manager Frank Buckley was particularly adept at spotting youngsters and gave them monkey-gland supplements because he thought it would sharpen their thinking. He also paired them up on the halfway line and made them dance to music played over the tannoy in order to improve their footwork. Few would argue with the Major, especially when all but three of the 1949 FA Cup-winning side were 'Buckley Boys'.

Chief Scout was Jimmy Thompson, no slouch himself on the football field, with 34 goals in just 42 games for Chelsea in the late 1920s. He is fondly remembered for his persuasive approach, which attracted the cream of talent to the club, often from the East End under the nose of West Ham United. His methods could also be unorthodox, but he was a superb judge of a footballer and enjoyed the sobriquet of 'Champion Rolling Stone'.

The driving force of the Youth Scheme was Dickie Foss, supported by Albert Tennant until he became first-team coach in 1953. By his own admission, Dick's development as a footballer was unspectacular. He played for amateur clubs Wood Green, Hitchin and Park Royal, and was skipper of the Southall team that made history in the FA Cup when playing through the qualifying rounds to reach the Third Round proper, finally losing to Watford. A shrewd reader of the game, Dick came to Chelsea in 1936 as a wing-half or inside-forward. He played the majority of the time in wartime football and one of his greatest ambitions was achieved in 1945 when he appeared in the Cup final-winning side against Millwall at Wembley. When Dick did not appear in Billy Birrell's post-war plans, the development of youth football was a natural progression and he was formally appointed Youth Manager in 1952. Dick's honest, disciplined style focused on exposing and eliminating errors, and his mantra of quality football was taken for granted and rarely discussed. His crucial efforts are felt by many of his protégés to have been understated in the history of the club. Dick continued to steer the youth side until retirement in the late 1960s.

The Juniors first played in February 1948, a London Minor Challenge Cup game against Durnsford Rangers. The programme notes were prophetically penned, 'It will be an occasion of pride and importance . . . may today be the first of many occasions which the future will hold when a number who joined the Chelsea Youth Scheme will enter our famous arena, later, we hope, as members of the Chelsea first eleven.'

Two youth teams initially played on Saturdays at the Welsh Harp, Hendon ground. The 'A' side played in the Harrow, Wembley and District Youth League, while the 'B' team were members of the Harrow Local Youth Committee League. It was 'Mr' Tennant or Foss, never 'Albert' or 'Dickie', who always tried to watch their pupils in action, subject to their Football Combination and Eastern Counties commitments. When unable to attend, they asked each boy to submit a written report on their own performance.

It wasn't always easy to assess which players would succeed. Teenagers might be conscientious trainers and good listeners on coaching techniques, but the simple fact is that some of them went so far and then, for various reasons (temperament, lack of determination, loss of form, uncertainty etc), suffered premature erosion. There were of course many natural footballers whose potential was always going to be fulfilled, Jimmy Greaves being the prime example.

The policy started to bear fruit in the 1952/53 season, when the youth side won the South-East Counties Cup. Jimmy Thompson's scouting net took him not only to all parts of London, but he also trawled the south of England from the south coast to East Anglia. The quality of intake can be measured from the South-East Counties League table, which the youth side headed for nine consecutive seasons from 1954/55, with the exception of 1955/56, when they finished a modest second. The South-East Counties Cup was won on four further occasions in the 1950s and the Southern Junior Floodlit Cup three times. Success was also secured at international youth tournaments in Holland.

Dick Foss's greatest triumph was to secure the FA Youth Cup, the junior equivalent of the FA Cup in the 1959/60 and 1960/61 seasons, after a long and patient wait. The 1957/58 side had a golden opportunity, winning the first leg of the final at the Bridge 5–1 against Wolves, thanks to Harrison (with 2 goals), Greaves, Block and Bridges. The second leg was a calamity, as Wolves ran out 6–1 winners and 6–5 on aggregate, Greaves scoring the consolation goal. In 1959/60 Chelsea were held to a 1–1 draw in the first game of the final at the Bridge by Preston North End, Bert Murray scoring. With Peter Bonetti replacing Barry Smart in goal and Terry Venables the driving force in midfield, the second leg was won in convincing manner. Bobby Tambling bagged a hat trick and a fourth goal from Gordon Bolland made the score 4–1. The following season Everton were the visitors to the Bridge in the first leg, with another 4–1 scoreline, this time a hat trick from Bert Murray and another from Bolland. Gillingwater scored in the return match as the youngsters went down 2–1.

The next step was the most difficult – for the graduates of Dick's prolific academy to break into Ted Drake's first team. Ted assured himself of a permanent place in the record books when he scored seven goals out of eight for Arsenal at Aston Villa in 1935: 'I had eight shots – seven went in and the other came back off the crossbar.' He managed Reading prior to his appointment at Chelsea in May 1952, long before a revolving door was fitted to the managerial office at the Bridge. At once he instigated a programme of change, designed to allow Chelsea to be seen as a more progressive club. He successfully rebuilt the side with a number of shrewd signings at a time when the key to the Stamford Bridge trophy room had not turned for fifty years. Ted also overcame the music-hall prejudices to secure the club's first League Championship, his outstanding highlight in football.

In the 1950s the Busby Babes, of course, shot to fame, and Matt Busby's scouts and talent spotters would watch more than 5,000 youngsters in one season. Ted was well aware that his reliance on experience in the Championship side would necessitate early change and, like Busby, Drake's Ducklings were a pivotal element in his strategy. Ted believed in catching them young: 'I have to, otherwise they either go to an amateur club, settle into a job and do not want to become a professional, or else they stop playing after leaving school and are lost to the game altogether.' Perhaps prematurely, Ted jettisoned too much experience for youth during the latter part of the 1950s in his desire to secure further success. It was asking a lot of youngsters to come straight into the First Division and survive.

Possibly because of his own background the most successful products of Drake's Ducklings were forwards. In September 1956 he blooded what was thought to be the youngest forward line in Chelsea's history against Leeds, earning a goalless draw. Frank Blunstone at 21 was the oldest and the only player who did not come through the youth scheme. The other starlets were Les Allen, at 18 making his League debut, Peter Brabrook (18), Ron Tindall (20) and Tony Nicholas (20).

In the 1957/58 season Ted bravely spurned the transfer market – not a single fee was paid out for a player. For the 2–2 draw against West Brom in September 1957, Mike Block made his first-team debut alongside Brabrook, Greaves, Tindall and Nicholas. With an average age of 18½, it was again Chelsea's youngest-ever forward line. Ted continued to place his faith in youth, and against Preston in February 1958 the average age of the forward line was 18 years 11 months, with Brabrook, Greaves, Allen, Block and David Cliss all graduating through the junior ranks, as had 27 others in a professional staff of 47. It was a proud occasion for Jimmy Thompson, all five being Thompson boys, the realisation of an ambition.

In 1958/59 Ted again turned his back on the transfer market, as more than a dozen teenagers appeared in the first team, and his confidence seemed justified when Chelsea climbed to second place at the end of September. Free of the contemporary baggage of managerial ego, Ted was more concerned with the youngsters demonstrating how good they could be, and in February 1959 took what he described as 'the greatest gamble of my career'. The much-vaunted tenderfoots were beginning to make their presence felt as once more he selected the youngest forward line which Chelsea – and probably any other First Division club – had ever fielded; Brabrook, who was 20; Cliss, 19; Bridges, 17; Greaves, 18; and Tambling, 17. For Barry Bridges and Bobby Tambling it was their first games in League football. And they were facing one of the most powerful sides in the country, West Ham. But both scored in a 3–2 win.

Despite (and perhaps because of) the commendable initiative, the side was unable to achieve any sort of consistency in the League and Ted ultimately paid the price when leaving the club in September 1961. In later years he became a director at Fulham and died aged 82, in 1995. His successor gratefully accepted an unprecedented windfall of excellent youngsters to form 'Docherty's Diamonds'.

LES ALLEN

A neat, constructive forward with a fine turn of speed, Les Allen first attracted attention when at 16 he assisted Briggs Sports to reach the semi-final of the Amateur Cup. He signed professional at Chelsea on his 17th birthday in 1954, and made his debut against Leeds United in 1956, playing outside-right instead of his usual position in the middle of the forward line. A fortnight later he moved to centre-forward against Birmingham City and by the end of the season had scored five goals in 19 League games. Les was unable to displace Ron Tindall from the number nine slot and, after 49 games and 11 goals, in December 1959 he moved to Spurs in exchange for Johnny Brooks. He was the final piece of the Nicholson jigsaw puzzle and became an integral part of Spurs' 1960/61 League and FA Cup double team, playing in every League game and scoring 23 goals. With an accurate right-foot shot and excellent positional sense, Les also had a calm temperament and was well respected for his sportsmanship.

After the arrival of Jimmy Greaves in 1961, Les found opportunity restrictive and eventually moved to QPR in July 1965 for £20,000 and was top Third Division marksman with 30 goals in his first year. He pulled off another double in the 1966/67 season, helping QPR win the Third Division title and defeating West Brom 3–2 in the League Cup final. His experience was vital as Rangers eased through the Second to First Division, and was the only player-manager in the First Division when appointed midway through the 1968/69 season. Les moved to Swindon Town in 1972, taking over the manager's job from Dave Mackay weeks after joining as Chief Scout. From a talented footballing family, son Clive and nephew Paul, of course, made names for themselves and Les, who lives in Hornchurch, is now a model-maker.

MIKE BLOCK

Mike was another winger who relied on pace to outwit his marker. He also scored many goals with his powerful shooting and direct method.

Jimmy Thompson saw me play at Selhurst Park for England Schoolboys against Wales. Len Darling, who played for Brighton, was the head teacher at my school at Cobblestone Road, Ipswich. He was in contact with Ted Drake and said I would go to Chelsea as soon as I left school. However I had actually signed for Ted Fenton at West Ham six months before my 15th birthday. He said he would put the forms in the safe as it was illegal to sign before you left school. Being a country boy I was young and naive – my head was spinning and all I wanted to do was play football. When I said I thought I'd made a mistake and signed for West Ham, Mr Darling went mad, and he and Ted Drake told Fenton they'd take West Ham to the FA unless he tore up my forms, which he did. So in 1955 I signed for Chelsea in my mother's fish and chip shop, one of 18 that joined that year, including Jimmy Greaves and David Cliss.

Within two weeks I played in an end-of-season friendly against Colchester for the first team. I used to get on the bus and watch

Ipswich play them, it was the local derby. It was very strange playing people on the tiny ground at Layer Road I had been watching from the terraces. My boots were the old-style ones, halfway up my leg, with rubber studs that lasted all year, and when Harry Medhurst picked them up he said, 'What the **** are these?' I followed the rest of the players out onto the pitch before the game, not even knowing what we were doing out there! When we walked back into the dressing-room all the kit was laid out. I went to the number 11 kit and huddled up in the corner with my head down. I had a jockstrap which I had never worn before, but managed to work out how to put that on! There were also two pairs of socks, and the second pair had a loop in it like skiing pants. I didn't know what they were for, so put the small sock in between my big toe. By the time I pulled it up from my toe, it came half way up my leg. I put my shinpad in, then I had a tie-up, which I hadn't come across before either – I was used to a thick piece of elastic. So you can picture me with these big boots on, pads that came above the socks, and tie-ups I put onto the pad. When I lifted up my head, the whole of the team were standing there with their mouths open! I didn't know what I was doing but somebody up there must have liked me, because within ten minutes I scored!

In the Youth Cup final we went to Molineux on the Thursday, two days after we ripped into them at the Bridge and thought it was a formality. They made a couple of changes, we played the same team, and I don't know what happened but we got done, it was unbelievable. Ted Drake was a very nice man, but a jack-the-lad and never got on with Wolves manager Stan Cullis, who was a church-goer.

Mike signed as a professional at the beginning of March 1957 on his 17th birthday, and in September 1957 an injury to Frank Blunstone paved the way for his first-team debut against West Brom.

When Frank broke his leg Chelsea were going to buy Cliff Jones for £35,000, which was a lot of money then. But when that fell through it gave Michael Harrison and myself a run in the side. When we played West Brom it was a dreadful night, raining hard. They were a pretty good side and Don Howe, who knew it was my first game, was my marker. He was saying, 'Come on son, take me on, have a go at me on the outside etc' and was really good to me.

Mike retained his place for the next game at Newcastle and scored in a 3–1 victory. Shortly after, he played under Ron Greenwood for England Youth against Romania at White Hart Lane and found the back of the net twice. Mike played 20 times for the first team in his opening season, scoring four times.

> My best Chelsea goal was the one I scored at Newcastle. I wasn't a great header of the ball, but it came from a Peter Sillett cross and I must have been on a trampoline, as I never jumped that high. I also scored in the 5–4 defeat by Arsenal at Highbury [March 1958]. I had the whole goal to aim at and pushed it through Stan Charlton's bow legs.

Mike played a further 16 times in the 1958/59 season and scored in the 6–2 victory over Wolves in August.

> The famous Wolves game was my most memorable one for Chelsea, although when we were one up my head was in a spin as I had sunstroke! I went off for about five minutes and when I came back on I think we were 3–1 up. We played really well and for one of Jimmy Greaves' five goals he picked the ball up inside his own half and scored, it was brilliant. I used to room with Jimmy and we were very close. I knew he was going to be a bit special within a year of going there, when we played in the youth team. He had that bit of pace you need, but more importantly his balance was the main quality. If he wasn't in the team you felt a bit depleted, as you could have a bad game but Jim would get us out of trouble.

Mike never quite fulfilled his early promise and was unable to retain his place when Frank Blunstone returned from injury. In his final first-team appearance he scored against Leicester in October 1961. Strangely it was the only game he played that season. The influence of Tommy Docherty was a telling factor.

> There were massive changes when Tommy came to the club. He injected enthusiasm for youth, but immediately didn't want the older players, like the Sillett brothers, who he got rid of. They were a similar age to him, had played against him and he felt nervous and threatened. As a result the players split into two and it had a bearing on the whole atmosphere. Jimmy Greaves, who wasn't a good trainer, sided with the older camp – he was the only one who was ever going to survive as he was so valuable. Tommy also got rid of Derek Saunders on the

strength of me. When we played a reserve game at Southend I pulled a tendon in my knee. Derek, who was the second-team trainer, pulled me off at half-time, as I couldn't stand up. Tom came in just after half-time and saw me in the bath. He said the following day, 'Nobody comes off the field unless they've got a broken leg.' Derek was all set to take over as first-team trainer, but Docherty got rid of him.

I remember my last game when I scored. Frank McLintock, who was marking me, got two and they won 3–1. Docherty and I weren't getting on very well and I knew I was on my way. A few weeks before my move Docherty put six studs down my leg in practice. He was trying to break my leg, which I thought was a bit stupid, especially as he was going to sell me. I was p****d off at the time and went to see the secretary and also Mr Pratt, the vice-chairman, as Joe Mears was out of the country. Pratt just shrugged his shoulders and said Docherty was a hard man, what could he do? It got to the stage where I was going home and not sleeping, but several clubs came in for me, including Brentford. I had children and didn't want to move from London, so I met the Brentford manager Malcolm McDonald in the secretary's office at the Bridge. I was also due a benefit from Chelsea and we agreed on financial terms for my move but, unknown to me, Docherty was listening behind the door to what I was saying. The next morning we were running round the track at the Bridge and he called me into the centre of the field. He said, 'I don't know who you think you are, but if you don't go you'll lose the [benefit] money from us. Don't ask them for any money or you won't get anything from us.' In the end McDonald came back and we sorted it out.

After 40 appearances with Chelsea, Mike became a Brentford player in January 1962; a fee of £5,000 was involved. He was an instant success, although the team suffered relegation to Division Four in his first season. The Bees bounced straight back as champions in 1962/63, Mike supplying much of the ammunition for the international forward trio of Johnny Brooks, Billy McAdams and John Dick. He was never afraid to test a keeper's ability and in the 1963/64 season received the Player of the Year award with 15 goals. Mike was a regular for five seasons, scoring 30 goals in 146 appearances.

I enjoyed my time at Brentford – when we were coasting at the top of Division Four it was almost like a practice match. Dave Sexton and Docherty actually asked me if I was interested in coming back to the Bridge, but they could have offered me two million and I wouldn't have played for him again! A highlight was scoring a hat trick of penalties in a 6–1 League win against Queens Park Rangers [in August 1965], which I don't think had been achieved before. I remember having to make my mind up three times which way to put the ball past Frank Smith, their goalkeeper. I was switched to the right-wing for the 1963/64 season, when George McLeod was put at outside-left. It was really enjoyable, as I then had two ways to go, cutting inside as well. Malcolm McDonald took us up from Division Four, then they became ambitious when Jack Dunnett took over as chairman. He got Billy Gray in as manager, but the club failed to get into the Second Division.

Following Brentford's relegation back to Division Four at the end of the 1965/66 season, Mike moved in September 1966 to Watford.

Ken Furphy remembered playing for Workington against me. He actually arranged a friendly behind closed doors, when I played for him against Alan Hawley and Mel Scott, who made me look like Di Stefano – they looked after me! Furphy was a difficult person to please and with hindsight maybe I should have moved further afield. I stopped enjoying my football under him, then Chelmsford came in for me. Although I had my coaching badges, I was preparing for the future at Watford by doing the knowledge for my London cabbie's qualification. We won the Southern League at Chelmsford, beating Wimbledon and I stayed there for four years.

Stan Lynn of Aston Villa was the toughest defender I faced, followed by George Curtis of Southampton. In the pre-match warm-up Stan would drift up to the halfway line and say, 'Michael, you'll be in the stand in the first five minutes!' He was built like the proverbial brickhouse and Curtis was also a very hard man, he was there to give you an almighty whack and stop you playing. On the wing when your back is to the defender, you would try to have a look and get a bit of space. If you could turn with your pace you were OK, but they would try to get you before you turned.

My cabbie work suits me, it gives me the freedom to play golf at Mill Hill, which is my passion. I have a handicap of four, played for Middlesex Seniors in 2000 and am the club champion at the moment. I have three children, Rosalind, Nicholas and Melissa, and five grandchildren.

DAVID CLISS

Lightweight Enfield boy David Cliss came from a footballing family and was nicknamed 'Twinkletoes' by his schoolmates because of his mazy dribbling skills. He came to prominence as a 14-year-old in 1954 when starring for London Boys in a 4–2 victory over Manchester Boys at a floodlit White Hart Lane, broadcast live on television. He delighted viewers with his close ball control and all-round display likened to Johnny Haynes as a schoolboy. David scored a 'Matthews'-style goal (his hero) when, collecting the ball from the halfway line, he weaved his way past five defenders to crack the ball home. Commentator Kenneth Wolstenholme remarked that he doubted if viewers would ever see a goal like David's again from such a young player. He even overshadowed his inside-forward partner Jimmy Greaves, although Jimmy scored one of the other goals. His sports master Mr Craggs phoned the Arsenal manager Tom Whittaker. 'Yes, Arsenal were delighted with David, a promising lad,' was the response. David said, 'I want to play for Arsenal. They look after their younger players.' Heaven knows what means Jimmy Thompson subsequently used to persuade him to join their deadly rivals!

In 1955 David became the first Enfield boy to win a Schoolboy international cap and celebrated with a goal in the 6–2 victory over Wales at Cardiff. The return leg a month later in front of 90,000 at Wembley saw another goal avalanche. Whilst he did not score, David had a hand in all six goals and was the 'controlling genius of the magnificent England side, showing superb ball control and in high-speed bursts'. Alex Dawson, later of Manchester United and Preston, scored two of the goals without reply. Shortly after, David made four and scored once in a 9–1 trouncing of Ireland.

In customary Thompson-style David joined Chelsea two days after leaving school. He was at the time the most sought-after schoolboy in England and made history when turning down the overtures of Arsenal. He signed pro in November 1956 and the same month gained the first of four England Youth caps.

With Jimmy Greaves and Barry Bridges, David was a member of the high-scoring Junior team in 1956/57, collecting 18 goals in 19 South-East Counties League fixtures. In September 1956 he made his debut with Jimmy Greaves for the Combination side in a 2–1 win over Bristol City at the Bridge, Greaves scoring one of the goals. After being nurtured in the Combination side David made his League debut against Preston North End at the Bridge in February 1958. The Ducklings, however, floundered in an ocean of mud and Preston ran out 2–0 winners. David tirelessly covered the pitch, searching for the ball, probing for openings and generally trying to inspire with his enthusiasm.

By the end of the season David had played nine times, scoring his only League goal in the final match against Manchester United, a 2–1 win at the Bridge in front of 45,000. His performance was said to be reminiscent of United's Ernie Taylor. When Greaves put David away in the 14th minute, Harry Gregg failed to hold his shot for Chelsea's opener, Les Allen clinching victory in the 24th minute.

David played three times for the first team the following season, but the grounds were so heavy he was rested to allow more weight to be added to the forward line. Ted Drake recognised the frailty in his young 'pocket-sized Hercules', which ultimately proved disastrous for his career. He made just four League appearances during the 1959/60 season and spent the summer of 1960 in New York playing in an international tournament, where his intricate ball skills delighted the excited onlookers. David made a total of 24 League appearances, but his Chelsea career ended when he broke a leg at the beginning of the 1960/61 season against Leicester City in a Combination fixture – he collided with the goalkeeper going for a 50–50 ball and it was a severe fracture. He never played another first-team game for Chelsea and in the summer of 1962 joined Guildford City, where Peter Sillett was manager. Whilst it was a lower standard of football, David never lost his latent ball skills, and a hat trick against Clacton Town included an audacious 35-yard lob over the goalkeeper.

David emigrated to Australia in 1968 due to the poor health of his daughter. He played about five seasons as a semi-pro for St George Budapest in Sydney, the highest Australian League standard at the time. He then moved to another Sydney club, Arncliffe Scots, for a couple of seasons as player-coach, until retirement from football. David took up employment as a truck driver, making local deliveries. When he eventually sold his truck, he worked as a storeman in a local food store in Sydney until retirement. He has two children, a son, Andrew, and a daughter, Debbie, who both live in Australia.

In common with many footballers, David had his cartilages removed some time ago. Then in about 1986 he had an operation on the leg that he broke. The doctor said that because of the way it was originally set, the leg healed at an angle and was bowed. It wore out his knee joint on one side, which undoubtedly explains why he was never the same player again. David lives in New South Wales and sadly suffers nowadays from Parkinson's disease.

MIKE HARRISON

Another pacy and direct left-winger, Mike Harrison was born at Ilford in 1940. At a mere 8-years-old he was playing for Newby Park Old Boys Club at an Under-15s League.

> I was a Jimmy Thompson signing, like everybody else. With his pin-striped suit, hat and umbrella, he used to get the mums and dads on his side and you had to sign for him. He first saw me play for Ilford Boys in the same team as John Lyall. I was lucky enough to have played at Derby in the England Schoolboys Under-14 team against Ireland at 13. We beat them 6–0 and it went on from there.
>
> My biggest influence and best coach was my father. He wasn't a footballer himself, but he gave me confidence, self-esteem and focus, although I didn't know what he was doing at the time. In those days there were about 80 players on the staff, including five outside-lefts, and I remember going home one day in tears. I was only 15 and my father told me to believe in myself and keep plugging away.

That advice was timely as, although Mike started just two South-East Counties League matches in the 1955/56 season, his progress was so rapid that within 12 months he made his first-team debut in a 1–0 defeat at Blackpool in April 1957, still a week short of his 17th birthday.

> Being a left-winger, I faced their right-winger on the halfway line, Stanley Matthews. He almost touched my shoulder, but I couldn't even look at him, I was totally in awe. I was up against Jimmy Armfield, but had a good game and held my own.

Mike had to wait a year before getting his second chance against Manchester United in the last game of the 1957/58 season. He was still a member of the youth team in 1958, which went so close to winning the Youth Cup, scoring twice in the first leg of the final.

> Losing the Youth Cup final was probably the biggest disappointment of my career, as we were the best young team in England. Then in my second game for the first team I played in front of a big crowd against United post-Munich. It was an emotional occasion and they had a collection round the ground. My first Chelsea goal against Newcastle

[September 1958 in a 2—1 win] was the best goal I ever scored. About ten minutes after the start I took a free kick almost out on the touchline. The wind was behind me and it struck the cross bar. Five minutes later I had another one from virtually the same position and I thought I would just crack it. It went in the far top corner past Ronnie Simpson and was my best strike ever from a dead ball. I remember scoring another from 35 yards past Jack Kelsey at Arsenal with a piledriver when the wind caught it [March 1962 in a 2—3 defeat].

Mike had an extended run in the first team during the 1961/62 season and played three times for England Under-23s. However, like Mike Block, he had the misfortune to be on the staff when Frank Blunstone was in prime form as the recognised left-winger.

When I won my first Under-23 cap I actually played a full practice match at Stamford Bridge on the morning of the game. Someone got injured and I had a phone call to go to White Hart Lane. We had a good team including Bobby Moore and Johnny Byrne, and beat West Germany 4—0 — I must have been fit in those days!

I remember going in to see Ted Drake asking for another £2 per week next year and he said, 'Are you playing for money, not love of football?' There were always plenty of jokes and jokers around, but it was a way to create team-spirit. We trained very hard and were really fit and serious trainers. On reflection I feel we were the first set of modern-day players who had developed through a youth side, with the help of Dick Foss. In the end I couldn't claim a regular place in the side and had a row with Docherty, who I didn't get on with. Jack Marshall, the Blackburn manager, watched me at Southampton and bought me a few days later.

After 64 appearances for the Blues, scoring nine times, Mike stayed in top-class football with a move to Rovers in September 1962 for £18,000. For five years he was a regular first-team choice, making nearly 200 appearances.

You can't really see what managers are trying to do when you are young, but Jack had the foresight to successfully juggle about seven players into different positions. He converted Keith Newton from a half-back to a full-back, Fred Pickering from full-back to centre-forward, Andy McEvoy from midfield to striker, switched Mike England around, and moved Bryan Douglas over with me to inside-forward. He also bought

Mike Ferguson from Accrington Stanley for £1,500 and we had a really good team, especially the forward line. We were always entertaining to watch and put eight past West Ham at Upton Park and also beat Spurs 7–2 at Ewood Park (both matches in the 1963/64 season). We more than held our own in the First Division and were great going forward, but we were getting hammered at the back. I had a great time there and still keep in contact with the club.

The year they got relegated [1965/66] I was transferred to Plymouth, but only had a few months there, before going to Luton. I saw a lot of good things happening and we had a superb team, with Bruce Rioch and Malcolm Macdonald coming through. I ended up with two good years at Dover in the Southern League. I retired for a couple of years, but when we moved to Lincolnshire I played for a while at Spalding.

Jimmy Armfield and George Cohen were the best full-backs I faced. I had some good battles against Jimmy, not only because he was quick, but he was one of the first overlapping full-backs, so I had to track back as well. I used to look at the fixture list at the start of the season and knew I could take nearly all of them on my pace, but would have to be very sharp against those two. Alex Parker, the Scottish international at Everton, was another. I'd get past him but he would always recover and catch me almost on the byline, so I had to get the ball in quick.

I coached Spalding for a while, and also coached in schools for about five years. I'm now a professional salesperson working for a broker, selling private health-care. I have three children, Greg, Gary and Sharon, and five grandchildren. I married a Brazilian girl, Priscilla, who is football-mad, on Copacabana Beach, Rio de Janeiro, in September 1999. We then had another wedding in Plymouth, where we live, and some of my ex-colleagues at Blackburn Rovers attended, including Ronnie Clayton and Bryan Douglas and Keith Newton's widow, Barbara. My interests nowadays are psychology, personal development and keep fit.

TONY NICHOLAS

The strongly built, blond inside-forward first attracted attention with the junior side and in September 1954, at the age of 16, he played for the

Combination team against Brentford. Tony Nicholas signed professional in May 1955 and enjoyed rapid promotion. In October 1955 Tony starred in his first youth international against Denmark.

> We beat Denmark 9–2 at Plymouth, when I scored three goals and should have got more, as I hit the woodwork three times. I also played against Holland and Hungary, which we won as well. The best player I ever faced was Duncan Edwards. We played Manchester United in the semi-final of the Youth Cup in 1954/55. We lost each leg 2–1 and Duncan scored all four goals and also headed two off the goal-line at Chelsea. He would have been one of the greatest players ever. Dickie Foss was a big influence, as he did a lot of one-to-one training with me, and made me run around like hell!
>
> I made my League debut at Sheffield Wednesday in August 1956 when we got hammered 4–0. Albert Quixall had a fantastic game for them that night. One of my most memorable games was scoring two in a 6–1 thrashing of Burnley at the Bridge in October 1957. Peter Brabrook helped me that day – he turned their full-back inside out and was unbelievable.

Tony was applauded off the pitch at the end of the Burnley match and, during a run of nine consecutive games, he also scored a brace the same month in a 4–2 home win over Aston Villa.

> My best Chelsea goal was at home to Tottenham in August 1958, when I hit a cross/shot that went just inside the far post and we won 4–2. The next game was when we beat Wolves 6–2 and Jimmy scored five. We could have been two up in the first five minutes, as I went past my marker Bill Slater, twice and beat the keeper but put the ball past the post. Then Ron Flowers and Bill Slater changed over, and Slater couldn't hold Jimmy.
>
> When you weren't doing too well, Ted Drake would come into the dressing-room and smash a few cups – sometimes they were thrown in my direction! I remember playing at Burnley [February 1958] and did everything but score, but the keeper pulled off a great save and I hit the woodwork, and we lost 2–1. I got a great write-up but on the Friday was the only one who was dropped. I stormed into Ted's office and, while I didn't hit him, I hit the door and put a hole in it. The next time I went there they had put an imitation football over it! You need to have a bit of luck in football and be in the right place at the right time and if anyone

got dropped it was usually me. In the end I went to Brighton to get away from Ted, then he got the sack. I would have been laughing with Tommy Docherty as I was a runner, but instead I went into obscurity.

It was Tony's misfortune to be a contemporary of Jimmy Greaves, and he never wholly fulfilled his potential at the Bridge. He was restricted to 63 appearances, scoring 21 times, yet it was surprising that he failed to make more of an impact with his subsequent clubs. When he signed for Brighton in 1960 the fee of £15,000 was a club record and in his first season Tony scored 13 goals in 27 appearances. The following year was a disaster for Brighton and at the end of the season most of the club's experienced players, including Tony were released.

Brighton were bottom of the Second Division when I joined them, but in my first game we won 2–1 at Swansea [November 1960] and, although I was marked by Mel Nurse, an international, I had a good game. We avoided relegation and had a good cup run, drawing 3–3 with League champions Burnley when we could have beaten them. The following season we needed new players, but George Curtis didn't have any money and we were relegated. George was a tremendous coach, but as a manager he didn't have a clue.

I went to Chelmsford for a couple of seasons. We had a very good team including Bobby Mason, who came from Wolves, and one year came second in the Southern League. In 1965 we played Leyton Orient in the final of the Essex Professional Cup, hammered them 5–2 and I scored a hat trick. I signed for Orient on the strength of that game but could never get on with Dave Sexton, who was manager at the time. I had a season with them and we got relegated. I went back to the Southern League with Dartford for a couple of years, then Folkestone and Gravesend. When I retired I played local football with my two sons. We also had Peter Collins who used to play for Spurs, so it wasn't a bad side and I really enjoyed it.

I have always been able to make things and started a DIY business in the sixties when I was at Chelmsford. It was very good until the conglomerates came in, when we diversified into fitted kitchens, bathrooms and bedrooms, called Nicholas Anthony, my name backwards. We now have three shops which my boys, Tony and Kevin, run. I have been retired about seven years and love my golf, which my wife Darlene plays as well. We live at Chelmsford and I play off a handicap of eight at the local golf club. We also enjoy spending time with our three grandchildren.

STRIKERS

GEORGE HILSDON – *107 goals in 164 appearances*

For many years if you glanced upward at the Bridge your eyes may well have focused on the weather vane perched on the roof of the West Stand. The silhouette of the footballer was modelled on George Hilsdon, the club's inaugural goalscoring centurion, and it is highly appropriate that the first in a long line of distinguished centre-forwards remains visible.

Born in 1885 at Bromley-by-Bow, Cockney George first made a name as a fearless centre-half for his Marner Street school team. He was spotted by West Ham playing in a Sunday League match on the eve of the 1904/05 season and promptly signed. His early appearances were for West Ham reserves in Division Two of the Southern League and, whilst still an amateur, he also played in the Western League. At the beginning of 1905 George suffered the indignity of being in the West Ham XI that lost 10–0 to Tottenham in the London Charity Cup, but a few weeks later demonstrated his potential with four goals in a 6–0 defeat of Bristol Rovers in the Western League.

Towards the end of the season George scored in his first-team debut against New Brompton. He was troubled by a foot injury which restricted his appearances, but played in a reserve match against Fulham towards the end of the 1905/06 season that changed the course of his life. It was Chelsea's first year in the Football League and player-manager Jackie Robertson was assessing another West Ham player, but George's performance heightened Robertson's determination to sign him. Negotiations were concluded in May 1906 for a move across London, without a fee involved. The transfer was something of a surprise as George was obviously a great prospect and had already scored seven times in 16 Southern League appearances for the first team. It was one of the most canny signings in Robertson's brief managerial tenure, as George became a cornerstone of his team-building plans.

George impressed during a pre-season continental tour and Robertson raised more than an eyebrow or two when the rookie 21-year-old was preferred to Frank Pearson, the previous season's top-scorer, for the first

League game. It was 1 September 1906, and all over the country the heat was so intense that matches became a feat of endurance after half-time, with many players retiring overcome by the sun. At Stamford Bridge in front of 12,000 sweltering fans George took the baptism in his stride and calmly scored five goals against Glossop. He created another four for his new team-mates as they ruthlessly exerted their authority to overwhelm the opposition 9–0. The debut feat still remains a club record and remained the highest number of goals scored by a Chelsea player in a League game until equalled by Jimmy Greaves. George was quickly tagged the 'Mushroom' centre-forward because of the way he burst onto the scene in such dramatic fashion.

George's old colleagues at West Ham were so delighted with his progress that the whole side witnessed him star in a South v North trial for the England team. Within six weeks of his Chelsea debut he was selected for the Football League against the Irish League and responded with a hat trick.

George was firing bullets from all angles, which also earned him the sobriquet of 'Gatling Gun'. He was equally adept with both feet and 27 goals in his first season were decisive as the team gained promotion to the First Division. George continued apace with 24 League goals in the 1907/08 campaign and 25 the following season.

Full England recognition was swift, with George making his debut against Ireland at Goodison Park in 1907. Over the next two years a further seven caps were awarded, with George finding the net an extraordinary 13 times. His highlight was four goals in 1908 at Budapest in a 7–0 win over Hungary, with a brace against Ireland at Bradford the following February.

In January 1908 an unsuspecting Worksop team arrived in town for the first round of the FA Cup. The directors had persuaded Worksop to switch the tie to the Bridge for financial reasons when they came first out of the hat. George opened the scoring in the first half and Chelsea went into the break 4–1 to the good. He bagged a further five goals, three in the opening five minutes, as Worksop were disembowelled 9–1. Their consolation was undoubtedly a share of the gate totalling £381. George's haul of six goals is another record so far unbeaten.

His prolific scoring continued with a hat trick in November 1908 against top of the table Everton at the Bridge in an exhilarating 3–3 draw. However, a leg injury suffered in the second game of the 1909/10 season restricted George to fewer than half the club's fixtures. He netted just three times and profligate finishing cost the Blues relegation. Again George revelled in the space afforded him in the Second Division, although he had to be content with 18 League goals, behind Bob Whittingham. His form had returned and the confidence in the side was reflected in an excellent FA Cup run. George played in all the rounds but disastrously sprained a tendon at Broadstairs, where the side were preparing for the semi-final against Newcastle. He was replaced by a partly-fit Vivian Woodward and his absence was felt to be a significant factor in the 3–0 defeat.

Then, as rapidly as the 'Gatling Gun' rose, the barrel started firing blanks. By this time he had become something of a cult figure in local circles and a familiar figure in the local taverns, where there was always another drink available for 'Our George'. George Hilsdon Junior defended his father's excesses: 'What wasn't widely known at the time was that my mother had chronic asthma. It affected her terribly and my father as well. He used to come home and see her suffering – it was not surprising that after a while he started taking a drink or two.'

It was a heavy burden and George's form declined as he neglected his fitness. His attributes had always been his physical strength – with broad shoulders he could hold his own against the strongest, winning tackles and brushing opponents aside. But his play was not solely based on brawn and sheer power. He had developed a shrewd positional sense and ability to lose his marker. However, with injury problems and his weight ballooning, George found it increasingly difficult to prise open defences. He was dropped after three games of the 1911/12 season and his subsequent loss of form (just one goal) was dramatic. In the short term the club supported George and a testimonial match at Easter 1912 raised £180 to supplement his pay of £4 a week.

A change of club during the summer of 1912 was however felt beneficial and George was released on a free transfer back to West Ham. He was only 26 and, while he never fully recaptured his form, his lively personality and good-natured humour did much to revitalise the Upton Park team. One of George's strongest games was back at Stamford Bridge when he scored twice in a FA Cup tie against First Division West Bromwich Albion, who were defeated 3–1. His experience was valued in the development of younger players, especially Sydney Puddefoot, later a legend at West Ham. George played 92 games for the Hammers, scoring 35 times up to the end of the 1914/15 season. Called up for military service, he was badly affected by mustard-gas poisoning, as explained by George Junior: 'Father was still an idol when he played for West Ham but the First World War put an end to all that. He joined the East Surrey Regiment, but it was not until the last year of the war that he had to fight. A kindly brigadier had kept him out of the trenches, because he was the king of the regimental soccer and cricket teams, but then came the last big German push, and father copped the mustard gas at Arras.'

George suffered terrible pain in his legs from the poison and never played senior football again. A job as player-manager at Kent League side Chatham Town proved some consolation, but by the time he retired in 1919 George was on the slide. A canary breeder, George survived on his wits in a variety of occupations between the wars, including a spell with Fred Karno's Troop, and time as a publican. After being evacuated from his East Ham home early in the Second World War, George died from tuberculosis at Leicester in May 1941, a month after his 56th birthday. The Football Association paid for the funeral, poignantly attended by just four people, including his son, and George was buried in an unmarked grave.

BOB WHITTINGHAM – *80 goals in 129 appearances*

If George was renowned for firing bullets, likeable Bob Whittingham had a reputation for despatching cannon-balls. One such was in March 1912 against Gainsborough Trinity, a thunderbolt delivered with such ferocity it knocked the goalkeeper off balance and over his line. Bob was moulded in the traditional way as a bustling, aggressive centre-forward. His strength was attributed to a well-developed physique and many goals came from long-range efforts. He revelled in picking up the loose ball from deep-lying positions and used his power to bear down on goal. Goalkeepers were apprehensive every time Bob muscled his way through, driving in spectacular efforts with aplomb.

Born at Goldenhill, Stoke-on-Trent, in 1889, Bob was the younger brother of Samuel, who he followed to his first club, Goldenhill Wanderers. He won North Staffordshire Alliance League and Cup medals with them, before embarking on nomadic spells at Stoke, Crewe and Port Vale. Bob became a professional in July 1907 at Blackpool, scoring a goal on his League debut at Stockport County in September 1907. It was a Division Two fixture and brother Sam was in the same side. Top-scorer with 15 goals in his first season, he was snapped up by First Division Bradford City for £750 at the beginning of 1909, having scored 28 goals in 53 appearances.

Bob's vigorous style continued to unsettle defenders and 21 goals in the 1909/10 season equalled the League record at Valley Parade. A hat trick against Chelsea at the beginning of April 1910 was no doubt a significant factor in his next move, as Bob joined Chelsea less than two weeks later for £1,300. With just three games to go the Blues were threatened with relegation to the Second Division. Bob scored a stunning goal in his second game to secure a 2–0 victory against Bury, but in the final match of the season a last-minute defeat by Spurs sent Chelsea down.

Alongside George Hilsdon and the stylish amateur Vivian Woodward, the trio enjoyed the reputation as one of the finest inside-forward lines in the country, but success remained elusive. Ever-present Bob's contribution in the 1910/11 season was 30 League goals, a record until eclipsed by Jimmy Greaves. It wasn't quite enough to regain Division One status as, with two points needed to secure promotion, the Blues lost the last fixture 3–1 at Gainsborough.

One of Bob's most notable games was on New Year's Eve 1910 at the Bridge against Derby County, when five goals were scored in the last six remarkable minutes. The legendary England international Steve Bloomer converted two penalties for the Rams. Bob and Angus Douglas replied, before Bob secured victory with a third penalty and seconds to spare. It was one of the occasions when Bob was favourably compared to Bloomer, who was said to put more power behind the ball than any of his contemporaries. Although the best player tag was a shade excessive, Jack Whitley, Chelsea's long-serving keeper, maintained that Bob justified his reputation as the hardest hitter of his time.

Another highlight was the fourth round of the FA Cup in March 1911, enjoyed by a record 77,952 spectators at the Bridge. Swindon, then of the Southern League, were soundly beaten 3–1, Bob helping himself to two goals. There was a more consistent feel about Chelsea the following season, with solid home form playing a key part. Battling Bob was a major factor, particularly in the prolonged absence of Hilsdon and Woodward. Despite the additional burden, Bob blitzed 26 goals as promotion was achieved – hat tricks against Forest and Clapton Orient inside a month in 1912 confirmed his value to the Blues.

Strangely, Bob's scoring return of the first two seasons was never subsequently approached and his career was disrupted by the outbreak of the war. He returned to the Potteries, guesting for Stoke during wartime and, after scoring 86 goals in 84 games, he was formally transferred there for £500 in September 1919. His tenure at Stoke was brief and, after just one season, Bob retired from professional football due to health problems. He managed 17 goals in his final year from 28 first-team games. In the autumn of his career Bob scored twice for the Football League against the Scottish League at St Andrew's (February 1919), and was honoured with a Wartime Victory international cap against Wales (October 1919), scoring again in a 2–0 win at the Victoria Ground.

Bob did play at Scunthorpe and Lindsey United in the Midland League for a while in 1921 and unsuccessfully attempted to revive his career with

Wrexham in 1922. With an impressive record of 147 goals in 249 appearances, he returned to Goldenhill Wanderers in 1924. Health problems persisted and Bob collapsed and died at his Goldenhill home in June 1926 from tuberculosis at the premature age of 37.

JACK COCK – 53 goals in 110 appearances

The 1960s and 1970s embraced the glamour and personality players at Chelsea and, with his fine singing voice, Terry Venables was the Blues' first crooner. Try telling that to Jack Cock! With flowing black hair and the striking looks of a film star, Jack supplemented his football income in the early 1920s as a music-hall singer. The young ladies at the Granville Theatre, Waltham Green, swooned as the dashing Jack serenaded them with his fine tenor voice.

Strong and perfectly proportioned, Jack was a natural athlete, the dashing hero of the newspaper cartoonists and the contemporary idol of Stamford Bridge. He was a deadly marksman with a powerful shot in either foot delivered with precision. Jack was also a fine header of the ball which brought him many of the 200 goals he scored in senior football.

Born in 1893 at Hayle, Cornwall, Jack started his League career with a short spell at Brentford in 1914. His fledgling reputation as a centre-forward of great potential persuaded Huddersfield Town, then a reasonably successful Second Division team, to sign Jack immediately prior to the onset of the war. During the enforced break, Jack returned to London, playing regional football for Brentford and Croydon Common whenever his military duties allowed, and he distinguished himself with the Military Medal in 1917.

When Jack returned to Huddersfield in the autumn of 1919, his club were experiencing severe financial problems and, with a heavy heart, he was transferred to Chelsea in October 1919. Jack had enjoyed his fractured spell at Huddersfield, with nine goals from just 18 League games, but the £2,500 fee represented good business and enabled the club to remain solvent. Not for the first time were Chelsea experiencing difficulties in finding the net, particularly in the absence of Vivian Woodward and Bob Thomson. Jack eased into the side with two goals on his debut against Bradford Park Avenue, followed by three more in a 4–0 victory over Preston North End in November 1919. There was an element of luck with the first goal when Nils Middleboe sent in a hard shot and the ball rebounded off one of the Preston backs into the net. The second goal, soon after half-time, was a curious one. Jack was credited, although it resulted from a defensive mix-up when he was right through. He was tackled by keeper Whalley, who, running out of goal, kicked the ball; it struck Jack and rolled slowly into the net. Jack was entirely responsible for completing his only Chelsea hat trick in style for one of the most emphatic victories of the season. He was the Blues' leading scorer with 24 goals from 30 games as the club reached the dizzy heights of third spot in the First Division. He was also a key member of the side which reached the FA Cup semi-final before losing 3–1 to Aston Villa in March 1920.

There appeared to be one flaw in Jack's make-up which may account for why he never quite maintained his excellent start. He was a man of moods and seemingly adopted a diffident approach to the game, good days being followed by barren spells. This may have created a false impression as Jack was a fine athlete and a glutton for work. According to goal keeper turned trainer Jack Whitley, he was almost over-conscientious and it was frequently necessary to dampen down his thirst for training; 'You've done enough for one day Jack,' he would say. But once Whitley's back was turned he would be hard at it, grinding out more laps round the greyhound track. Nonetheless his output of goals fell away during the subsequent two seasons to 28 in total, although he remained the leading goalscorer. Indeed, for the 1921/22 season Jack's 13 League goals were key as the Blues were only able to find the target 40 times.

But for the outbreak of the war Jack would surely have made a bigger impact on the game and added to his two full international caps. His display for England against Scotland in the Victory International at Sheffield just before he arrived at Chelsea, scoring twice on a waterlogged mud heap, one with virtually his first kick, was lavishly described as 'the best centre-forward exhibition ever'. Then in 1920 he scored the decisive goal against Ireland in the very first minute.

With Dave Calderhead wrestling with the problems associated in a struggling side, Jack was transferred to Everton in the early part of 1923. Despite a feeling that his career was on the wane, it was always on for a good pro like Jack to 'dip his bread' and he gave the best possible rebuttal with 30 goals in 72 games for the Toffeemen. His career was extended with a brief spell at Plymouth Argyle in 1925, before finishing on a high with Millwall. His 92 goals in 135 appearances, plus a Third Division South Championship medal in 1928, were a marvellous way for Jack to conclude his League career. He had short spells at Folkestone in 1931 and Walton & Hersham in 1932 before retiring. In 1944 he returned to manage the Lions and was in charge when losing 2–0 to Chelsea in the wartime 1945 League South Cup final. Jack retired in 1948, after over 30 years in the game, and later became a publican in New Cross. The final years of his life were spent in south London, where he remained a popular figure, and he died in April 1966 at Kensington, aged 72.

GEORGE MILLS – *124 goals in 239 appearances*

The tall amateur footballer worked in the city during the week, so could only train in the evenings. The week before Christmas 1929, a new name appeared on the Blues first-team sheet at number nine in the form of G.R. Mills, a raw young man whose scoring feats with Bromley had been brought to the club's attention. Dave Calderhead was again desperately seeking the right formula upfront to kick-start a disappointing season and the effect was dramatic in the home game against Preston. Just 33 seconds into his debut, George's approach work paved the way for a simple chance for Jackie Crawford and goals from Rodger, Bishop and Miller (2) completed a resounding 5–0 victory.

A Deptford boy, George was born in 1908. His first club was Emerald Athletic, but it was at Bromley that he set the pulses racing with his clinical finishing. Whilst he only came into the side midway through the 1929/30 season, George justified his signing-on fee of ten crisp £1 notes by finishing top-scorer on 14 goals. This was a remarkable feat, given the intense competition for the number nine shirt, with Sid Elliott and Reg Weaver initially ahead of him in the pecking order. George's goals were a significant factor in the Blues' successful quest for promotion to the top level after an absence of six seasons.

With Calderhead appreciating the need to strengthen the side for the challenges of First Division football, Hughie Gallacher's signature was secured and George's place was in jeopardy. He wasn't given another opportunity until December 1930 and only played a handful of games during the season. That established a trend for George as at times he was used sparingly over the years, deputising first for Gallacher and then vying for the number nine shirt with another international Joe Bambrick. Nonetheless he always maintained his enthusiasm and was a popular team player who never let the side down, continuing to score in an understated manner. He even had a spell at inside-right, which, whilst not his favourite position, added a new dimension to his game.

George's form peaked in 1936/37, when he scored 22 times in 32 appearances. He continued in the same mode with a hat trick on the opening day of the following season when Chelsea blitzed Liverpool 6–1 at home. George scored his first goal early in the game and soon after Billy Mitchell deceived the goalkeeper with a dipping shot from long range. Then Harston eluded Bob Griffiths to score for Liverpool with a low hard drive. George again put Chelsea two up just before half-time, which was also his 100th for the club. He celebrated with a third in the second half and two further goals from Harry Burgess and Jimmy Argue left Liverpool in a hopeless position. The trouncing in front of 42,000 delirious spectators remains Chelsea's best opening-day victory.

George also convinced the England selectors that he was worthy of international consideration and didn't let his country down. A sensational debut hat trick at Belfast against Northern Ireland in a 5–1 win in October 1937 was followed by two more caps that season. George had at last secured the centre-forward slot for his own – how ironic that the war should intervene at the height of his powers. Wartime appearances for his club became infrequent, and in 1944 George decided to retire in order to concentrate on his business interests.

George worked his way up to the position of sales director with a London printing firm and remained with them until his death. He never fully severed his ties with the club and coached the 'A' team for a period after the war. In the 1950s George reported on the opposition for the first team and recalled having watched Blackpool 23 times during the 1952/53 season, as invariably the Tangerines' opponents one week were Chelsea's the following. For many years up to his death, Gentleman George actively supported the club with the enthusiasm of his playing days. He died in July 1970 while on holiday in Torquay, leaving a widow and son. Three months earlier, George had witnessed his beloved Chelsea triumph in the FA Cup final.

HUGHIE GALLACHER – *81 goals in 144 appearances*

He peaked at five feet five inches, short in stature, but long on reputation, when he signed for Chelsea. Hughie Gallacher was one of the legendary figures in the game and considered the most clinical centre-forward in the first half of the last century. He had pace, an abundance of courage, exceptional ball control and a terrific shot with both feet. Although he preferred the ball at his feet, his spring gave him the ability to out-leap taller men and brought him goals few other men of his height could have scored. Hughie was one of the most colourful and explosive characters football has ever known and became the most-discussed forward in the country. On the pitch he was fiery and a brittle temperament got him into trouble with opponents and referees. During his long spell at the top he scored 386 goals in 545 League matches, and 24 in 20 international appearances for Scotland. Old facts, but they still resonate. He was probably the tiniest man ever to win world fame as a centre-forward and had everything, but ultimately lost everything.

Hughie was born in 1903 at Bellshill, ten miles from Glasgow, and attended Bellshill Academy. At ten he played in goal in place of his brother John, who broke a leg tripping on a skipping rope. Despite his lack of height, he saved a penalty, the school won 2−1 and Hughie gained his first medal.

As a teenager during the First World War, Hughie worked in munitions factories at Mossend, then was subjected to long hours in the coalmines, a harsh upbringing that toughened him for the challenges that lay ahead. He also loved boxing and regularly sparred at a local gym, mixing with opponents taller than him. In 1920 he turned up to watch his local side Bellshill Athletic, when they were one short. Hughie was invited to make up the numbers, netted in a 1−1 draw in front of nearly 5,000, and signed for the club soon after. The same year, at the age of 17 Hughie married a Bellshill girl, and their first child sadly died less than a year old. The marriage did not last and, after a second child, they separated in 1923. Queen of the South soon spotted Hughie's potential and signed him; it represented a step up and Hughie was delighted with the signing-on fee of £30 and weekly wages of £5. Goals were easy to come by and he registered 19 in just nine games and soon attracted Scottish League scouts. A spectacular overhead kick in 1921 against Airdrie reserves was enough to entice the Division One club to move for Hughie. However, his career and life stalled, almost terminally, when he was rushed to hospital with double pneumonia and was on the danger list for a few days.

At the time of signing Airdrie were a mid-table side and young Hughie was gradually integrated into the first team. His opening season saw seven goals in 15 appearances, with a first senior hat trick in a 4−1 win over St Mirren. Scoring 49 goals in two seasons was more than enough to warrant selection for the full international side, and in March 1924, with his 21st birthday just behind him, Hughie ran out in front of over 30,000 for his debut at Celtic Park in a 2−0 victory over Northern Ireland. Shortly after, the most important match in the club's history was staged, when Airdrie took on Hibs in the final of the Scottish League Cup. Hughie's 'terrier-like attitude' wreaked havoc with the opposition and Airdrie were 2–0 winners in a one-sided affair. His reward was a bonus of £8, plus a ride through Airdrie town centre in an open-topped bus.

Hughie had established himself as a deadly marksman, reflected in a further 35 goals during the 1924/25 season. However, it was not without cost, as he had developed a reputation as having a somewhat short fuse, which defenders regularly ignited. He also clashed with referees for arguing, and in a match against Partick Thistle was sent off in an unseemly brawl which continued in the tunnel. He was suspended for five matches, the first of a series of altercations he had with the authorities. The international selectors were more sympathetic to him and a second cap against Wales at Hearts saw a superb performance from the little man, bagging two goals in a 3–1 victory. The second was a trademark solo run when he effortlessly eased past five defenders before casually lobbing the ball over the goalkeeper's dive with his right foot, and tapping the ball into the empty net with his left foot. He considered it his best ever and said, 'As I turned to walk back I saw the Welsh players applauding me.' Another brace against England in front of 92,000 at Hampden Park in April 1925 established his position as Scotland's premier forward. After 100 goals from only 129 games, in December 1925 Hughie embarked on his English career by signing for Newcastle United for a recorded fee of £6,500.

The Tyneside press was in no doubt that the determination of the Newcastle board in securing their man was 'the smartest stroke of football business that has been transacted in modern times'. In the first nine games he scored 15 goals and that special rapport between Newcastle supporters and their centre-forward was already bonding. With an expression of confidence bordering on the outrageous, at the start of Hughie's first full season (1926/27) the directors appointed him captain. Leading a five-pronged attack with an average height of five feet seven inches Hughie relished the responsibility, and for the next three seasons was arguably at the zenith of his career. His success continued to court controversy and he became such a marked man that he started to wear a half-inch thick pad of cotton wool under his shinpads to protect himself. Among a record of 29 goals in 41 matches in his first year, a superb individual effort at Blackburn was the highlight. The season culminated in a 1–1 draw with West Ham to clinch the Championship, the last occasion Newcastle have enjoyed such success in the League.

Hughie's vitriolic words again got him into trouble when he complained to the referee in a Huddersfield fixture at the end of 1927 that he wasn't being sufficiently protected. His anger boiled over when the ref awarded a penalty that secured victory for the opposition. After the match Hughie approached the ref to apologise, but the red mist descended when he found the ref bending over to get into the bath, kicked out and, in a manner anything but friendly, pushed him in! Hughie was reported to the FA, who handed him a six-week suspension without a personal hearing. He was not allowed to train with his colleagues and received no wages. However, he earned more money writing for a Scottish newspaper on Scottish Cup ties during this period. The incident caused the Newcastle board to strip him of the captaincy for the 1928/29 season.

By now Hughie was the most talked-about figure in the game, and off the field was seen immaculately dressed around town in expensive suit and a white hat or bowler. He was invited to open functions and wallowed in the celebrity status accorded him. He was not averse to flashing around wads of money to impress, even if much was cut from paper!

International success peaked with the 5–1 destruction of England in 1928 on Hughie's first visit to Wembley. The Scottish players, including his childhood pal Alex James, were nicknamed the Wembley Wizards for their sorcery. Then in February 1929 he scored five times in a 7–3 victory against Northern Ireland at Belfast. Hughie's soft-hearted nature came to the fore on the morning of the fixture, when out walking with goalkeeper Jack Harkness. At one street corner an unkempt man was standing beside a barrow, loaded with rosettes and other favours for the match. Hughie patted the old chap on the back, felt how soaked his jacket was, immediately took off his own raincoat, a new Burberry, and handed it to the barrowman. 'Put that on or you'll get the death of cold,' said Hughie and walked off – a typical gesture. He scored twice against Wales in the mud at Cardiff later in 1929 and many observers rated one of the goals the greatest they had ever seen. Hughie reportedly beat eight men in a run from his own half before walking the ball around the goalkeeper and into the net as simply as posting a letter.

His last season at Newcastle was again dogged by incident and when, after the final game, he was confronted by Chelsea chairman Claude Kirby and scout Jock Fraser, he knew his days at St James' Park were over. The patience of the directors had been exhausted and, to the dismay of the supporters, their idol came south in May 1930 for a fee of £10,000, having netted 143 goals in only 174 games. Whilst he had mixed feelings about moving to London, Dave Calderhead continued to accumulate a sizeable number of imports from north of the border, which made Hughie feel at home.

By a quirk of the fixture list Hughie made an early return to St James' Park for the second game of the 1930/31 season. The Londoners were unprepared for the extraordinary reception accorded to their new signing. A 'storm of cheering' greeted his arrival, a scene Hughie acknowledged later was the most emotional moment of his life – never in his football career did he feel so much like crying. An estimated 10,000 were locked out and hundreds sat on the stand roof, in trees or anywhere they could gain a vantage point to witness the return of their idol. The result was no fairy-tale ending as Chelsea were defeated by a single goal in front of a record crowd of 68,386.

Hughie's first home game saw over 55,000 enjoy a 6–2 victory over Manchester United. Hughie scored twice and helped Alec Cheyne bag a hat trick in a superb all-round display. However the team of ten internationals failed to live up to expectations and the talented individuals struggled to blend as a unit. To exacerbate problems, some fierce tackling from the Grimsby defence in December saw Hughie retaliate with a wandering elbow, and use abusive language in the direction of the referee. A further lengthy period on the sidelines was inevitable, this time for two months and, as he later said, 'Once again my hasty tongue had got me into trouble.' Hughie still finished top-scorer with 14 goals as the side languished in mid-table, but found it difficult to settle and at the end of the season requested a transfer, which was declined. Indeed such was the confidence of the directors that they installed him as captain for the 1931/32 season, a responsibility he failed to carry with him off the pitch. In September, after a night out to the cinema he was confronted by a mob intent on goading him. He became embroiled in an argument at a caféewith some Fulham fans, which took a turn for the worse as Hughie suffered a black eye. Flailing fists prompted a call for the police and Hughie was bailed to appear at West London Police Court the following morning. The authorities were sympathetic and instructed him to place ten shillings in the poor box. Chelsea were not so lenient and he was dropped for the next game at his beloved Newcastle. Hughie was very upset with the press, which went to town, and the club, who he felt treated him unjustly. 'I think that started our break-up,' he said. He increasingly turned to drink to escape the pressures of life, although his performances on the pitch were not the slightest impaired as he blazed a trail of 30 goals, taking the side to the brink of the FA Cup final before losing, almost inevitably, to Newcastle in the semi.

A further cause of animosity with the board came during the summer of 1932, when Andy Wilson and Alec Cheyne were tempted to play in France for wages beyond the maximum permitted in England. Hughie felt the level of wages in football an injustice and called for a lifting of the maximum wage. 'I believe a footballer should be paid like all artists, according to his drawing power,' he wrote prophetically. The plea fell on deaf ears and as a consequence Hughie was not averse to accepting illegal payments from various sources, although match-fixing was never in question.

For the tenth consecutive season, in 1932/33, Hughie was again top-scorer for his club, bagging 19 goals. He played for Scotland in 1934 after a five-year absence, when the Scottish authorities excluded anyone outside the Scottish League. In September 1934 he also married for the third time but the following month, as a consequence of a protracted and messy divorce, Hughie was declared insolvent in the bankruptcy court, with debts totalling £787, a substantial amount in the 1930s.

Hughie became increasingly unsettled in London, and didn't see eye to eye with new manager Les Knighton. At the start of the 1934/35 season he lost his place to George Mills and, after a handful of games, moved to Derby County in November 1934. The fee involved was £2,750 and included a £200 payment to the bankruptcy court in order to discharge his liabilities. It was also alleged that he was paid a signing-on fee of £300 in order to satisfy his financial demands.

It was felt in some quarters that Hughie was past his sell-by date at 32, but he confounded his critics yet again in the best possible way. Manager George Jobey handled the complex character with tact and persuasion and Hughie responded by netting 24 times in 30 games. He also won his final international cap when helping beat England 2–0 at Hampden Park, watched by an entirely jaundiced crowd of nearly 130,000. The 1935/36 season saw Derby runners-up to Sunderland, their best League placing for years. Hughie's contribution was again significant with 16 goals in 25 matches, only to find himself out of the starting line-up the following season. Reserve-team football was no good at his age and a move to Notts County followed in September 1936, for a fee of £2,000. Despite Hughie's best efforts (25 goals in 33 games), no doubt spurred on by a massive incentive from a local businessman to pay him £800 if promotion was secured, Notts County finished runners-up in Division Three South. It was Hughie's biggest disappointment in the game, but he returned to the First Division in January 1938, when Grimsby paid £1,000 for his services. It was his first unsuccessful spell in football and he again fell foul of the police after being involved in a traffic accident. He had been drinking and was fined £12 and banned from driving for 12 months, which accelerated another transfer.

When Gateshead of Division Three North offered Grimsby £500 for his signature in June 1938, Hughie jumped at the chance to return to the North-East. He defied his age (36) with a further 18 goals skilfully converted with ease. Fittingly, he scored in his final League match against Carlisle in May 1939.

Hughie said of his own play, 'Undoubtedly there were faster centre-forwards at the time, but I think I was the most skilful. I did not believe my job was solely to score goals, although naturally smacking the ball in the net was an important part.'

During the war Hughie played in several exhibition matches and was a member of the Air Raid Precautions, driving an ambulance. He worked in local munitions' factories and moved on to various manual jobs once hostilities had concluded. His desire to return to football was restricted to a column in the Newcastle *Evening Chronicle* covering local matches. He delighted crowds with regular appearances in veterans' exhibition matches during the 1940s and 1950s. His turbulent life took a devastating turn for the worse in 1950, when his wife Hannah died from a heart complaint. Her death affected Hughie badly; he became depressed and was never the same person. His health took a turn for the worse and he started to drink heavily.

In May 1957 one of his sons, Matthew, was taken into council care after the NSPCC alleged cruelty by Hughie. He lost his temper and threw an ashtray at the 14-year-old boy, which caught him on the side of his head. That spontaneous action broke Hughie's heart, as he idolised Matthew. He was summoned to appear at Gateshead Magistrates Court on 13 June – an appearance Hughie never made. He felt humiliated by the incident, which was covered in detail by the media, and on the morning of 11 June walked to the local railway line. As the York–Edinburgh express train approached, Hughie tragically jumped in front of it and died instantly; he was 54 years old.

A verdict of suicide while the balance of his mind was disturbed was returned at the inquest. A letter Hughie had posted expressing his regret was handed to the jury by the coroner. A journalist said that he had visited Hughie at his request on 10 June. Hughie said, 'I'm in big trouble. It's no use fighting this when you know you can't win. They have got me on this one; my life is finished now. Drink has been my downfall. If I could have kept off the drink I would have been a different man and this would never had happened.' He also called at his sister-in-law the same day to see Matthew. He told the boy, 'These are the last words. Look after your Aunt Dolly. She has been a good pal to you.'

TOMMY LAWTON – *35 goals in 53 appearances*

Another of football's most famous centre-forwards, Tommy Lawton, was a brilliant header and skilful ball-player, with most delicate footwork for such a big man. He was magnificently built, the towering athlete, his heavily slicked hair greased back with an immaculate centre parting, his features unmistakable. What separated him from other centre-forwards of his time was the balance and quickness off the mark which left centre-halves trailing.

Above all there was the headwork, the capacity to leap a fraction ahead of his marker, hang in the air and connect with the ball in devastating fashion. Tommy scored 231 goals in 390 League matches. Including wartime and victory internationals, he played 45 times for England and scored 46 goals, figures that speak for themselves. Had his international career not been truncated by the war, when he lost seven seasons between the age of 19 and 26, his goal-count would have reached awesome proportions.

Born in 1919, Tommy was a pupil of Tonge Moor School in Bolton where he first showed signs of natural ability as a sportsman, and his outstanding potential was reflected in an astonishing haul of 570 goals in schools football. On leaving school, Tommy took a job at Walker's Tannery, like Nat Lofthouse after him, making golf clubs, before Burnley offered him a position on the groundstaff as assistant-secretary in May 1935. Tommy was encouraged to hit the ball accurately with both feet by picking out the 'B's' in the 'Burnley's Beer is Best' advertising hoarding. He practised his heading with the ball hanging from a rope at varying heights, and in an early game against Derby reserves he encountered Hughie Gallacher, who offered him advice he never forgot.

> I was having a bad match and, as I walked off disconsolately at half-time, the little Scot said to me, 'Look, son, you must learn to cover the ball with your body. If you are being tackled on your right, keep the ball at your left foot, then your opponent will have to come across your leg to get at it. And it's the same when you come on your left.' I was rather overwhelmed and stammered, 'Thanks very much, Mr Gallacher.'

Within a year Tommy made his first team debut at 16½, the youngest centre-forward to play in League football, when he faced Doncaster Rovers in a drawn match at Turf Moor in March 1936. Goal number one, naturally a header, came in the following game at Swansea. Tommy's sporting talents extended to cricket, where he excelled as a batsman for Burnley in the Lancashire League during the summer.

In October 1936 Tommy signed professional forms on his 17th birthday. He celebrated the following day with his first senior hat trick against Spurs in a 3–1 home victory. His scoring feats soon attracted the attention of First Division clubs and negotiations for Tommy's transfer to Everton were handled by his grandfather, who was handily placed as Burnley's groundsman. The sum involved was £6,500, a record transfer fee for a boy under 21, whose role was to understudy Goodison legend 'Dixie' Dean.

Dean's first words on meeting Tommy were, 'Youngster, you've come here to take my place – anything I can do for you I will.' A magnanimous gesture, which Tommy was to find epitomised the great man. The 1937/38 season proved significant in his burgeoning career, when the campaign started poorly and skipper Dean made way for Tommy against Manchester City. It was a monumental decision for the board and marked the end of Dean's career – he played once more for Everton. Tommy beat Frank Swift (who later became his greatest friend in football) early on as Everton ran out 4–1 winners, and later in the season had the satisfaction of scoring the only goal in his first derby match at Anfield. Tommy missed just one more game (due to injury) and ended the First Division's top-scorer with 28 goals in his first full season.

Tommy blazed a trail of glory the following year, as Everton won the League Championship. They stole an early lead on their rivals with a record six consecutive wins, including their best performance of the season, a 2–1 victory over Arsenal at Highbury in front of 68,000. Tommy scored the second with a crashing left-footer past the hapless Swindon. It was a vintage display described in the press as some of the best football ever seen in the capital.

Tommy made his England debut in October 1938 at Ninian Park, shortly after his 19th birthday. Wales spoilt his big day by winning 4–2, although he did have the satisfaction of scoring a penalty. April 1939 saw Tommy fulfil one of his ambitions when he led the line to victory at Hampden Park, sharing Dean's distinction of scoring the only goal with a quality header from a Stanley Matthews cross in front of 150,000.

> The ball went in the corner of the net, with the outstretched fingers of the diving Dawson inches from it. I almost turned a somersault in mid-air as I turned to congratulate Stan.

His joy was short-lived when war interrupted Tommy's progress and he was posted to a 'Footballers Battalion' in the Army Physical Training Corps. He appeared in hundreds of charity matches, helping to raise vast sums for the Red Cross. A personal milestone was achieved when Company Sergeant Major Instructor Lawton was the first centre-forward since Vivian Woodward to be appointed captain of England. A 2–2 draw with France at Wembley in May 1945 was Tommy's stage, finding the net in the second half.

In the knowledge that his wife Rosaleen had been unwell for some time, after the war Tommy was advised to move south for her benefit. He had no desire to uproot from Everton, but his form had been affected by Rosaleen's illness and he reluctantly requested a transfer. Billy Birrell was quick to respond and, in November 1945, Chelsea paid £11,500 for Tommy's services.

TOP LEFT: Bobby McNeil in 1935 as trainer with Hamilton Academical FC on left, with Bertie Harrison and David Wilson, the most celebrated player in Accies history. (© Peter McLeish)

TOP RIGHT: Jackie Crawford

ABOVE: The Chelsea forward line of February 1939; Dick Spence, Joe Payne, George Mills, Jimmy Argue and Alf Hanson. (© Scott Cheshire)

RIGHT: Top of the table clash with Wolves at Stamford Bridge in April 1955. Eric Parsons crosses ahead of Bill Shorthouse.

BELOW LEFT: Charlie Cooke in majestic full flow.

RIGHT: January 1964 Bert Murray celebrates after scoring with a looping header over the despairing Spurs keeper John Hollowbread in the F.A. Cup at White Hart Lane.

RIGHT: Clive Walker unleashes the spectacular winner against Bolton at Burnden Park in May 1983 to prevent relegation to Division Three. (© Scott Cheshire)

ABOVE: One of those mazy dribbles from Pat Nevin as he eludes Watford's John Barnes and Wilf Rostron at Stamford Bridge in October 1984.

LEFT: Tommy Lawton in action for Chelsea at Stamford Bridge. (© Sport General)

ABOVE LEFT: George Hilsdon.

ABOVE RIGHT: Bob Whittingha

LEFT: Jack Cock
(© Scott Cheshire)

ABOVE: Hughie Gallacher in combative mood as a goal is disallowed for off-side by referee Denton in the West Brom fixture at Stamford Bridge in March 1933. George Mills joins in the arm waving behind Gallacher.

BELOW: Sheffield Wednesday goalkeeper Dave McIntosh is struck by a full-blooded shot from Roy Bentley in the last home game of the Championship winning season (April 1955).

TOP: Peter Osgood converts Charlie Cooke's cross in the 1970 F.A. Cup final replay at Old Trafford. (© John Moynihan)

ABOVE: Ian Hutchinson clashes with Leeds United's Norman Hunter at Wembley during the 1970 F.A. Cup final (© Monte Fresco).

OPPOSITE PAGE:

TOP: John McNichol challenges Manchester City's Bert Trautmann as the ball runs loose at Stamford Bridge in October 1955.

MIDDLE: Bobby Tambling torments Mick Wright during Aston Villa's 6–2 defeat ██████ September 1966 at Villa Park. Bobby scored five of the goals.

BELOW: Barry Bridges beats Ipswich's goalkeeper Jim Thorburn with a spectacular header at the Bridge in February 1964.

ABOVE: Kerry Dixon is foiled by Portsmouth goalkeeper Alan Knight at Stamford Bridge in January 1988.

LEFT: David Speedie celebrates his hat-trick goal with Kevin McAllister in the Full Members' Cup Final against Machester City at Wembley in March 1986.
(© Shoot Magazine/ Phil Bagnall)

Tommy had incredible drawing power and the crowds came flocking back after wartime to watch the resumption of soccer. His first match, days after the transfer, was one of the most remarkable seen in England, when Moscow Dynamo embarked on a short tour of the UK. With an official attendance figure of 74,496 (unofficially 100,000 plus), it seemed all London had taken the afternoon off. It was the biggest crowd ever seen at the Bridge, with spectators on the hoardings, over the greyhound track, on top of the stands, and someone even fell through the roof of the stand.

> When the team lined up for the National Anthems, we could see that each Russian player carried a posy of flowers. At a word of command from their trainer, they stepped smartly forward and with a bow handed us a bouquet. The crowd roared and I felt like a film star at a premiere. They looked for all the world as if they were dressed wearing old-fashioned bathing costumes. They were one of the fastest teams I have ever seen in my life and showed brilliant teamwork, speed and ball control. They should have been four up in the first 20 minutes, then we got started and scored twice in ten minutes.

In the 25th minute Jimmy Bain crossed from the left. Tommy went up for the ball with keeper Khomich, and it fell to Len Goulden, who made no mistake. Six minutes later Reg Williams unsettled left-back Stankevich into an error, when an attempted clearance crashed against Williams and the ball rebounded into the net. Two goals in the second half enabled Moscow to draw level, before Tommy exquisitely headed a long, high ball past the advancing Khomich with eight minutes remaining. Chelsea were diplomatically denied victory in the dying minutes when Bobrov flashed the ball into the net when conservatively five yards offside as the game ended 3–3.

Tommy struck up a friendship with Reg Williams at the Bridge and harboured high hopes of fulfilling his remaining ambition in football, that of playing in an FA Cup final. His hopes were dashed in the 1945/46 season when the team lost to Aston Villa in the fifth round: 'At Villa Park Reg put in a wonder shot, only for the ball to bounce off the crossbar. The luck was against us.'

In the 1946/47 season Chelsea's best chance of success again lay in the FA Cup. Arsenal were waiting for them in the third round at the Bridge. In front of 70,000 Leslie Compton marked Tommy efficiently and Chelsea secured a draw through a lob from Tommy Walker. Two replays were fervent tussles, with Tommy equalising Ronnie Rooke's goal in the first at Highbury, and dominating the second with two devastating goals at White Hart Lane.

> After beating Arsenal we all felt there was quite a chance that Chelsea's name would be on the Cup. But it was not to be, yet we nearly beat Derby County, the holders. At Stamford Bridge I had a good goal disallowed and, with us leading 2–1 and only 90 seconds to go, Raich Carter got a freak goal to square the match. Following a scrimmage in the goalmouth, Raich managed to force the ball into our net with his thigh.

On a frozen baseball ground Jackie Stamps scored the only goal in extra-time as Chelsea failed to convert any of the numerous chances created. Tommy played his part to the full in the League with 26 goals in 34 games.

A severe winter meant the 1946/47 season was the longest in the history of football, lasting from August to June. It was the most successful internationally for Tommy, chosen on eight occasions to lead the forward line and finding the net ten times. The end of the season saw England tour Switzerland and Portugal, where the home side were trounced 10–0 at the Stadium of Light in Lisbon. The ball had been in play 13 seconds when Tommy met a perfect cross floated over by Wilf Mannion. In the 22nd minute Tom Finney, playing for the first time at outside-left, with Matthews on the other wing, dribbled 50 yards before coolly lobbing the ball over the keeper with his right foot, and cracking it into the net with his left. 'The goal of the century,' said Tommy, who scored four times, as did Stan Mortensen. The trip had exhausted Tommy, who, on his return, was desperate for a break from football. However, a club tour of Sweden started just two days later.

Tommy rang Chelsea and promised to report for training on the Thursday. During the night he was taken ill with food poisoning. Following a visit from Billy Birrell and the club doctor, Tommy agreed to travel the following Sunday, three days later. Tommy was again violently ill on the Thursday night and his own doctor's view was that Tommy would risk his health if forced to travel, an opinion shared by a specialist. At the insistence of one of Chelsea's directors, Tommy was again visited by the club doctor and a further specialist on the Saturday. Despite his and wife Rosaleen's protestations, he was pronounced fit to travel, but refused to do so. Instead Tommy spent two months resting with his family in Broadstairs and, batteries recharged, reported for training a month before the start of the new season. On seeing Billy Birrell he was asked why he did not join the tour party.

> I repeated all that had happened but apparently my explanation didn't appear to be satisfactory. From then on things went from bad to worse and the situation between Chelsea and myself became impossible. So

at last I asked for a transfer, feeling that this was the best thing to do to ease the unrest. My first two requests were refused, but eventually the club announced they were prepared to receive offers for me. I never regretted the move to Chelsea and it was only the differences of opinion with the management that forced me to ask for a transfer.

Tommy was determined to leave despite pressure from his fan club, but only played a handful of first-team games amidst rumours of dressing-room disorder. He had a reputation for speaking his mind and didn't suffer fools gladly. There was enough time for a fabulous goal at the end of August 1947 against Derby. Ken Armstrong won the ball and passed to Tommy, who trapped it in an instant, side-stepped a tackle and simultaneously hit a scorcher into the top of Townsend's net for the winner. However, relations deteriorated to the extent that Tommy was told by a reporter that he had been dropped to the reserve side shortly after being placed on the list.

I didn't mind being chosen for the reserves at all, but I did object to the underhand methods of the Chelsea officials in notifying the world before me. I played in the reserve side at Highbury the following Saturday (in front of 20,000) and really enjoyed myself. I scored with a header and helped the lads earn a ten-shilling bonus that day. A week later I figured in a thrilling international match against Ireland at Goodison Park. Three minutes from the end I crashed in what seemed to be the winning goal from a perfect centre from the peerless Stanley Matthews, only for Peter Doherty to nod one past Frank Swift 40 seconds from time to equalise.

Tommy attracted interest from a number of clubs, including Arsenal, Portsmouth and Derby, but in November 1947 signed for Notts County of Division Three South for the first-ever fee of £20,000. At the time he considered it the best move of his life, though on reflection in later years expressed deep regret dropping out of the First Division at such an early age. His greatest pleasure was retaining his England place, and in May 1948 Tommy scored in one of England's finest team performances, a 4–0 win over Italy in Turin. Though still in his twenties, a 0–0 draw with Denmark later that year was his final international.

Notts County were fourth from bottom when Tommy joined and in grave danger of having to apply for re-election. By the end of the season they had risen to sixth place and in 1949/50 the average gate increased from 9,000 to 35,000 as the club secured promotion. Tommy played for County until 1952, when he signed for Brentford, with a brief spell as player-manager. Nearly two years later Arsenal, urgently needing a focal point to their attack, took him back to the First Division at the age of 34. Though he did not score with his old panache, the footballing brain and flicked headers were still powerful weapons. He stayed at Highbury almost three years before moving to Southern League Kettering as player-manager in 1956. A successful start appeared to point the way to a fruitful new career, but a return to Notts County as manager was unsuccessful and he was sacked in April 1964, although appointed a club director. He had a spell as County's coach and was Chief Scout from October 1968 to April 1970.

Tommy also took over a pub, but his reputation for financial hard-headedness in football was not replicated in his business life. He later wrote a newspaper column, but his remaining years were spent in more or less straitened circumstances. There was a string of court appearances, where he was treated leniently for minor financial offences. Both Brentford and Everton staged testimonial matches without doing more than easing the burden for a time and he had to sell his England caps to repay debts. From the early 1970s he suffered from poor health, having sustained a heart attack at the age of 50, and the death of Rosaleen in 1988 was a blow from which he never really recovered. For the final years of his life he lived in a nursing home at Nottingham and died in November 1996, aged 77. At his funeral a collector lent the family the England cap he won against Holland in the 1940s. At the service the Reverend acknowledged Tommy would be remembered with pride, a man who brought honour to the game.

ROY BENTLEY − 150 goals in 367 appearances

As captain of the Championship-winning side, Roy Bentley has a special place in Chelsea's history. He was an outstanding forward with all-round skills, who injected cunning and special awareness into the front line with his roving style of play. A superb header of the ball, he was Chelsea's leading scorer and star for eight consecutive seasons. Born at Barrow Hill, Shirehampton, in 1924, Roy's exceptional sporting skills were recognised at Portway Senior Boys' School, where he was captain of both the cricket and football teams.

> I come from a family of five boys and two girls, and my father, who was a rugby player and also a bare-fisted boxer, hoped one of us would

play sport. I played in every position in the Football League except goalkeeper and have my Dad to thank in particular for making me play with two good feet. My brother Arthur had a lot of talent and was a terrific footballer. He used to shove me at outside-right and look after me in senior games when I was still a kid at school.

In 1938 Roy scored the third goal for Bristol Schoolboys in a 3–1 victory against Cheltenham Boys at Ashton Gate in the English Schools Divisional Final. He scored over 100 goals for Bristol Boys, captaining them in his last year and earned high praise in the press.

I wasn't too disappointed I failed my 11-plus, as I left school at 14 to play football, but my only regret taking football as a career is that I never finished my schooling. As a manager I always used to tell my players to prepare themselves for the future, and was coaching at Thatcham when I said to Maurice Evans at Reading, 'I've got a good boy for you who wants to go to university – he's too intelligent to be just a footballer.' He was Lawrie Sanchez who was looking ahead and didn't do too badly – of course, he's in management himself now.

I joined Bristol Rovers from school in 1938 and was on £1 per week as a groundstaff boy. However, they almost went bankrupt and Joe Davis was playing snooker charity matches to help them out. I was told for the coming [1939/40] season my pay would be reduced to ten shillings a week and my dad wasn't having that.

I was introduced to Mr Jenkins, the Bristol City chairman by a City scout. I went to see him with my dad at his pub/hotel in Eastville and they signed me for at least twice what I was getting at Rovers. I was shown by Billy Mitchell at City how to look after myself without being dirty or going over the top. Then the war started, but at 16 I was playing war-time football at outside-right in the first team with five or six internationals until 1942, which was a great experience. I went into the Navy and was posted to a destroyer on convoy duties and must have crossed the Atlantic 20 times. When I was in Toronto they wanted me to have a baseball trial – after all I'd played most other sports!

Roy rejoined City after the war and at the beginning of the 1946/47 season Newcastle United signed him as an inside-right for £8,000. It was a step up from Division Three, but not to the League he expected. Coaching was non-existent, so Roy looked to senior pros like Tommy Pearson, Jack Fairbrother and Joe Harvey for advice. He never found out who actually chose the team, which baffled players and supporters alike, with the selection usually announced at the last minute, and often details were heard first from the local news reporter. Roy played for a season and a half, scoring 22 goals in 48 matches, but requested a transfer as the strong air didn't agree with him. His weight reduced from about 14 to 10½ stone, which left him without any stamina and affected his game.

> I found out just before I went to Newcastle that I was joining a Second Division club, not a First Division one! Before I went there I trained for three weeks to lose over a stone, as I had been in the Navy, and was surprised with the lack of professionalism, especially the equipment we worked with. Of course it was just after the war, and we had big ex-marine white polo shirts for training or had to bring our own gear. I was in digs with a wing-half from Bradford called George Bradley, a nice guy. He said that people who came to the north-east had reacted to the climate, as it could be bracing and took a lot out of you, which is what the doctor eventually told me. As a young lad of 22 I should have been running all over the place, but I had a bad time football-wise and got very tired as the season wore on. I was even struggling to finish a round of golf! I also married Vi in 1946, and the extra responsibilities could have been another reason for losing weight, as within a year she was expecting. I was trying like mad in the first team, but George Martin, the manager, wasn't very understanding and never gave me a chance to explain the problem. He did send me to Scarborough though, where Vi and I stayed in the best hotel. They gave me Guinness with every meal to build me up and I started to feel better. In the end Newcastle were advised to let me go, otherwise I might have contracted tuberculosis.
>
> When we lost 1–0 to Charlton in the semi-final of the FA Cup at Elland Road in 1947, we trained at Scarborough. On the Friday we went to a spa for a special peat bath and it was like having a hot poultice put all over your body. Jackie Milburn and a few others refused to have it. It was supposed to tone our muscles and relax us, but we had rubber legs and could hardly get out of the bath. I'm not trying to find a reason why we lost, but I don't recommend having it the day before a semi-final! It was my biggest game and disappointment at Newcastle.

Roy returned south to Chelsea in January 1948 in an £11,000 deal, where he was converted to a centre-forward. He regretted Tommy Lawton's transfer just as he joined the Blues – it would have been a great thrill to have partnered his hero.

Tommy always impressed me with his heading. I won school cups at athletics, including the long jump and high jump, which helped me get up for the ball in the air. Although the most important thing is timing, I also used to bring my feet up and jump to bring the body higher and above goalkeepers. Tommy's last international before the war started was against Scotland, when he scored a brilliant goal with his head. I remember watching it on the Pathé news in the cinema and wanted to watch it again and again. Tommy was not at his best at Chelsea, but when I was told I was taking over from him it gave me an added incentive to perform.

I was the first player to have a medical before the club decided to buy me, and was also surprised at the lack of professionalism at Chelsea. I expected some form of discipline, but there wasn't a lot of order, which I was used to, especially having been in the Navy. In my first game at home to Huddersfield, Peter Doherty, their captain, went over the top of the ball to me, which I don't think was intentional, he was not that sort of player. I saw him coming and tried to ride with him, but was a split second too late, and he just caught me enough to strain my groin. The following Saturday we played Manchester City in the cup and I went through a training session at Manchester, when it was all right. Halfway through the second half I was feeling it, we lost 2–0 and I had a poor game. I shouldn't have played but didn't want to let anyone down. Then I was told by a spectator, 'You're no good, get back to Newcastle, we don't want you here.' I'm glad he said that as I thought I'd show him. At the time I was down to ten stone and not fit.

Billy Birrell took the credit, but it was Len Goulden the coach, who converted me to a centre-forward. He said I was, 'two-footed, had pace and didn't mind getting stuck in'. Billy agreed to Len's suggestion when I was trying to take Tommy Lawton's place, but not succeeding. That was against Everton in September 1948 at home, we won 6–0 and I scored a couple. Len came in and said, 'You'll never play anywhere else and will be in the England side inside a year.'

At the end of the 1950/51 season Roy requested a transfer for a number of personal reasons. Roy and John Harris were in dispute with the club, so they missed the first six games of the new season.

People don't know the real truth about Johnny Harris and I going on strike. For the first three years we fought relegation and I had been told year after year that a lot of money would be spent to bring new players in. Johnny and myself and a few others were getting fed up – the rest were not that bothered if we won, drew or lost. Unknown to me Johnny Harris had been promised the assistant manager's job, to take over after Billy Birrell and he'd also been let down. It was against my character to do anything about it, but coming away from the ground one day I said to Johnny, 'I'm not going to sign,' and he was going to do the same. It wasn't that I wanted to leave Chelsea, but promises were never fulfilled over a long period. Johnny put on a cloth cap and spectacles to disguise himself and we watched Chelsea play from the terraces. It was hurting us as much as anybody and lots of things were being written in the papers that were untrue. In the end we weren't being paid and couldn't hold out any longer.

Roy was successfully utilised as a roving centre-forward, an unorthodox method at that time, employing a degree of mobility which frequently saw him raiding down the flanks. The renowned Hungarian Nando Hidegkuti had been familiar with Roy's tactics and in 1953 Roy watched the deep-lying forward star in the thrashing of England.

I watched Hidegkuti when Hungary beat England 6–3 in the famous victory at Wembley. He said to me at dinner after we played Red Banner in 1954 that he had copied my 'rover' style of play, which I was very chuffed with. Being a centre-forward himself Ted Drake and I talked a lot about the way I should play. I was making as many goals as I was scoring and asked him how I could keep up my form, when defenders couldn't work out my 'rover' style. I just played normally in a game to start off with, then mixed it up. It was trial and error and just seemed to work. I only stopped when I was no longer young and fit enough to do it.

The papers were full of centre-halves saying how they would stop me, which always did me a world of good. The physical side of it never worried me, I could look after myself. I always thought it harder to follow than to be followed, so felt I had an advantage over a defender. I had the pace over 10–15 yards to get away from them anyway. The best defender I played technically was Neil Franklin. He wasn't terribly fast, but he was a good thinker and read the game well. Leon Leuty of Derby County was another good defender, he should have won more caps but was competing with Neil and Billy Wright.

The most physical defender I faced was Harry Johnston of Blackpool, hard but fair. Malcolm Barrass of Bolton was a good player, a hard man, but I never really gave it a thought. The most consistent centre-half and anchor in the side I saw was Frank Brennan of Newcastle, big but quick for his size. He was injured playing for Scotland and missed our FA Cup semi-final, which cost us dearly. Fred Hall of Sunderland was the hardest man I played against, not dirty. He didn't turn a hair and said very little.

Roy's 21 goals in 1954/55 were a decisive factor in clinching the League Championship, and he felt the signs of a side starting to gel in the previous season against West Brom. Whilst Roy's most memorable game of the Championship season was the 5–6 thriller against Manchester United, a personal highlight was his 100th Chelsea League goal, again versus West Brom.

When we played top of the table West Brom at the Hawthorns [October 1953] we decided to play a particular system but got beaten 5–2. We were disappointed with our performance and expected a roasting from Ted, only to be greeted with, 'Well done lads, it's nearly there, keep at it. You won't be playing a West Brom side every week.' He could see what we had been practising was coming. The biggest thrill was when we beat them 5–0 in the return game and it ruined their championship hopes.

Every goal was a good one – I worried when I wasn't scoring and went through periods between December and February, when the ball wouldn't come through cleanly and I didn't have so many chances. My 100th goal [October 1954 in a 3–3 draw against West Brom at the Bridge] was a big thrill for me. Just as he said he would, Eric Parsons sent across a low centre for which Jim Sanders dived, but failed to reach. The ball came to me and I tapped it into the back of the net.

During the era of the 'W' formation there was not a great focus on goalscoring duos. Roy's telepathy with inside-forward Johnny McNichol was the nearest approach to a partnership. They were the perfect foil for each other, with Roy's ubiquitous wandering and Johnny carving out openings. Whenever Johnny got hold of the ball, Roy's stride quickened – nonetheless Roy asserted the importance of teamwork.

Johnny and I had a terrific understanding; we first played together in the reserves at Newcastle and knew each other's play. But Ted would emphasise that's how it should be with all the players. It didn't always happen, but you hoped it would work with one of the forwards during a game. Les Stubbs was good – he loved it when I moved wide, as he would go into my space and wait for the crosses to come in. John would be more inclined to be the one to give the ball to the wide players. It was, of course, a different system in those days, but you should never go onto the field trying to link up with one player more than another, as the opposition would soon realise it.

My best Chelsea goal was against Manchester United in the quarter-final of the FA Cup in 1950. Billy Gray sent me a clever back-heeled pass which put United's defence out of their stride. The ball came to me at the ideal height and I let fly from just outside the 18-yard box. The ball curled all the way into the top corner and I knew it was a goal as soon as I hit it, thanks to Billy.

The story did not have a happy ending. Chelsea drew the first semi-final 2–2 against Arsenal. Roy scored two early goals, the first a beautiful lob over Swindon's head, the second a glided header just inside the post. Arsenal won the replay in extra-time against a side weakened by injuries. Two years later Freddie Cox was again the Blues' Achilles' heel as Chelsea were defeated 3–0 in a second semi-final replay.

In January 1950 Walter Winterbottom selected Roy to be included in the 'B' international squad for the game against Switzerland at Sheffield. Six minutes before half-time he created history by becoming the first English international substitute when replacing Chelsea colleague Billy Gray, who had damaged a cartilage. At the end of the 1949/50 season Roy became the first Chelsea player to appear in a World Cup finals competition, winning caps against Chile and in the infamous 1–0 defeat by USA in Belo Horizonte.

I made my England debut in 1949 against Sweden in Stockholm, when Walter Winterbottom tried to play with three centre-forwards. I was playing my roving role and, as soon as I moved away, both Stan Mortensen and Jack Rowley would come in and want to play upfront through the middle. Stan was like lightning, Jack was more physical, but a good goalscorer. They let me do all the fetching and carrying and it was never going to work. But it was my first cap and I wasn't going to turn it down! They were more experienced than I was and you couldn't expect them to change their game, but why did the powers-to-be pick us?

My best game for England was when I scored in my first home international in 1950 and we beat Scotland at Hampden Park to get to the World Cup finals. About 30 minutes from time Bobby Langton, my left-wing partner, whipped down the touchline. I received a low cross from him and, although goalie Jimmy Cowan got his fingers to it, the ball entered the net over his left shoulder. Thanks to Bobby I had scored the only goal that put us on the road to Rio.

The World Cup was overshadowed by getting beaten by the USA, which I've only talked about in the last few years. Our team on paper was as good as you can get including Tom Finney, the best all-round player I ever saw, a gentleman on and off the field. He was skilful, could head a ball, kick with both feet, was the strongest tackling forward I've seen and took the most amazing knocks. We prepared professionally and didn't underestimate them, but the ground was a bull-ring, bumpy with very little grass. I hit the crossbar four or five times and it was just one of those games that happens occasionally in football. Their goalie was an ice-hockey minder, but he did a good job on the day and carried the luck. As soon as the game finished we walked back to the changing-rooms at a nearby school. By the time we got there, we had been told not to talk to the press, which we weren't allowed to anyway.

After being a pivotal figure at Chelsea for almost nine years, Roy moved to the adjacent parish of Fulham in August 1956 for £8,500. He played 143 games, scoring another 23 goals but again suffered the heartbreak of losing in the FA Cup semi-final.

I went to Fulham, which was a very friendly club, as a centre-forward and switched to inside-right when Maurice Cook was bought – Johnny Haynes played at inside-left, which was great. Then I went to right-half, where I played when Fulham drew against Manchester United in the 1958 cup semi-final at Villa Park, and lost the replay at Highbury. I played in seven semi-finals of the FA Cup, including replays, and lost them all. There is no worse feeling in your stomach than to lose in the semi-final.

We won promotion to the First Division in 1958/59 and when the two centre-halves, Derek Lampe and Joe Stapleton, were injured, Bedford Jezzard, the manager, asked me to play there. I was happy about that and really enjoyed it. We had Alan Mullery at right-half, George Cohen at right-back, Jimmy Langley at left-back and Eddie

Lowe left-half. When Bedford took over I knew he would be intimidated by managing players more experienced than him, so said on behalf of the team, 'Everybody's behind you.'

Roy moved to QPR in June 1961, where he played 45 games and had a spell as full-back before retiring. Roy was capped 12 times for England and scored 208 goals in 656 appearances in total. He successfully moved into management with Reading in 1963, then Swansea in 1969.

I wanted to play until I was 40, but had a bad stomach injury and had to retire at 38 when I was still enjoying it. The manager at QPR was Alec Stock, who could get any side going. Without a shadow of doubt he was the best manager I played for, not necessarily on the tactical side, but more with his man-management. He could lift a player at half-time inside three minutes and I learnt so much from him.

I wasn't originally going into football management as while I was at Chelsea I took different jobs in commerce. Being Roy Bentley obviously helped me, but it was also a hindrance, as I was never quite sure if I won orders because I was doing my job well or because I was well-known. I spoke a lot to Johnny Harris at Sheffield United, who convinced me I could do a manager's job and some of my colleagues suggested I try it. Reading were a good club but there were financial constraints, which came to a head when we were about fourth in the table with twelve games to go, and Tommy Docherty had two players I wanted, one a centre-forward, the other a wing-half. While I couldn't guarantee promotion, three weeks before I had been to the directors and asked £10,000 for a couple of players. I said even that might not be enough, as I wanted players who were not only good enough for the Third Division, but also for the Second and First Division. Tom said he would let me have them for £20,000 and I knew he was doing me a favour. I saw the chairman the next day and asked for another £10,000, which he declined. Subsequently Tom collected £20,000 for the centre-forward alone and £15,000 for the other boy. On the last day of the season Oxford needed a draw to go up in second place, which they got with a penalty in the last few minutes. We won 2–1 at Workington but stayed third.

At Swansea we got promotion from the Fourth Division [in 1969/70] and I only bought one player, Barry Hole from Aston Villa. However, there were some funny things going on off the field in connection with the building business – some of the directors were property developers, solicitors etc and they let me down badly. They said they were not going to renew my contract on the basis I hadn't got the right players at the club, which I didn't agree with and I left.

I was secretary at Reading and Aldershot, and for Ron Harris's golf club in Swindon. I ran a shop just outside Reading and was also manager at Thatcham Town for a while. I have always enjoyed golf, reading and gardening. I now play as much golf as I can, off an 18 handicap nowadays. We have two daughters, Lorraine and Jane, and six grandchildren.

JOHN McNICHOL – 66 goals in 202 appearances

In his autobiography *Yours Sincerely*, Ron Greenwood wrote, 'John McNichol was the first player I saw really curve shots and passes with the outside of his foot. He was a player who made things happen and was famous for his "Bovril" ball, as we called it, a long pass hit towards a Bovril advertisement in one of the corners for Eric Parsons to chase.' If Roy Bentley was the star of the side, Johnny McNichol was one of the unsung heroes. There is little doubt he would have graced most premiership sides given the skills he exhibited among the cream of the First Division nearly fifty years ago. Born at Kilmarnock in 1925, Johnny came from a sporting family.

> My older brother Felix was a good goalkeeper and played in the equivalent of the Southern League in Scotland and, like everybody else, went into the Forces. My other brother Danny sadly died in the war.

During the war Johnny served with the Fleet Air Arm, mainly in Scotland. He came to Newcastle's attention with Hurlford Juniors, just outside Kilmarnock, and signed as a part-timer in August 1946.

> In the old days professional clubs used to have the first team playing the seconds a couple of times before the start of the season, and a Newcastle scout invited me to play for the reserves in a pre-season trial. Newcastle had just signed Frank Brennan, Roy Bentley and Joe Harvey, who had come out of the forces and played for the firsts. The reserves were quite good, as during the war miners didn't go into the

forces, they stayed in the mines, so there were four or five who had been playing regularly in the first team. Even Jackie Milburn was not certain of a first-team place at that time! There has always been fantastic support at Newcastle and 30,000 people watched the practice game – we were beaten very narrowly 3–2. They wanted to sign me and asked me to come back for the second game, which we did well to draw, and most of the players like Norman Dodgin, Tot Smith and Charlie Crowe went on to play for the first team.

I never trained in the morning the whole time I was at Newcastle – I trained with about half a dozen other part-timers in the evening, which was not much fun in the middle of winter! Because of the number of postponements my second season actually went on to June. My son was born on 6 June 1948 – it was also the day of my last game at Newcastle, which we won 6–1. When I got home my wife was in labour and the woman from next door, who was a qualified midwife, told me to get down to the nearest phone-box and ring the doctor. By the time I got back John had been born, then 20 minutes later the doctor arrived!

Footballers were a cheap commodity in those days, and there were at least three teams packed with professionals, so opportunities for young Johnny were slim.

The standard of the Newcastle reserve team was as good as the Third Division and it was very difficult to break into the first team as an inside-forward. As well as Roy Bentley, Len Shackleton was an inside-forward, together with George Stobbart, who cost a lot of money, Ernie Taylor from Blackpool and Tommy Thompson, who played for England.

In the end Johnny left St James' Park over a contract dispute. At the time he was a trained motor mechanic, earning money outside the game, and the manager thought this justified offering him a lower wage.

As a part-timer my contract was £6 per week for the first year, and I would get £1 per annum rise, which I did the second. The third year the manager George Martin told me I'd done well, would probably be in the first team next year and ready to go full-time, then he said my contract was still £7 per week. I thought he'd made a mistake, as it should have been £8. He said, '£8 and you're part-time working, you're getting more money than a first-year!' I said, 'But I'm doing two jobs,' so made up my mind not to sign, as it was in breach of my contract. That extra £1 would have paid my rent.

At the time Norman Dodgin's brother Bill was the manager at Southampton. Bill came regularly to the north-east as his parents lived there, and in passing Norman recommended me to him. It was agreed that when Bill was next in the north-east I would talk to him and see if I was interested – Norman would have been with us as well. I was unsure as, working part-time and playing, I was just as well off as a full-timer, and getting used to my job after three years in the forces. In the meantime there was a Newcastle reserve called Laurie Nevins who was transferred to Brighton. He must have recommended me to the club, as the Newcastle manager wanted me to see Don Welsh, their manager. I thought I was in trouble now, although my meeting with Bill wasn't done illegally, more as Norman was my best friend. The day Bill was on his way to see me, he was on the railway platform in London when he bumped into Don, a million-to-one chance. Bill obviously couldn't say anything when Don told him he was on his way to Newcastle to see a young man called McNichol!

Don Welsh, who was a good coach, wanted me to sign full-time, and offered me the maximum wages I could have had in those days, with first-team money even if I wasn't in the first team. It meant I would be getting the same amount for one job as I was for two jobs, so I left Newcastle and signed for Brighton because of £1.

Johnny joined during the close season of 1948/49. Against a backdrop of post-war austerity it was surprising that Brighton were prepared to splash out a club record of £5,000 on a player yet to play in the League, but Welsh convinced his directors that Johnny was well worth the investment. Johnny's ball-playing style was first displayed in a typically tough Third Division South battle at home to Swindon in August 1948. Fresh players generated so much interest that the gate of 21,500 for the 1–1 draw was a League record. Johnny didn't start as a scoring sensation – he was not initially considered a natural goalscorer. Two goals from 33 starts didn't deflect interest being shown by other clubs.

I had been injured towards the end of the season at Swansea, and was decorating the flat that belonged to the Albion when Don Welsh called one day to say, 'I have Jock Thomson, the manager, of Manchester City in the car, he's interested in signing you.' I couldn't believe it – here I was, at the end of my first season, I said I didn't think I had done that badly! He was even offering me wages which were worse than I was on at the Albion, if I wasn't in the first team. He had been offered a lot of money for me and the club were hard up, but I turned him down flat and enjoyed my time with the Albion.

With nine goals Johnny top-scored the next season (1949/50), and he again finished leading striker in 1950/51 with 14 in League and Cup. He was also the only ever-present and had a superb year, playing a brand of football that won him the reputation as the finest inside-forward in the Third Division and brought scouts flocking to the Goldstone. The highlight was a 9–1 thrashing of Newport County in April 1951, breaking all Brighton's goal-scoring records – four of the goals came from Johnny. By 1951/52 Johnny had been appointed skipper and scored twice in the Albion's finest display of the season, holding Division winners Plymouth to a 2–2 draw at Home Park. Success continued to elude Brighton and in the summer of 1952, after 39 goals in 165 appearances, with a £12,000 plus cheque, Jimmy Leadbetter took 27-year-old Johnny to Chelsea – he was Ted Drake's first signing.

I had played during the season at Reading, where Ted was manager. The Albion beat them 4–1 and I scored three goals, so obviously he must have been impressed on that game alone. He got in touch with Alec Wilson the Albion trainer, who he used to play with, to see what sort of player I was over a season. Alec openly told me he had recommended me and I signed for Chelsea.

Despite having played all his League football in the Third Division, Johnny was undaunted by his extraordinary debut on the opening day of the 1952/53 season against Manchester United at Old Trafford. The game was 12 minutes old when, advancing 20 yards into the United half, Sid Tickridge put everything into a kick that would have landed the ball in the goalmouth had not an opponent travelling at speed in the opposite direction hit the ball at the same time. Tickridge's right knee took the full impact and his ligament was badly damaged.

Without substitutes I had to play at right-back, and playing left-wing that day was Roger Byrne, who was making his way in the game and, of course, became the England left-back. It was a quite amazing debut – they had won the League the year before and had some great players and we were beaten 2–0.

It was Johnny's first outing at full-back and he adapted magnificently, with quick interceptions and clever use of the ball. One other game sticks out in his memory from the first season.

> I'll never forget my first FA Cup tie for the Blues. It was in January 1953 when we were drawn away to Derby County. With 20 minutes left we were 4–1 down but pulled back to 4–4 and I got the equaliser. We won the replay at the Bridge by the only goal – Eric Parsons scored it in extra-time. For me it was a cracking cup tie in more ways than one, because I cracked two ribs in the first game but didn't know about it until after the replay!

Johnny is remembered as playing an integral role in the Championship side – he was able to spot an opening in a split second. With 14 League goals in the 1954/55 season he became a regular goalscorer as well as a creator of chances, especially for Roy Bentley.

> Roy was a great header of the ball and very fast. He was a hard man as well, who could mix it if a centre-half wanted to mix it, which you needed. He was so good that Bobby Smith couldn't get a game.

The coruscating home fixture against Manchester United in the Championship-winning season was one of Johnny's most outstanding memories for Chelsea, as it was for a 24-year-old Bishop Auckland amateur footballer travelling down on the Friday overnight train from Newcastle. Seamus O'Connell was careful not to lose sight of the brown-paper parcel he brought with him containing a pair of football boots that he wore to score a hat trick on his Chelsea debut. You couldn't have written the script (other than reversing the scoreline) of one of the most remarkable matches ever seen at the Bridge, when cautious football was swept aside by a giant broom.

> It was one of those games you don't forget, them being in front, us coming back from 2–5 down, then pushing up – it was very open. Some of the goals shouldn't have happened, as you were attacking when you should have been defending. They were a good team then coming up to greatness. Tommy Taylor, their young, lean tall centre-forward, was beating Ron Greenwood in the air all the time and at half-time Ted had a go at him for conceding all these balls in the air. Ron, who of course became one of the top coaches in the game, said to Ted, 'What do you want me to do, stand on his feet!' Seamus

O'Connell, who had a great eye for the ball, had a good job as an amateur – I don't think that would happen nowadays!

Johnny also recalled the two contests against nearest challengers, Wolves.

Up at Molineux we came from behind to snatch an exciting 4–3 win in the closing minutes, after a lot of the home supporters had left for home. I remember walking off the field with Ron Flowers, the England wing-half who had been marking me that day. He was certainly not looking forward to confronting his manager in the dressing-room. 'Stan Cullis will go bloody wild,' he prophesied.

Then in the return fixture four months later, when the 1–0 win virtually clinched the title, Johnny recalled the day for an entirely different reason.

I travelled up from Brighton and went to the match on the underground, which was absolutely packed. When I got to Fulham Broadway station I literally had to fight my way to get off the train and up the stairs. This was a couple of hours before the start as we had to be there at least an hour before kick-off. When I asked what was happening someone said they had shut the gates so, instead of turning left, I had to go round the houses and come round the back way. Everything was shut with thousands locked outside and I had trouble getting in the ground myself! The ground was packed and you couldn't help looking at the crowd sometimes – there would be a ripple of movement and a wave of people going down the terracing – it frightened the life out of me.

Johnny was involved that season in one of the strangest goals ever scored – Chelsea's second in a 3–1 home victory over Leicester City. After Eric Parsons had fired the Blues into an early lead, a shot from Johnny hit the bar. The ball rebounded between two Leicester players, Stan Milburn and Jack Froggatt, who, desperately trying to clear their lines, simultaneously kicked the ball high into their own net.

As the ball came over I made firm contact and my header hit the underside of the crossbar and I think might well have bounced down over the line anyway. In the scramble that ensued two Leicester players came rushing in and appeared to make contact with the ball at the same time, forcing it into the net. It was quite impossible to divide it so they had to shoulder the responsibility together – each angrily blaming the other!

Thus, the records show 'Milburn and Froggatt shared own goal'. Johnny scored Chelsea's third and also remembered a brace at Tottenham in April 1955.

> We had a depleted side as Ken Armstrong won his only England cap. A young Alan Dicks played in his place and Peter Brabrook stepped in for Frank Blunstone, also on England duty. It was a big game for us, we won 4–2 and I always seemed to do well against Spurs.
>
> After we won the League we were probably over the top, with about seven players thirty-plus, although one shouldn't slide away so rapidly. Season 1955/56 wasn't going too well and what Ted did was bring in too many youngsters at once. When I see the age of some players now, I wonder if Ted sold the experienced players too early. I was 12th man when a young fella called Jimmy Greaves took my place at Spurs – of course he scored a goal and the rest is history. Peter Brabrook took my place initially and when he went to the right-wing I regained my place. Then we played Darlington in the fourth round of the FA Cup at home in January 1958, thought it would be a doddle, but went 3–1 down. We brought it back to 3–3 and I scored the equaliser. The replay was my last game and, although I scored, we were beaten 4–1. So I scored in my two last games before being transferred.

Johnny appeared on Chelsea's team sheet more than 200 times over six years, for several seasons he was second-highest scorer to Roy Bentley. He recalled relaxing trips to the Kent coast.

> There was a period when we won the League that Ted would take us for special training to Broadstairs. Three or four times we played away on the Saturday and the following week went training there. We also played golf but by Wednesday the players were bored to tears. Big six feet three inches Stan Wicks was an excitable and nervous chap. When little Frankie Blunstone once climbed up and knocked on his window, Stan got the fright of his life! I remember in the 1955/56 season we played at Hartlepool in the third round of the FA Cup. We were leading 1–0 when I ran in hoping to get a rebound. I went right into the goalie who got a knock, the referee blew for a foul and I got the bird. The

crowd then started giving the whole team a load of stick and big Stan came running to me and said, 'It's all your fault.'

When Johnny first joined Chelsea, he kept his house in Hove and bought a newsagent's shop in the town. After sending the paper boys on their round, he caught the 8.15 from Hove and arrived at Stamford Bridge by 10 a.m. for training.

When we won the League I was 31 and already thinking about what to do after football, so bought a post office/newsagent. I wanted to make sure I had something after football, as I didn't want to go back to being a mechanic. When I bought my shop I don't think Ted was very pleased, and from then on I was in and out of the team. I eventually sold it in the early 1960s.

In March 1958 Johnny moved to Crystal Palace; a fee of £2,000 was involved.

In fact just before I went to Palace Ron Greenwood, who when he retired managed Eastbourne United, wanted me to play for them. They were in the Metropolitan League, so it was a big step down. He was my room-mate when we played away and offered me £20 per week, which was pretty well what I was getting at Chelsea. I thought I would have two years at Palace and ended with five and enjoyed it. I captained the side and we got promotion from the Fourth Division [in 1960/61]. By that time I had also been converted to a full-back, which helped prolong my career. However, I had my jaw broken and broke my arm, and in my last game for Palace had my cheekbone fractured for the third time. Maybe the injuries were caused by being just that split second slower than I was five years earlier. In the side was Johnny Byrne, who was a very good player, taking on big centre-halves week after week in Division Four and getting a lot of stick. If he had been three or four inches taller he would have been a world-class player.

Johnny played over 200 first-team matches and, although he spent most of his Palace career in defence, managed another 15 goals. In May 1963 he signed as player-manager of Tunbridge Wells in the Southern League, but in 1967 had the misfortune to break his leg, when one of his players couldn't make the game. It marked the end of Johnny's playing career, but he stayed in football.

Palace chairman Arthur Wait approached me and said they were
starting a new fundraising programme. I said I never knew anything
about the pools, but the Southern Area manager of Littlewoods helped
me. I thought I might have a chance of getting back into football but
never got anywhere near the footballing side. I stayed until 1979,
when I was approached by Tony Millard to move to Brighton on the
commercial front, as it was nearer to home. I stayed at Brighton until
about 1992, when I retired.

Johnny remains a keen follower of the game and his appetite remains
insatiable. Sometimes he watches Chelsea, more often than not he is happy to
take in a local game. He lives at Saltdean with his wife Connie in a bungalow
with a picturesque sea view.

My hobbies include gardening, which I enjoy. My son does gardening
for a living and now and then I help him, doing the easy bits like the
lawn. I have two children, John and Margaret, three grandchildren
and one great-grandchild.

JIMMY GREAVES – *132 goals in 169 appearances*

Tuesday morning at Chelsea was always the first team versus the reserves. One
week there were a few injuries from the Saturday, so three groundstaff boys
from Hendon were sent for by Albert Tennant, who would stand on the
touchline giving instructions. After about 20 minutes, a kid that the players
had never seen before picked the ball up in midfield and set off on a run. He
went by one, then another and Albert shouted, 'Get rid of it.' He went by
another one, carried on and drew Reg Matthews out. He dipped his shoulder;
Reg went one way and he rolled it the other side. He strolled back to the
halfway line, then turned to Albert and shouted, 'You didn't tell me when!'
Later on when Jimmy Greaves was clean through in practice games, Reg, a
vastly experienced England goalkeeper, would turn his back, as he knew
Jimmy would take the mickey out of him.

   The doyen of cricket writing Neville Cardus once wrote that the
characteristics of a classical style were precision of technique and
conservation of energy. Jimmy would enjoy that analogy as he amassed goals
with the same hunger Don Bradman accumulated runs. A quick eye, allied to a

razor-sharp brain and sudden feet, Jimmy's keen sense of anticipation invariably kept him ahead of his marker. While many of his goals appeared straightforward, to other players they wouldn't even be half-chances as he made goalscoring look so easy.

Born at East Ham in 1940, Jimmy left school at 15 in April 1955, aspiring to two of his idols, Tommy Lawton and Len Shackleton. Jimmy Thompson was able to lift the spirits of Ted Drake on the evening of the Manchester United 5–6 defeat in October 1954. Thompson rang Ted as usual to be told he'd missed a cracker of a game. 'Never mind that,' enthused Thompson. 'I've found an absolute cracker this morning. He's 14 and the slipperiest goalscorer I've ever seen, a real little diamond. Leave it to me, guv'nor, I'll make sure he comes to Chelsea.'

'What's his name?' asked Ted.

'Jimmy Greaves,' replied Thompson.

While his father wanted him to enter the printing trade, Jimmy signed for Chelsea in October 1955 as a groundstaff amateur – his main job was a telephone exchange operator. Dickie Foss was soon in raptures over his young charge: 'Perfect balance, perfect timing. He needs no room to shoot.' Special weight-lifting exercises were arranged to develop his muscles and add inches. In his first full season (1956/57) he hit an astonishing 114 goals, scoring in all games, mainly in the South-East Counties League, earning him the nickname 'Wonder Boy'.

The harmless looking Duckling, with just three reserve-team appearances to his name, scored on his League debut, a 1–1 draw against Spurs on the opening day of the 1957/58 season. His performance exhausted the media's lexicon of superlatives: Charles Buchan wrote in the News Chronicle of the lad with close-cropped hair and shorts down to his knees; 'Young Jimmy Greaves gave such a brilliant display against the mighty Spurs defenders that I think he may rival the performance of Duncan Edwards, Manchester United's left-half, who became the youngest player to play for England. Only 17-years-old, Greaves showed the ball control, confidence and positional strength of a seasoned campaigner. It was the finest first-ever League game I have seen from any youngster.'

A month later Jimmy starred for England Under-23s against Bulgaria at Stamford Bridge. Although he missed from the penalty spot, Jimmy twice found the back of the net, as did Johnny Haynes; 'best inside-forwards since Carter and Mannion,' wrote the critics. His 13 goals in 12 Under-23 internationals is a record.

After 16 League games Ted Drake left him out of the side to play Sunderland at Roker Park as the heavy grounds arrived. 'You're getting too much football,' said Ted. 'Go home and forget about the game for a fortnight. Don't come near the ground, don't watch football, just rest.' Unleashed back in the team on Christmas Day, Jimmy scored four times against Portsmouth in a 7–4 victory. He finished leading scorer with 22 goals in 35 games and just missed out on a place in the 1958 World Cup squad for Sweden. Despite bursting onto the scene in such a spectacular manner, Jimmy was not immune to criticism from his esteemed boss.

> I was, of course, very much in awe of the great Ted Drake. He was one of the old brigade of managers, strictly a collar and tie man, and one you seldom saw near the training pitch. The great man kept himself to himself but on occasion wasn't averse to giving a fair bit of stick. I remember one occasion I got it hot and hefty and I wasn't even playing! It was when we drew Darlington in the FA Cup [January 1958]. The first match was at Stamford Bridge and we had a nightmare, only drawing 3–3. It was a bit of a disaster and I was dropped for the return match. The replay wasn't much better but at the end of 90 minutes the score was 1–1 and, of course, everyone expected the fitter, more experienced First Division side to go on and clinch things in extra-time. We finished up losing 1–4 in one of the sensations of the season.
>
> Without substitutes I was the travelling reserve in case of emergencies and when I went into the dressing-room the boss was giving the lads a real roasting. I felt relatively safe; after all I hadn't been part of the debacle, but he spotted me turning and gave me my first ever dressing down, roaring at me: 'And as for you Greaves, it shows what kind of ****ing player you are, you can't even get in the side!' I was 17 and on the way to realising that football can do funny things even to gentlemen.

Jimmy was earning £17 per week at the time, living in a one-room flat and driving a 1937 Opel Convertible, before upgrading to a dilapidated 1938 Standard 8, which the Sillett brothers, Peter Brabrook and Ron Tindall, piled into after training to save the bus fare. It would frequently break down, but he was the only one with a car.

In August 1958 Jimmy became 'The Man who tamed the Wolves', scoring five times in Chelsea's 6–2 defeat of the new champions. Ron Flowers tried to contain him in the first half, Bill Slater in the second. Both were hugely experienced players marshalled by Billy Wright, but Jimmy tore the defence to pieces. And all this after Chelsea went one down after two minutes with a goal from Bobby Mason. If Jimmy was the executer that day, Peter Brabrook and Mike Block were flying on the wings. Jimmy's superb opportunism constantly caught Wolves' defence square and he even had a sixth goal disallowed for off side. He was also involved in the fluent passing movement which led to the other goal, scored by Block, and a penalty converted by Slater was hollow consolation for the visitors.

'I've been told that I was the reason Billy decided to hang up his boots at the end of that season,' said Jimmy poignantly. Stan Cullis enthused, 'What a player. They say he doesn't run around enough, he wouldn't have to for me. I'd tell him to stand around and wait – that would be enough.' Years later, Cullis endorsed his comments by saying, 'Jimmy Greaves was the greatest finisher of all time.'

Jimmy set a new club record of 32 goals, beating Bob Whittingham's 48-year-old mark. Chairman Joe Mears presented him with an illuminated address recording the feat. Jimmy later remarked, 'It was one of my proudest moments.' It's a quirky thought that both the FA and the Football League had to be asked permission for the presentation!

> It was a lovely club to work for – we were the 'all the best' club. The players just used to say 'All the best' to each other as they ran out onto the field. That's where that came from. To be honest I thought that was quite normal; I didn't know anything different. Ted was a nice, honest guy, who I thought probably, as far as modern management goes, wouldn't qualify because he just used to sit in the office. I never really saw him in a track-suit apart from maybe a session where press and photographers were there.
>
> Ted was a lovely man – maybe all managers were like that in those days. Maybe Bill Nicholson, possibly Bill Shankly and one or two others, were the first of a hands-on management that has seen the game progress to what it is today. At Chelsea the team were coached, if that's the word, by Albert Tennant, and we had a trainer called Jack Oxbury, and it was really a matter of doing a few laps and having a kickabout behind one of the goals there, that was about it. Of course in those days there was an enormous running track, a dog track and there was plenty of room behind the goals to play. So we used to train at the back, with the dogs. The dogs used to beat us – that was the trouble!

By the winter of 1960/61 Jimmy was earning the maximum wage of £20 per week when he first asked Chelsea for a move to satisfy his ambition. But for his goals, which included a further haul of five in the 7–1 demolition of West Bromwich Albion in December 1960, the club would have had even more of a struggle to survive in the First Division. He was not looking to venture abroad, but AC Milan manager Giuseppe Viani stepped in with an option to buy Jimmy at the end of the season, and in June 1961 Chelsea were £80,000 to the good. Jimmy secured a £10,000 signing-on fee and readily admitted he was seduced by the financial terms offered. He was a passionate advocate of enhanced wages for players and, in an ironic twist, shortly afterwards the maximum wage was abolished in England. He attempted to have his contract cancelled, but to no avail. Years later, Jimmy was to learn that Chelsea made no real attempt to fight his corner – they needed the money. Milan were so keen to have him on their books they increased the signing-on fee to £15,000, and Jimmy was on his way.

It was a difficult time for the family and, shortly before the transfer was sealed, Jimmy and his wife Irene were dealt a devastating blow with the death of their first son, Jimmy Junior, from pneumonia, at the age of four months. Jimmy later acknowledged that the precise moment he started his downhill path to alcoholism was when he signed for Milan and turned to comfort drinking as a release.

That last season (1960/61) he scored 41 League goals, a club record that still stands. Jimmy was in lethal form in an otherwise average side. He bade farewell to the Stamford Bridge faithful in the most appropriate way by scoring four times against Nottingham Forest in his last match. The fans caught the spirit and carried him round the pitch, but sadly the split with Chelsea ended in acrimony. Jimmy refused to go on a meaningless end-of-season tour of Israel, and was promptly suspended for 14 days. What made the decision particularly galling for Jimmy was that he was also forced to miss an England match.

Life did not improve for Jimmy when new manager Viani had a heart attack, which prompted his retirement. In his place Milan appointed Nereo Rocco from Padova, an infinitely harder individual. Jimmy, who at Chelsea was not averse on cross-country runs to hitching lifts on milk floats and tractors, found the incoming coach a brutal man. Despite scoring in his first game, a 2–2 draw in June with Bogota at the San Siro, his future was already uncertain. Several battles later Jimmy scored a typical goal against arch-rivals Inter-Milan. After ghosting past three defenders and planting the ball into the back of the net, Jimmy gave a double V-sign in the direction of Rocco. Soon after, Milan announced they would receive offers for him.

Bill Nicholson had no hesitation in breaking Spurs' club record to capture the homesick outcast in December 1961. Whilst Chelsea had a clause in the contract giving them first option, secretary John Battersby was despatched to Milan to negotiate for Jimmy without signing him. He was said to have made a secret pact with Spurs to prevent an auction spiralling the price beyond them. Identical bids of £92,500 were submitted and Spurs, being Jimmy's preferred choice, were left to progress the signing. A fee of £99,999 was agreed, Nicholson refusing to burden Jimmy with the pressure of being the first six-figure signing in British football. After nine goals in 14 appearances for Milan, it was a merciful release.

In December 1961 Jimmy celebrated his Tottenham debut against Blackpool at White Hart Lane with a hat trick. The most memorable goal he ever scored came in this match.

> Dave Mackay took a long throw-in on the left, Terry Medwin flicked it on and I connected with a left-foot scissor-kick despite the attention of centre-half Roy Gratrix. The ball flew into the roof of the net and from that moment the Spurs supporters were happy to accept me as a member of their 'super' side. Late in my career as a midfield player with Barnet I scored with a 35-yard volley against Grantham, but as nobody believes me, I couldn't choose that goal!

His acquisition was in time to help Spurs reach the 1962 FA Cup final, scoring with devastating nonchalance against much-fancied Burnley after three minutes. Bobby Smith added a quality second goal and Danny Blanchflower wrapped it up with a penalty late on. It was the era of European Cup football at White Hart Lane, and in 1963 Jimmy netted two goals to help Spurs lift the cup with a 5–1 victory over Athletico Madrid in Rotterdam.

> The Cup Winners' Cup final will always stand out as my greatest footballing moment. Not just because I scored two goals but because on that May night we became the first ever British club to win a European trophy. It was an experience I'll never forget.

Jimmy proved a classic Nicholson signing – he had filled a gap that no one but he had seen. To rub salt into the wound, Jimmy played in the FA Cup final in 1967 against the Blues.

> Actually the whole thing was a bit of an anti-climax following the press build-up. Bill Nicholson had rebuilt the great side of the early sixties, but with Dave Mackay as skipper we feared no one. It has to be said dear old Chopper kept me quiet throughout. On the day that

didn't matter too much. We were far too good for Chelsea. We got a morning morale boost when some of the Chelsea youngsters seemed nervous when interviewed for television. It was one of the first finals television covered in a big way and it certainly worked to our advantage.

Jimmy Robertson scored a fine goal to put us one up at the break and halfway through the second half Frank Saul, with his back to the Chelsea goal, swivelled to connect with a Mackay throw-in and Peter Bonetti was caught by surprise. Bobby Tambling did get one back near the end, but we held on comfortably to hear the 'Glory Glory' chants ringing round Wembley again – marvellous moments, moments no footballer forgets.

Between 1961 and 1970 Jimmy scored a club record 220 League goals in 321 matches. His subsequent move to West Ham was one of the biggest mistakes of his life. Suspecting that his reactions had slowed because of illness, Nicholson dropped Jimmy after an FA Cup defeat at Crystal Palace. It was also the time that Jimmy was diverting his energies towards motor trials in readiness for the 1970 World Cup rally to Mexico. On transfer deadline day in March 1970 Nicholson agreed a £200,000 transfer for Martin Peters, with Jimmy accounting for £54,000. A telephone call confirmed a change of club, though not in the way Jimmy would have liked.

I loved my nine years at Spurs. I had wonderful companions, some fantastic moments and an abundance of good times. The fans were superb and if it was me who got the goals every other player deserved credit for them too. I was in paradise. What striker could fail with the back-up I had? Naturally I have my favourite memories but winning the three cup medals has got to take pride of place. I had only two regrets – that I never won a Championship medal and that the club never won the European Cup. Our team in the early sixties was certainly good enough to win it.

Like my earlier move to AC Milan I was unhappy at moving to West Ham. I was happy at White Hart Lane and would have readily played out my senior days there. It was a shock of the first order when I got a phone call [from Bill Nicholson] to say, 'Get your boots – you're going to West Ham.' I did feel tired although I felt I had more goals in me for Spurs. I was bitter at the way I was informed that I was to be part of the deal which took Martin Peters to White Hart Lane. I realise that footballers are expendable at all times but I would have thought that anyone giving the kind of service I gave to Tottenham might have been given the hard news in a softer manner.

The Hammers were having a hard time – relegation threatened, and the fine team of the sixties was beginning to go over the hill. Martin Peters wisely saw the signs and it was back to the old Chelsea days of trying to avoid the drop. Ron Greenwood put me straight in the side and we went to Maine Road to play Joe Mercer's Manchester City. We smashed them 5–1 and I got a couple. That sparked a little revival which eventually got us clear of trouble. Ron suddenly had that nice grin he always had as a player at Chelsea when I was a lad there. Mind you he wasn't smiling a year later when Bobby Moore and I got involved in the ill-fated Blackpool incident – something which cost the Hammers a cup tie and which pointed me towards the Exit Door of top class soccer.

During the summer of 1970 Jimmy teamed up with Tony Fall for the Ford Motor Rally, which gave him his favourite sporting memory. Starting at Wembley Stadium, they survived 16,000 miles of rough road on two continents to finish a highly respectable sixth out of 96, in Mexico City.

In January 1971 Jimmy and Moore were suspended by Ron Greenwood for two weeks for having a few drinks at Brian London's nightclub in Blackpool on the eve of the FA Cup tie. He netted nine times for the Hammers that year and at the end of the season made his biggest mistake by announcing his retirement at the premature age of 31. In 516 matches, Jimmy scored 357 First Division goals, and 492 in all senior matches. Whenever he donned a new strip he obliged with a debut goal. He was the First Division's top-scorer a record six times – twice with Chelsea, four times with Tottenham. Statistics may be the stewed tea of sport, but the peerless goalscoring legend freshened them each time he took to the field.

Jimmy celebrated his first full cap with England's only goal in a 4–1 defeat by Peru at Lima in May 1959. Some of his finest performances were with Bobby Smith, and in the 1961 England–Scotland match at Wembley Jimmy was unstoppable, scoring three goals and, with Smith and Haynes both striking twice, inflicting a record 9–3 victory. It was Jimmy's view that the 1961 side was the strongest England had produced since the war.

Seven months before the 1966 World Cup Jimmy was handicapped by a bout of hepatitis which caused him to miss five months of the 1965/66 season. It robbed him of half a yard of pace and drained him of his energy, but he still played in the opening game of the World Cup, a 2–0 win over Mexico. He retained his place against France but at a cost. He always maintained absolutely no bitterness towards Alf Ramsay as England conquered the world with Jimmy sidelined, and scotched rumours of being dropped from the side.

> The truth is I suffered a very bad shin gash, the marks of which I have to this day, and had three stitches put in the wound after we beat France. Having been asked by Alf if I felt fit enough to face the Argentinians he later branded as animals, I truthfully had to answer 'no'. The rest is football history. Geoff Hurst played well against Portugal in the 2–1 semi-final win and Alf elected to say 'same again' for the final. The lads had played marvellously well against the Portuguese – Eusebio and all – and deserved the right to represent their country on its greatest day. I might have been considered the best goalscorer in the squad but I had no divine right to a World Cup place. Being injured and omitted from the final was the saddest day of my life. I was thrilled for Alf and the team but when I slipped away before the party that night it was not a snub, it was just to hide the hurt in my eyes.

Jimmy's final international was against Austria at Vienna in May 1967. Between 1959 and 1967 he scored 44 goals in 57 full internationals. He came out of retirement in the 1970s to play non-League football for Barnet, where chairman Dave Underwood was a good friend. He was still in love with the game and realised that he had finished too early. He had also made a semi-serious comeback with Brentwood, then Chelmsford and Woodford Town, but by that time had turned to full-time drinking. In the winter of 1977 Jimmy was taken to the alcohol unit of a mental hospital in Colchester. His drink-related problems were publicised in the media and Jimmy's life had reached a low ebb.

> Prominent in my thoughts at the time was the haunting knowledge that right through my football career I had been compared with Hughie Gallacher. They said I scored goals like him. Was I going to follow in his path to the graveyard? The thought became something of an obsession and when everything was going to pieces around me I used to make sure I stood at the back of a railway platform in case I got the sudden urge to run forward and end it all under a train.
>
> But I was luckier than Gallacher. I had friends and people around me who cared. The dearest amongst them was Norman 'Speedie' Quicke and his lovely wife, Jean. Norman was a Fleet Street sports photographer who had been one of my closest pals for more than 20

years. He and Jean were always on hand to help nurse me through my most desperate periods and they were the people Irene would turn to for help when I was getting out of control.

Happily Jimmy conquered his alcohol-related problems to became a popular columnist with *The Sun* and a television analyst for many years, introducing himself to generations who were too young to remember his genius as a player. He acknowledged Irene's decision to divorce him saved his life by finally bringing him to his senses and they are back together. The Greaves have four children, Mitzi, Lyn, Andrew and Danny, who also played professional football. What Jimmy treasured most was the fun, the glories shared with colleagues and the camaraderie. He looked back on his favourite player and six other footballers who clearly made a lasting impression.

In the sixties we recognised George Best as the greatest, but Denis Law was always my favourite, and to this day we're good friends. When I first came into the game at Chelsea, Bolton were the team everyone feared for their sheer brute force. Their 'Savage Six' are still imprinted firmly in my memory: Eddie Hopkinson in goal, full-backs Roy Hartle and Tommy Banks, centre-halves John Higgins and Bryan Edwards and wing half Derek Henning. Those guys were undoubtedly the meanest, toughest men ever to pull on a pair of football boots and the Leeds team of the sixties/seventies were a bunch of fairies in comparison! Every one of them was seven feet wide and no matter what the weather was like, and it was usually raining and cold in Bolton, they always wore short sleeves. Tommy Banks used to say to Peter Brabrook, 'If thou tries to get past me today, lad, thou will get gravel rash!'

For the final word Jimmy reflected on his own special brand of football:

Here's an honest assessment of myself. I was born with a natural gift for striking the ball in the net, and wasn't interested in doing much else. I would rather have played badly for 89 minutes and score the winner than play well for 90 and not hit the net. As far as coaches were concerned, I was often a nightmare player, because work-rate hardly existed in my vocabulary. My favourite era was the mid-fifties to the mid-sixties, before the game became too defensive. Once they decided it was more important to stop goals than score them the game lost a lot of attraction for me. I got out when I wasn't enjoying it any more but now, looking back, I wish I'd gone on and had a crack at Arthur Rowley's magnificent scoring record [of 434 League goals]. If I could go through it all again, I'd give Italy a miss and play out my career with Spurs.

RON TINDALL – *70 goals in 174 appearances*

With football occupying the calendar for almost 12 months, gone are the days when a professional all-rounder could combine the country's winter sport with cricket in the summer. Ron Tindall was one such dual sportsman who successfully accomplished that feat. Born at Streatham in 1935, Ron came from a family of sportsmen and attended Camberley Grammar School. The tall, strong, speedy centre-forward joined Camberley Wanderers, where he quickly attracted League scouts.

My father was an amateur goalkeeper and played for Mansfield at some time. Ours was an extended family i.e. three boys born before the war, and a girl and boy after. The three before the war were all good at sport and I was the middle one. I was invited to trials with Ted Drake at Reading. I was invited back but wasn't sure whether to go as I had just signed as a professional cricketer for Surrey. Then out of the blue Ted was appointed manager at Chelsea and I was invited there as an apprentice. Surrey's home was Kennington Oval and Chelsea's was just across the Thames – how lucky can you get? From 1953 to 1955 I did my National Service and was signed as a full-time professional just prior to that.

I was very nervous initially as an apprentice. All the other apprentices had played for their country at schoolboy level whereas I had only represented Surrey, but Bobby Smith took me under his wing and helped me. It was sad when he went to Spurs even though I would have eventually been competing with him for a position in the first team. I had to sweep the terraces once a fortnight on the Monday after home games. The terrace opposite the main stand had more than 100 steps and I was thinking that I would rather be training!

Other apprentices helped the groundsman but I was given the job of working in the office doing general administration. I helped Ted's secretary Mrs Metcalfe, who was the typical middle-aged secretary, very efficient and overseeing everything. When I was elevated to a full professional and the office work ceased, I regularly went into the office for a chat. That was when I became aware that copies of all the photographs, which had been taken at the home games, were sent to the office. When I made my debut in the first team she gave me a photograph and from then on regularly gave me photos, and I was able to build a good collection. In addition I discovered that the club compiled books for every season made up of all the programmes – they were bound with hard covers, first and reserves. I was supposed to keep this secret, but somehow John Mortimore found out and managed to get one as well!

At the start of the 1955/56 season Ron embarked on a prolific goalscoring run in the reserve and A teams with 19 goals, including two hat tricks, in 14 fixtures. He fully merited his opportunity for the first team in November 1955 at the age of 20, when he scored a debut goal in a 2–0 win over West Brom at the Bridge. The Chelsea coaches were invaluable support to Ron during his formative days, as was his manager.

Dickie Foss and Albert Tennant were big influences who nursed me through my early days. Compared to today coaching was different. We played three-a-side matches in the greyhound area at the back of the South Stand and the training lacked variety in comparison with the modern era. We were not allowed a ball from the Thursday, so you would be hungry for it on the Saturday. However Peter and John Sillett, Peter Brabrook, Jimmy Greaves, Frank Blunstone and myself would steal a ball from the cupboard and disappear every Thursday. It was great fun, a wonderful learning environment and the best kept secret at the club! Ted was always a friend and gentleman who spoke little about his achievements as a player. He had a tendency to lose control sometimes on the bench but quickly recovered. He hated losing to Wolves when Stan Cullis was manager. I once scored the winning goal at Molineux against Wolves in the last minute and he virtually carried me off the field. We organised a 'This is Your Life' for him at the Xmas party one year with me being Eamonn Andrews. Several of the players played cameo roles of past players coming back to speak to him. Pick of the bunch was Jimmy Greaves playing a renowned hard man from those days.

During an extraordinary period in February 1956 seven games were played

ABOVE: The youngest forward line in Chelsea's history prepare with manager Ted Drake for the Leeds match in September 1956 – Drake with his ducklings Les Allen, Peter Brabrook, Ron Tindall, Tony Nicholas and Frank Blunstone. (© Scott Cheshire)

BELOW: More of Drake's Ducklings for the West Ham game in September 1958 at Upton Park – Peter Brabrook, Jimmy Greaves, Ron Tindall, Tony Nicholas and Mike Harrison.

ABOVE LEFT: Dick Foss proudly holds the F.A. Youth Cup after victory against Preston North End in 1960.

ABOVE RIGHT: Mike Block

BELOW: David Cliss collides with Preston keeper Fred Else during his first-team debut at Stamford Bridge in February 1958.

ABOVE LEFT: Eric Parsons

ABOVE RIGHT: Frank Blunstone

BELOW LEFT: Peter Brabrook

BELOW RIGHT: Bert Murray

ABOVE LEFT: Charlie Cooke

ABOVE RIGHT: Clive Walker

BELOW: Pat Nevin teasing Charlton Masters
at the London Arena in July 2000.
© Action Images

Mike Harrison on his wedding day
with Priscilla in Rio de Janeiro,
September 1999.

Les Allen

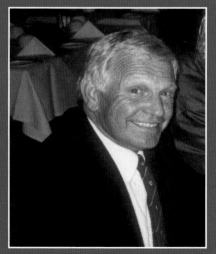

Tony Nicholas

Mike Block

ABOVE LEFT: Roy Bentley

ABOVE RIGHT: Johnny McNichol

BELOW LEFT: Jimmy Greaves

BELOW RIGHT: Ron Tindall

ABOVE LEFT: Bobby Tambling

ABOVE RIGHT: Barry Bridges

BELOW LEFT: Peter Osgood

BELOW RIGHT: Ian Hutchinson

ABOVE: Kerry Dixon
© Keith Mayhew

ABOVE: David Speedie with
team-mate Jimmy Case in
Liverpool Masters team,
October 2000.
© Action Images

BELOW LEFT: Gianfranco
Zola is presented with the
supporters' Player of the
Year trophy for the 1998/9
season by Ron Hockings.
© Ron Hockings/Francis
Glibbery.

BELOW RIGHT: Mark Hughes

in 18 days, dominated by five FA Cup ties in the fourth round against Burnley.

> In those days we only possessed one pair of boots and had to knock the studs in with a hammer. There had been a recent innovation where you could get rubber studs for hard grounds. You could also get small leather studs to hammer in the ordinary studs if the pitch was very muddy. We were travelling by train to the second replay at Birmingham with all the playing kit, boots etc in a basket in the luggage van. The boots had ordinary studs in as we were expecting usual conditions. As we travelled north conditions got worse with signs of flooding etc. The trainer started to panic and, as Peter Brabrook and I were the junior professionals of the side, we were seconded to the luggage van to put tops on the leather studs. Once the job was completed we went back to our seats. Halfway on our journey conditions outside changed. It was frosty and icy so we had to go back to the luggage van, take the studs out and put rubber ones in. We returned to the seats, but closer to Birmingham conditions changed so we went back to the luggage van to change to normal studs. When we arrived at the ground we had to put the leather tops on, as the pitch was very, very muddy. Would the current players be expected to do what we had to?

In 1957/58 Ron had established himself as first-choice centre-forward and was proud to be selected for the Football League in a 3–1 win against the Republic of Ireland at Leeds in October 1957. With 13 goals in 29 League games the 1958/59 season got off to a breathtaking start.

> As a cricketer my agreement between Chelsea and Surrey was that I played the whole of the cricket season. This meant my finishing soccer in mid-April and returning August/September depending upon the season. Chelsea's first match was away to Manchester United when I was playing for Surrey. It was the last cricket match of the season and I was due back at Chelsea on Tuesday August 26th. Manchester United beat us 5–2, which was not a good start. On Monday 25th August I had a phone call at the club from Ted asking me how I felt about playing against Spurs on the Wednesday. Not having kicked a ball since the previous April I had my doubts but said, 'If you are game, I am.' I did some training on the Wednesday morning and at 7.30 that evening ran onto the pitch in front of a full house.

After 20 minutes we were winning 2–0 and I had scored both goals. That was great but I wasn't! The adrenaline had been pumping so much I was running all over the place and with no training I could hardly breathe. Help was close at hand however in the form of Reg Matthews. After thirty minutes Reg collided with Bobby Smith and was winded. After 35 minutes Johnny Brooks and Bobby Smith sent piledrivers into Reg's ribs and he had to be carried off. Guess who was substitute goalkeeper – yours truly. I kept a clean sheet until the 51st minute when Bobby Smith scored. At that moment Reg returned and Jimmy Greaves made it 3–1. Then Spurs goalkeeper Ted Ditchburn dislocated a finger and had to go off with Ron Henry going into goal. Ted was off for five minutes and on his return Terry Medwin made it 3–2. Tony Nicholas made it 4–2 in the 75th minute and we held on from there – what a game!

Another remarkable match followed a month later, when Ron scored at the Bridge in a defeat of Newcastle United. After 20 goalless minutes of a lacklustre affair, a doleful voice in the crowd pleaded, 'Somebody do something.' By the end, a multitude of cigarette packets had been strewn on the terraces as a nerve-racking contest unfurled.

It was not my greatest goal but it set up the most extraordinary result. With ten minutes to go the score was Chelsea 4, Newcastle 5. Chelsea scorers were Brabrook, Greaves 2 and Nicholas, and Newcastle replied with Wright 2, White, Franks and Davies. At this stage Newcastle goalkeeper Stewart Mitchell played a short goal kick to the edge of the penalty area. Unfortunately for Newcastle at that precise time Bob Stokoe, who was the intended recipient of the pass, turned his back on the goalkeeper. The ball hit him on the backside, bounced off to me and I scored. Five minutes later I scored again with a diving header just prior to the whistle blowing for full-time to make it 6–5.

A versatile player, at the start of the 1959/60 season Ron had a run of nine League games at left-back. He then reverted to centre-forward, but his figures for the season were reduced to six goals in 24 matches. During this spell he faced one of the toughest defenders of his career.

In the December we beat Athletico Bilbao 5–3 at the Bridge, then lost 1–0 in Spain. In those days the centre-halves were big and strong and not the sort of players to dribble the ball out of the penalty area.

Bilbao's Jesus Garay was one of the first players I came across who marked you tightly, was really quick and could read the game well, but also brought the ball out of defence and used it intelligently. Bob McKinlay of Nottingham Forest was similar, also Billy Wright when he moved from right-half to centre-half. Jack Charlton of Leeds United was more like the traditional centre-half, very good in the air, but when you thought you'd passed him his long legs came out!

In 1960/61 Ron had to wait until the end of October for his first League outing, but by April had notched up 16 goals in 25 games. At six feet his height contributed to a rare achievement in November 1960, a hat trick entirely of headers, when Chelsea beat Newcastle at the Bridge.

I always saved my best performances for Newcastle and this was a great game. The first two were from corners and the third was relatively easy coming from a Greaves cross, which left me with just the goalkeeper to beat. We won 4–2 and Len White scored the Newcastle goals, also from headers. Then for the return match in March 1961 Newcastle goalkeeper Dave Hollins made his debut and conceded six goals in 28 minutes as follows: 54 minutes Tindall, 57 Greaves, 61 Tindall, 69 Greaves, 75 Greaves, 80 Greaves. The final result was Newcastle 1 Chelsea 6 and their fans were still singing 'The Blaydon Races'!

Ron had a reputation of being a raconteur, particularly when Chelsea travelled by train to away matches. He could be relied on to fill in a good part of the journey with a flow of tales, and recalled spearheading the attack with Greavsie.

Peter Brabrook, John Sillett, Johnny Brooks and Frank Blunstone were the characters in the side and I also recall Reg Matthews being very nervous. Ted used to allow him a fag in the toilets before a game. The leather balls and laces which we played with were so different from today. The laces played havoc with your forehead. On wet days it took a great kick to send a corner into a dangerous position and a run-up to the ball was necessary. Nowadays you can take one pace and kick the ball to the far post. Jimmy Greaves was a big influence on me simply through the experience of playing with him. I rate him up there alongside the best finishers of all time, for example Muller, Romario, etc. He had a unique ability to read the play and was very quick off the mark. No-one ever managed to clobber him – they couldn't catch him. He was very innovative and always gave credit to the player alongside him. I would also describe him as a tormented genius. I remember his first match at Spurs when he was not nervous and took all the hype comfortably. I can still picture his goal – he pounced upon it just before I got there. The newspaper picture the next day included the text: 'Get out of the way Tindall, this is mine!'

After seven seasons Ron became aware of changes once Tommy Docherty joined the club. In November 1961 he moved to West Ham in a part-exchange deal, one that enhanced his knowledge of the game.

When Tommy was appointed he did not see me as a regular player in the squad. Andy Malcolm was looking to leave West Ham, who had shown some interest in me in the past. It was an easy change-over with Chelsea giving me and £10,000 for Andy. I learned more about football during my short stay there than I had in my lifetime. Ron Greenwood, Phil Woosnam and the other West Ham players were virtually player/coaches and big influences on my football career for their ability to engage in clinical debate on coaching and tactics.

When I went to West Ham I still wanted to live in Camberley, keeping my Surrey cricket qualifications etc. This meant a trip totalling one hour 45 minutes, which I could cope with, but the West Ham training ground moved. With the train, tube and pick-up by Bobby Moore to the training ground I was spending approximately five hours travelling to and from work every day. Given the fact that my first daughter was born in October of that year meant she was asleep when I left for work as well as when I got back.

In addition I was awarded my county cap that year and decided that I would make cricket my priority. This led to a problem I had not come across before. At the beginning of the football season Johnny Dick was in dispute with the club and was not picked for the team. They wanted me back from cricket to fill the vacancy, but I was unable to do that as I would be breaking my cricket contract. This led to problems for Ron Greenwood which could not be easily solved. What happened in the short term was that he put his right-half to inside-left and this proved successful, that player being Geoff Hurst. Once cricket was over I returned to West Ham but the situation could not be resolved, so regrettably I was transferred to Reading.

When I signed for Reading I made sure my contract was squeaky clean. Harry Johnston and the chairman agreed to release me for cricket. However that same season Harry got the sack and the chairman died. Roy Bentley of all people was the new manager. The 1963/64 season was the coldest on record and in fact was extended to play the games that had been postponed. By the time I was due to go to cricket in mid-April Reading still had several games to play and were in the relegation zone. When I informed Roy I was leaving for cricket the following week he had not been told of the arrangement. There was a real dispute in place but I left to go to the Oval. I was eventually suspended and given a free transfer.

I was in the process of going to South Africa to take on a coaching job when I was invited to a cricket benefit match in Hampshire. A good friend of mine Jimmy Dickinson was playing and suggested I got in touch with George Smith, the Portsmouth manager. I ended up signing a two-year contract for the 1964/65 and 1965/66 seasons. Early on I played centre-forward and then moved to left-back and centre-half, playing 187 games. George taught me so much about the game, management and coaching. In addition he trained me to take over from him which was approved by the Board of Directors. In fact, I took over a year earlier than planned as he had a brush-up with some supporters and the Board. He moved to general manager in 1970 and I was appointed team manager, a position I held for three years, then general manager for one. I will always be indebted to George's assistance in developing me – he had a knowledge beyond the reach of most managers.

One of the highlights at Portsmouth when I was manager was when we played Arsenal in the FA Cup the year they won the Double [1971]. At Portsmouth we played really well and drew 1–1 with an equaliser late in the game. At Highbury we drew 2–2 and were beaten by a very dubious penalty just before the end of extra-time. After the game several of the watching First Division managers said it was a very poor decision, but the way the team played did our supporters proud.

I learnt a lot from George Smith about the tactical side of the game and we had been working one week on a different system in preparation for a game at Preston. I found when players were on a bit of a downer they were more likely to concentrate when they had different roles to play. I designed a system which was a mixture of mine and George's, and put it into place at Deepdale. We were just managing to hold out and, although it was working all right, we weren't getting anything out of it. Most of the time I would sit in the grandstand and get a better view of how the game was going. About 15 minutes before half-time I made my way to the bench to revert to our normal system. Halfway down I heard this roar and thought Preston had scored but when I got to the bench Preston were kicking off! So I quickly returned to the stand and we ended up winning the game 5–0. I learnt from George to be prepared to gamble and spent a lot of time on the blackboard looking at different systems.

I bought an excellent lad from Plymouth, Norman Piper, and also Ray Pointer from Burnley, who did a really good job, linking well with Ray Hiron. Just before George left we reverted to a one-squad team for financial reasons and our reserves were scrapped. We only had a squad of 18 and if the players weren't in the team they didn't play at all. We needed a second goalkeeper and, through my connections with West Ham and cricket, I brought Jim Standen in. Towards the end of one of the seasons John Milkins was injured and Jim came in over the Easter period. He hadn't played for about 20 weeks other than in practice and did really well to help us avoid relegation.

As manager I was also doing a lot of office and financial work, with Jimmy Dickinson assisting me as secretary, but with only 18 players it wasn't like most clubs. When the new chairman John Deacon was appointed we started to move back to reserve and youth teams, so we needed someone to manage all that. Deacon, who had strong connections with Southampton when John Mortimore was there, offered John the manager's job and me the post of general manager. When I heard it was John I was quite happy with the arrangement and spoke to him in Greece, where he was at the time.

With his four clubs, Ron played 370 League matches and scored 90 goals. Including cup games, he passed the century mark. As a cricketing all-rounder he joined the Surrey groundstaff in 1952 and played 172 matches from 1956 to 1966. The formidable Championship-winning team limited opportunity in his early years, but Ron gained a regular place in 1958. He enjoyed extended runs in the county team in the early 1960s until recalled to football duties. His most successful season was 1963 when he exceeded 1,000 runs and hit his highest first-class score, 109 not out against Notts at the Oval.

While I was with Surrey I recall a stand of over 200 with Peter May in 1958 against Somerset when I made 71 not out and he was 150 plus. We were getting close to a declaration and he kept asking me between overs, 'How are we going Ron? How many more overs should we be looking at, Ron?' The captain of England asking the novice? I learnt in later life what he was doing.

Other highlights include the Man of the Match award in a Gillette Cup tie against Northants in June 1965 and playing in the final that year at Lord's against Yorkshire. I did not like the result [Yorkshire won], but was top-scorer with 57. Also representing the MCC against Scotland in Glasgow, my maiden century at Taunton against Somerset and a stand with Ken Barrington of more than 100 against Yorkshire at the Oval on a very difficult wicket. Ken scored 80 odd and I got 52.

Ron had a break from football in 1975 for two years to manage Waterlooville Golf Club. Then, out of the blue, he received a letter from the Soccer Federation of Western Australia.

They were looking for a Director of Coaching and I had been recommended to them. If it had been any country other than Australia I would not have considered it. However all cricket poms have a desire to go to Australia. After long family discussions it was agreed that I would try it out for six months and if it was what I wanted then the family would come out. I left England on 1 January 1977 to stay with Tony Lock who also lived in Perth. My family [schoolteacher wife Ann, daughters Sarah and Deborah and son Robert] came out in June. All three [children] are now married and we have seven grandchildren. I have always had an interest in coach education and this has been my role in Australia both at state and national level. I left soccer after ten years and have been concentrating on the teaching of principles of coaching and have written books on soccer coaching and general principles' coaching. Over the last ten years I have won the Eunice Gill Coach Education Award for 'The recipient's outstanding contribution to coaching in Australia' and a special award from the Australian Coaching Council 'In appreciation for your services to coaching'.

I like to play golf; however I had two hip replacements in 1993/94 so my play is not too good. I have been coaching the state Under-16 soccer team for the last two years and am enjoying that. We played in a Singapore Tournament in June 2000 and National Championships in September. I have a pool at home and do a fair amount of swimming to keep the hips healthy. I am on a soccer development committee and am a season ticket holder for Perth Glory, Perth's team in the National Soccer League. I also watch the first-class cricket matches played in Perth.

BOBBY TAMBLING – *202 goals in 370 appearances*

When Bobby Tambling scored against Burnley in April 1969, few supporters realised it was the last time they would see their goalscoring hero find the back of the net for the Blues. It was goal number 202, a Chelsea record unlikely to be approached, let alone beaten in the future. Bobby was born at Storrington in 1941, one of six footballing sons of a farm worker, and moved to Hayling Island at three years of age.

> Although we came from a big sporting family the only time my father ever kicked a football was on an ice-covered river when someone broke their leg! I went to Hayling Island Primary School and played for the Under-15s at ten years old – I must have been a minnow. The highlight was scoring a goal to get us to a cup final. The week before the final we were playing horseback around the fields of our home, when I fell off and fractured my wrist. I wasn't allowed to play and was heartbroken – they gave me a medal but it wasn't the same. I moved to Warbleton Secondary School, Havant, when I was 11 and wanted to play football all the time.
>
> As a kid I was a mad Blackpool fan and, as we didn't have the luxury of a television, listened to all the games on the radio. Stan Mortensen was my hero, I read an article about him in a football annual and followed his career. I watched the 1953 FA Cup final on a television in an electrical shop. When it was 3–1 to Bolton with about 20 minutes to go I couldn't watch any more and cycled home. When I got home the family thought I would be delighted, and told me Blackpool were winning 4–3 – I missed all the action! I still look for their results and even when I played them it stirred something inside me.
>
> I went to Hampshire Under-15 county trials when I was 13 although for the first year I was not selected. I remember meeting Harry Johnston, who was one of my heroes in the Blackpool side. He came round to our house and, as he had just signed a Portsmouth lad, tried to persuade me to join Reading. He told me not to play locally as there would be many well-meaning people giving too much guidance, which may have complicated things – it was a good bit of advice.

Jimmy Thompson was also knocking on Bobby's door, and he joined Chelsea as a junior in July 1957, after some gentle persuasion from brother Ray, a Blues fan.

Portsmouth, Arsenal and Wolves were also interested in me. Ray persuaded me Chelsea was the right club and I was suitably impressed with the set-up – mind you, being a country lad, that wasn't too hard! Jimmy Thompson said he had been watching me, I'm not sure he had but he made me feel important. You didn't have to sign anything before you left school, as it was illegal to be associated with professional clubs. However the last year I was at school he said, 'Just sign this, you can keep the form but it's to realise that it's Chelsea for you.' About six weeks later he turned up at the door with Ted Drake. Ted said, 'Give it to me, I know you've signed a form for Jimmy.' I didn't know what to do as Jimmy told me not to tell anyone. I dug out the form, Ted ripped it up and said, 'I'm confident you've made the right choice in joining Chelsea.' I was convinced then it was the right club for me but wonder now if it was the biggest con trick out.

Bobby was captain of East Hampshire Schools from 1955 to 1957 and further recognition followed when selected in a Junior international against Ireland in 1956. He then played alongside Nobby Stiles at Wembley for England Schoolboys against Wales in 1957 (despite the programme mis-spelling his surname as Tamblin).

Playing at Wembley was wonderful. I had seen and heard so much about it, and to walk out on the turf is a memory I will never forget. The game itself wasn't great for me personally and I thought I would be lucky to retain my place, but we went to Northern Ireland, beat them 3–1 and I was fortunate enough to score two goals. The biggest memory for me was in 1957 beating West Germany's Schoolboys at Stuttgart in front of a huge crowd and I scored a couple. We then watched Germany, who were the World Champions, play Scotland in a full international.

In his first season Bobby scored 33 goals from 25 games, including no fewer than seven hat tricks, as well as five goals in a game against Southend. In October 1957 Chelsea beat Woodford Youth 14–0 in the first round of the FA Youth Cup at the Bridge. Bobby's personal goal tally that day was three, with several assists to the six scored by Barry Bridges. He typically put everything into the match, long after it had been won. Bobby signed professional in September 1958 and won an FA Youth Cup winners' medal in 1960.

I had a great time in digs with Barry Bridges and Barry Smart, it was a fantastic life and I thoroughly enjoyed what I was doing. I struggled with homesickness to start off and for the first few weeks I needed to get home and see my family. Ted Drake was a shrewd man and knew if he stuck to the norm of letting me go home just once a month I would not have returned. But he told me to go home every week if I wanted. Barry helped me make the transition and is a genuinely nice guy. He had already been through it, as he was a year ahead of me and knew what it was like to come from the country and just survive. The Sillett brothers were from Hampshire and spoke the same language as me, which in the early days was wonderful. The apprenticeship didn't do me any harm and made me realise I had a long way to move up the ladder.

Within six months of signing as a pro, in February 1959 Ted Drake blooded Bobby and Barry in the first team against West Ham. Bobby had only played in youth football, he hadn't even started a reserve team match. But 14 minutes into the game he scored his first senior goal, leaving his marker John Bond for dead.

I remember Mr Drake calling me up to his office. He told me the club had lots of injuries and, whilst there were left-wingers in Frank Blunstone, Mickey Harrison and Mickey Block, he told me to make myself ready for the game on the Saturday. That was on the Thursday and I don't know if that was a good or bad thing. We had two days to think about it and wondered if it really would happen. I remember not being too nervous until the team talk was held in the snooker hall above the offices. I sat there listening to all Mr Drake's instructions and thought I couldn't do half of what he wanted. I remember running out and playing against what seemed to be massive giants and thought John Bond would trample all over me. West Ham must have thought they were playing the Youth team. I got a lucky chance to shoot fairly early in the game, it took a slight deflection and went in at the near post. It was a wonderful feeling and, with Barry scoring as well, was the stuff that dreams are made of. I knew my legs had gone by the end of the game but we justified our selection. It might have been deliberate to play both of us to help each other. If I'd have played on my own I don't think I would have done as well. We caught the tube home with the supporters and the rest of the day is like a blur. I remember the next day the phone went and someone pretended to be a reporter from a Sunday newspaper wanting a quote from us. Being youngsters we were caught by it and didn't realise it was Peter Sillett on the other end of the line! The next week I was straight back into the Junior team which put my feet firmly back on the ground. Ted was canny – he brought the youngsters in, let them play a few games and before they could get carried away let them learn their trade back in the reserves.

You need to have skill to be a professional footballer but in my case it was all about attitude. I was determined to become a professional and, while I may not have been the most exciting or skilful player, I worked hard at it. Many people owe so much to Dick Foss – he helped us learn our trade and definitely kept our feet on the ground. I scored three in a Junior match once and Dick planted himself next to me on the coach back and said, 'I suppose you think you've played well.' I said, 'Yes, I'm quite happy with life.' He told me then what I didn't do and made me realise there was more to the game than just scoring goals. He was an uncomplicated man with no frills, but knew what the game was all about.

For two or three seasons I only played a couple of games in the first team, then I got a run and played in 1960/61 with Jimmy Greaves. We were inside-forwards together and I learnt a lot from Jimmy but we were completely different players. Jimmy was incredibly calm and when he got the ball was like an eel going through defences from the halfway line. I remember watching him play against Wolves when he scored those five. They were incredible goals, like the volley from the long cross Mickey Block put in from the left.

To follow Greaves was a difficult task, and for some time Bobby suffered through invidious comparison. He responded to the pressure with 22 goals in his first full season (1961/62), but couldn't prevent relegation to Division Two.

When he left I was labelled the new Jimmy Greaves and people expected me to be like him. I was happy to be compared with a genius but said to reporters my style of play was completely different – I relied on hard work and my shooting ability. At the start of the Docherty era he saw the future in the youngsters and we saw our future with him. The year we were relegated was blamed on Jimmy's departure, but Tommy realised he needed to change things quickly and was lucky he had the youngsters to step up. Barry and I scored 42 goals between us, so there were already signs that youth would hold the key.

Bobby operated in partnership with Barry Bridges, chasing balls played over the top or into the channel. In Terry Venables they had a regal midfielder capable of dictating play, an operator who delicately lanced passes through the defence with unerring vision.

> Although the two of us were bracketed together, mine was a completely different speed to 'Bridgo'. I didn't have his blistering pace but I was strong and hard to get off the ball. I had more power and people used to tell me the further I went the stronger I got. I felt running with the ball was as easy as without it and we automatically ran into different areas that really came with playing together – we didn't practise it, the partnership worked well. Barry must have terrified sides with his sheer pace – he scored and also missed some unbelievable goals. He moved so fast he found it difficult to control the ball sometimes.

At the start of the 1962/63 season, Docherty symbolically heralded a new era by making Bobby, at 21, the youngest skipper in the English League.

> I was surprised when appointed captain but it was an honour and I loved the feeling, although confidence is something I lacked and I could be difficult to deal with. If the players had all been older my confidence in being able to do the job would have been worse, but there was a terrific spirit in the club. I know I found it difficult talking to the press, although it wasn't a big part in my day. Everyone is different and Ronnie Harris was probably the quietest captain you could get on and off the field, but he led by example. Confidence in front of goal probably explains the spells I had when I knocked in a lot of goals. Tommy had a wonderful gift of making you feel good, although he could also flatten you. He seemed to boost Barry, Ken Shellito, Terry Venables and my career at different times, funnel it and then move on to someone else.

Bobby enjoyed one of his strongest seasons with 35 League goals, including four in the 7–0 defeat of Portsmouth that confirmed an immediate return to the First Division. He looked back on the last two games and acknowledged the role of one senior player, whose experience was invaluable during the tense run-in.

> Docherty made some amazing changes for the game at Sunderland,

including Frank Upton lining up at centre-forward. We had to win to stand a chance of going up and it was an incredible match. In the first half I took an inswinging corner from the right-hand side of the field, bent it in and little Tommy Harmer, the smallest player on the field, knocked it in with a certain part of his anatomy! In the second half we played against a howling gale and the wind was so strong Peter Bonetti couldn't kick the ball outside the penalty box. Virtually everything was played in our last third of the pitch and we hung on and pulled off the unbelievable. We had been told Sunderland printed their evening paper in pink when they were in the First Division and when they were relegated it was printed in black. They only needed a point and had already printed it in pink for that night's edition and had to change it! That left us needing to win our last game against Portsmouth.

We brought in Derek Kevan, a famous goalscorer who hadn't scored for us, but the one he scored against Portsmouth inside the first 20 seconds was so precious. We were very tense being young and could have struggled if the game hadn't gone our way. We ran the legs off an ageing Portsmouth side, the perfect opponents on the night and the feeling of relief and joy between the players and supporters was wonderful. I remember Tommy Docherty was shaking so much he could scarcely open the champagne bottle! Tommy Harmer, old enough to have forgotten emotional moments, couldn't speak, and Ken Shellito and Ronnie Harris celebrated by throwing trainer Harry Medhurst into the bath complete with tracksuit. You hoped at that stage of your career it would often happen, but little did I know it would be the only time.

Every time we took to the field we thought we would win and when I scored it encouraged me to want to score a second, then three. People think I must have been on a goal bonus, but my contract was no different from the other lads. Bertie Murray, who played out wide putting crosses in for us, worked his butt off and Frank Blunstone was a tremendous pro who had a double blow with injuries, but when we played alongside him he was incredible. He could do things with the football we could only dream about, helped the youngsters along and was the steadying influence we needed.

With the heart of the side bearing Dick Foss's imprint, a resurgent team finished fifth in the First Division at the end of the 1963/64 season. Bobby's form dipped along the way, which caused him a certain amount of angst.

When I had a long spell without a goal I didn't think the captaincy was on my mind and holding me back; the fact that I wasn't scoring goals was and became a self-inflicted pressure. We were doing well as a team and when they took the captaincy from me [in October 1963], we went to Ipswich and I scored two goals, albeit one was a gift from the goalkeeper. Perhaps on reflection it did affect me psychologically.

The impetus continued the next season with success in the League Cup final over Leicester City. The side looked set fair for greater things, provided the nucleus stayed intact.

The League Cup final was all about the first game at the Bridge. We put in a good performance and then did a professional job in the return leg to stop them getting into the game. Two-legged finals are not the same as a one-off and it was a shame the competition did not enjoy a spectacular climax at Wembley. We really had a good side in the mid-sixties and promised so much. When we got knocked out of the FA Cup semi-final twice though, we did wonder how many more chances we would get. When the players started to move after the Blackpool incident it broke up the spirit of the club and those who remained were affected by it.

Charlie Cooke came in and was a fabulous player, but his was a completely different style to Terry Venables. Charlie was all about close ball-playing skills and Terry was about vision. You knew if you made a run, Terry would find you. Probably without realising it we had to adapt our game when Terry left. Terry was a great character and there was always something happening when he was around. I remember we used to go into pubs where he would make fun of Graham Moore, who pretended to be a bit on the simple side, and waited for the reaction of people around him! Then we spent a lot of time in airport departure lounges. A favourite trick was to drop coins alongside a passenger who was obviously in a hurry, so that it appeared he had a hole in his pocket. Every time he moved on we would drop more coins beside him! We would also confuse innocent passengers by pretending out loud the flight we were waiting for was going to a different destination and fake concern it was late!

Despite the break-up of the side, Bobby continued to score prolifically, and, in November 1965 against West Ham, became the fourth Chelsea player to complete a century of League goals. His most outstanding game was in

September 1966, when he scored five times in a 6–2 triumph at Aston Villa, limping off the field after the fifth.

> Villa Park was a happy hunting ground and it goes unnoticed that I got a hat trick with my right foot. For one of them George Graham shot, the keeper made a good save, it came straight out to me and I knocked it in with my right peg. For the last one Johnny Boyle went waltzing past the defence on the right as if it was a training exercise, the keeper came to the near post and all I had to do was side-foot it in with my right foot. Villa were woeful and it could have been much higher as we both missed chances as well. It appeared so easy to score and I regret going off with about 20 minutes to play. At the time you don't think but I was within two goals of Ted Drake's record and must have had a chance of equalling it [and only one away from George Hilsdon's record]. I could have stood on my head and scored that day!

After 13 England Under-23 caps, scoring 11 goals, Bobby's exploits were recognised at full international level. He was typically modest about his first England cap at outside-left in 1962. He played so well that in his next international he was selected as first choice in a more familiar inside-forward role.

> In the early sixties I thought I had a chance to be picked for England, and remember looking up to people when I first got into the international squad and feeling inferior, wondering if I was entitled to be there. That was in my make-up and was difficult to change. For my debut against Wales I was called up late when Bobby Charlton was injured and, as it was the morning of the match, they looked around London for someone to play on the left. To me that was a chance international cap. My second cap against France was warranted on my club performance. I scored a goal, another header, which should have been the crowning glory of my career, but it was such a whopping defeat in the Nations Cup [2–5] it took the edge away. We had a forward line of Bobby Charlton, Bobby Smith, Jimmy Greaves and myself, all goalscorers but playing out of position, and not a lot of thought was given to the selection. Alf Ramsay was given the responsibility on the night but it was a team picked by the committee with no balance or shape. We were incredibly bad, the pitch was like concrete and it just didn't suit our game.
>
> I had a strong second half of the 1965/66 season leading up to the

World Cup, and must have caught the eye sufficiently to get back into the England squad after three years in the wilderness. The last cap against Yugoslavia was just before the World Cup and my performance was good enough at club level to warrant selection. Of the three I probably deserved two, but the third was a smiling grace from somewhere! Deep down I never felt I would be an established international. I was always an honest person, too honest sometimes. I thought some players had their heads in the clouds, maybe mine was too much in the trenches.

Bobby made the World Cup squad of 40 and was a regular in the 1966/67 Chelsea side, culminating in a desperate 2–1 FA Cup final defeat to Spurs.

You would think the Cup final would have been another highlight, but it was an anti-climax, even though I scored the Chelsea goal. The ball just hit me on the head – you would have thought with all these headed goals I was actually good in the air! You felt sorry for the supporters, as we had a chance to do something about it, whereas they sat there and suffered. I can't explain what happened – our form was lacklustre and there were no battling qualities – maybe the occasion got to us. Even when we scored with ten minutes to go, we didn't seem to be able to raise our game and the Spurs camp must have felt it was a comfortable win. There was a problem with lack of tickets leading up to the final, which maybe affected our morale, but you dream of these things and Wembley was the last place you wanted it to happen.

Bobby underwent two abdominal operations, which caused him to miss much of the 1967/68 season, but he fought back to full fitness and the following year saw some of his best form. However in the autumn of his Chelsea career he experienced the ultimate disappointment of missing out on the 1970 FA Cup win, playing only a handful of games leading up to the final.

Up to the 1967 Cup final my injuries had been confined to hamstrings, then I got a run of injuries and didn't know what they were. In the end I had trouble with my stomach which turned out to be a pre-hernia and had the same operation twice. Each time I felt it would be that much harder to regain full fitness and get back in the side. The last season was really disappointing, as in the fourth game I had an innocuous tackle with a West Ham player and damaged my cartilage. For three weeks they thought it was ligaments before they realised I needed a cartilage operation. I was out for seven weeks and Alan Hudson and Peter Houseman took their opportunity well. The injuries forced on them actually made the team click and I knew time was not on my side.

I was happy we won the FA Cup, but remember watching the lads in the bath thinking this was the crowning glory and I was looking from the outside. I'd battled through ten years of good cup runs and the best I got was a runners-up medal. People say I missed out on the World Cup in 1966 when I didn't make the final 22, but this was more disappointing.

Latterly in his career Bobby was employed along the left-hand side, where he revelled in the more open spaces. He was particularly effective in plundering runs down the line and cutting in. More importantly, he had a fantastic eye for goal. His style was based on a sudden burst of acceleration, taking the shortest possible route to goal, and an immensely powerful left foot.

The goals either seemed to go in all at once or not at all – it was for me something about feeling good at the start of a game. A good touch even if it was a simple one got me involved. All my life I have loved scoring goals, the more I scored the better and fitter I was. I had a lot of power and was a good striker of the ball, which came with confidence. I didn't score many spectacular goals but they were at an important time of the game. A goal I remember was against Sheffield Wednesday in the FA Cup one night at the Bridge [April 1967]. It was a swirling free kick going round the wall that we practised in training. I also chipped the keeper in one game, it didn't look spectacular but I meant to do it and was a confident goal.

I also remember the third round FA Cup tie in January 1966 against the holders Liverpool. They jolted us with a goal in the opening seconds but Peter Osgood pulled us level. Midway through the second half we broke from defence with a move involving all our forwards, starting with me out on the left. I played it inside to Terry Venables and then moved into the Liverpool half. George Graham was the last man to play the ball out on the right and he fired a deep cross into the Liverpool area. I jumped and sent a header looping into the net. While it wasn't a classic, what was so enjoyable was that it was the winning goal. We played them off the park and got what we deserved.

Tony Dunne was a difficult defender, one of those you wouldn't mentally look forward to playing against. Likewise the Leeds side of the sixties, even Les Cocker came on with a sponge and gave you a kick! I also found it difficult to get away from John Marsh at Stoke, who didn't have a big reputation but almost blotted me out of the game. I let drop to Ollie Burton at Norwich once that I thought I was having a comfortable afternoon. The next thing I knew his elbow whacked into my cheek and flattened me, so I didn't do that too often afterwards!

A glorious Chelsea career was drawing to a close. Bobby had comfortably become the highest goalscorer in the Blues' history, a wonderful achievement considering he played most of his football as a winger or inside-forward. He was loaned to Crystal Palace in January 1970 for three matches and transferred the following summer at a fee of £40,000.

I went on loan when I came back from my cartilage operation to get some first-team football. I enjoyed it, but at the end of the season remember the utter despair I felt of being out of the club I loved and having to come to terms with moving. I knew Palace would never be a team to challenge for trophies, but realised I had run my course and it would be easier to get a game there. As happy as I was at Chelsea, not to be part of the first team was a bitter pill to swallow and I didn't want to live on my reputation. I found it difficult to break my duck to start with, then I had a run of goals, but my two years were beset again with injury problems. It was also hard for me to get motivated – when you have a reputation to live up to as a goalscorer at Chelsea, you rise to the challenge, but I didn't feel it was so important at Palace. Bertie Head was manager and the middleman in the sense of buying and selling. George Petchey, who I had a lot of time for, was the coach and did the tactics and training, while Bert picked the team. It was a happy club, but you had the feeling the players brought in were there to stave off relegation each year. Dave Sexton told me it would be like a cattle market and he was right.

A Palace highlight was when we knocked Arsenal out of the League Cup the year they won the Double. We drew at home, played well and I scored. Then we won 2–1 at Highbury and I scored again. The same night I pulled my kicking thigh muscle, which ruptured and I was out for about three months. Then I had an Achilles tendon operated on and two-thirds of it was rotten as a result of all the cortisone injections I'd had in the past.

The following summer I went to South Africa for six weeks with Celtic in Durban and was treated like royalty. They were disappointed when I said I wanted to go home, but the pitches were wrong for me, they were bone hard and my wife couldn't stand apartheid. When I went back to Palace, Bert had gone and the new manager Malcolm Allison didn't even know I was on the books! I played two or three friendlies and scored a couple of goals from midfield, but the pitches turned hard and my heel started to flare up. I lost my edge in training and Malcolm said he would let me move on a free.

Bobby played 80 senior games for Palace, scoring 20 goals, before leaving early in the 1973/74 season for Ireland.

I wanted to go to the south coast and Paddy Mulligan fixed me up at Cork Celtic. I didn't know at the time that, of the two teams in Cork, I went to the one bottom of the League. The other, Cork Hibernians managed by Dave Bacuzzi, was top! However we shot up and won the Championship, finishing with an unbeaten 19-game run. I was commuting from London at the time, as I couldn't sell my house – it was enjoyable and almost like a holiday. I then felt ready to accept their offer as player-manager, but didn't realise there was so much to management. I had two or three seasons playing, coaching and managing and one year actually travelled to America with them for three weeks. It was a marvellous tour, but while we were away the club went defunct, which is not unusual in Ireland! I moved down to Waterford, had a good season with them, but at that stage knew I was on borrowed time. Then my last season was at Shamrock Rovers with Johnny Giles, Ray Treacey and Eamonn Dunphy playing with a lot of youngsters.

For all his goalscoring feats, Bobby never gained the rewards in terms of medals that he deserved. For someone with such a fantastic record, Bobby remains exceptionally modest and unassuming, a credit to his profession. Off the field in 1967 he had bought a sports goods shop in Havant.

I built it up into a good business which was going to be my future after soccer. However I lived over the shop and decided after three years to go back to London because of the travelling. I sold it to one of my brothers at cost price and he made a good living out of it.

I came to Ireland with no trade at all, but have never been frightened of work. I've done a lot of work in the building trade and twice managed a sports shop for a successful supermarket chain. I got fed up with being indoors though, especially in the summer and went back to outside life. I returned to England for a while, which was difficult – I couldn't find any work other than as a labourer on a building site. I wasn't too proud to do it, embarrassed maybe when people found out who I was. I eventually came back to Ireland and love it.

I have now been coaching Crosshaven, a local boys' side, for three years. We went to Majorca with them in the summer of 2000 and they were fantastic. My stepson Jamie is in the team and they give me so much enjoyment. 2002 will be their last year before they move on to senior football and I don't know what I will do without them. They are a great bunch of lads and realise winning is not the be all and end all – enjoyment is far more important.

I have been with my girlfriend Val for the last 15 years and feel I'm not bothering anybody and am very happy. I have two sons, Gary and Glen, and a daughter, Sharon, from my marriage. I would never want to change from the time I played, and I was proud of my career and what I achieved – I don't think there was a happier time. People say how lucky I was to get paid to do what I loved, and the players and people I met were fantastic. We don't see much of each other but the memories will never fade.

BARRY BRIDGES – *93 goals in 205 appearances*

George Graham described him as 'the fastest thing on two feet, quick enough to catch pigeons'. Barry Bridges was seriously quick, arguably the fastest player of his generation, and also scored goals, over 200 during his career with five League clubs. Born at Horsford in 1941, at the age of 13 Barry played for Norwich Boys Under-15s and at 15 won the All-England 100 yards sprint championship. After trials with various clubs he decided on Chelsea in 1956.

During my first two years I also joined the London Athletic Club. Harold Abrahams, who was friendly with Ted Drake, encouraged me and I used to watch Gordon Pirie and Derek Ibbotson train at Motspur Park. I found it very hard with football training, then athletics two or three times a week, and when I turned pro I stopped the athletics and never ran another race. I had lots of clubs after me, including Arsenal and West Ham. As a kid of 14 Highbury, with its marble walls and bust of Herbert Chapman, frightened me to death. Norwich were also after me and my father, who was a butcher, was offered a butcher's shop, but they were in the Third Division at the time. Although Chelsea had just won the League, they hadn't been a particularly fashionable club, but everybody was friendly and in the end my father left it for me to decide – he just said to go where I felt happy.

When I was 13 Jimmy Thompson turned up one day and said, 'Can't tell you where I'm from, but I'm a football scout, can I come in?' So he sat down in our tiny terraced house and said to my parents, 'I've watched the boy play and want him to sign for my club.' He shouldn't have approached kids of that age, but after a couple of visits we found out it was Chelsea and he came down every month to Horsford with a little present for me, like a pair of football boots. He was a tremendous fella and the greatest scout you will ever meet. The other scout who used to watch me was Wally St Pier at West Ham. My mother has always been house-proud and the lounge in the front room was only used on a Sunday. I remember we were sitting in the front room with Jimmy one Sunday afternoon when a big car pulled up and Ted Fenton, the West Ham manager, got out. Jimmy said, 'I'll stay in this room, you keep him in the other!' Fenton stayed for ages and we went between the two rooms and he never found out Jimmy was hiding in the other! Fenton wouldn't give up and one day I was competing in the All-England sports. I won the final, went through the tape and he was standing on the track as I ran into his arms, still trying to convince me that West Ham was the club to sign for!

Barry scored 168 goals in 85 youth-team appearances, a record for the club and acknowledged the influence of Dick Foss.

Dick was a really decent bloke who knew the game. He wasn't necessarily a great coach, but a perfect father-figure to be your first manager and lead kids into professional football. I also respected Ted Drake, who treated my parents well when I signed. He was a tough guy who could lose his temper, but he was a lovely man as well, very honest. We played in the third team, then the Metropolitan League against clubs like Hastings and Eastbourne United. We used to get kicked to pieces, but as a 16-year-old playing old pros of about 40, it was the greatest grounding in the world.

Barry, at 15, was a year younger than his team-mates when selected in February 1957 for England Youth against Luxembourg at Upton Park alongside Jimmy Greaves. In October 1957 he scored the winning goal for England Youth against the Netherlands in Amsterdam and the same month accumulated seven out of 12 goals against Grays Athletic in the FA Youth Cup. Barry signed professional terms in May 1958, shortly after his 17th birthday.

> When I was 16 Roy Bentley watched me play in a youth-team game. He called me to one side afterwards and said, 'Never pretend you are something you're not. You've got pace to score goals, use those strengths and don't kid yourself you're anything else.' Then in 1965 I was picked for the Football League against the Scottish League, which in those days was like a trial for England. On the pitch I thought I shouldn't just be a grafter, I must be a bit special so tried little fancy flicks and had a nightmare. It was 0–0 at half-time and Alf Ramsey, who was in charge, didn't bawl, he sat beside me and said, 'What are you trying to do? I picked you for one reason, you know your strengths, don't pretend you're something you're not, go out there and play your own game.' I went out, scored a goal and was in the England team within six weeks. So I had the same guidance nearly ten years after Roy and it was the best advice anyone could have given me, which I never forgot.

Ducklings Barry and Bobby Tambling were fast-tracked towards their first-team debut in February 1959.

> I played in the third team the week before and, after sweeping the terraces for about four hours one morning, Ted Drake told us we were both in the first team for Saturday. We couldn't believe it – I had only played five games for the reserves. Chelsea were struggling from a lack of goals and to play West Ham, who were a lovely footballing side with Ken Brown at centre-half, was a dream. He would say, 'Well done, son,' if you did anything half-decent. We were thrown in at the deep end, but it was a wonderful day in front of a big crowd and we played well. The following season my only game was against Bolton, the toughest defence you will ever come up against. I flew past John Higgins in the first five minutes and he said, 'Right, son, that's the last time you do that.' When I went again he smacked into me, I rolled over and bruised every bone in my body! I realised

this was my welcome to the First Division. That was it for a couple of seasons, it was unrealistic to be ready just yet for first-team football.

By 1961 the 20-year-old had earned a regular place in the first team, with his devastating burst of speed, cheeks puffed out as he swept past defenders, although he had a painful experience at the end of the 1961/62 season.

I broke my wrist at Wolves, and Bobby and I painted out the dressing-rooms and offices during the summer. My wages as a pro were initially £15 in the season, £12 in the summer, then we had a rise to £20 and £17! It was my left wrist, so I was able to paint with my right hand and made an extra £10/15 per week. Dave Sexton, one of the most inventive coaches in the world, was also painting and decorating. It was part of his job, he didn't get time off and we teased him unmercifully. It was Dave who taught me how to make diagonal runs and take defenders away to leave space for others to come through. We used to spend hours with him on the training pitch until it became second nature to us.

When Ted Drake left, Tommy Docherty threw all the youngsters in and we came back a better team. When we played Luton on Boxing Day 1962 we were ten points clear in the Second Division. The game was nearly called off at half-time because of the snow and we didn't play again until February. We went to Malta for three weeks, had a ball, came back and lost the first five games. We were promoted on the last day of the season and, if I have a regret, it's that the side was broken up too early. I'm sure we could have become one of the best teams in the world if we had stayed together, but we weren't given the chance to fulfil our potential. We were all great mates having grown up together – we didn't really even need a manager when we were back in the First Division. I know they've had good sides after us, but I still believe we would have been the best Chelsea team ever.

Then the Blackpool incident came along, which Docherty over-reacted to. I know we were wrong but if he had fined us £100 and kept it within the club, it would all have been forgotten. Instead we were on the front pages and that was the beginning of the end. I had just got picked for England for the first time to play the Under-23s at Highbury and asked Alf how the incident might affect me. He said, 'I don't want to know, you behave yourself with me and you'll be all right,' which I thought was tremendous – Alf was one of the best managers I played for.

Of the memorable Chelsea games I remember three FA Cup ties against Spurs, one of the best sides I ever played against. In the first we drew 1–1 at White Hart Lane in January 1964 and brought them back on the Wednesday night. We reported for the game at six o'clock and had to leave our cars with the police, as we couldn't get anywhere near the Bridge. There were 70,000 people in the ground, and about 30,000 locked out and we beat them 2–0. The following season we drew them at home in the fifth round of the Cup. I got the winning goal, which was the only time in over a dozen games I scored against big Maurice Norman. Like me he came from East Anglia and it meant a lot to do well against him – after all he played for England. He was one of the most difficult opponents I played against and used to kick me a bit, but we had good tussles.

I know I would have scored even more goals if I had been a fraction slower. My pace took me too quickly into positions and I used to stray offside a lot. If my brain had been a bit quicker than my body I might have delayed my runs. When I was having a bad time at Chelsea, playing well and doing my bit but missing goals, Docherty called me into the office one day and the club doctor was with him. He said, 'Barry, we think we've come up with a solution to you missing goals. We've got some tablets to slow you down!' I thought he was winding me up and said, 'You're kidding, I'm not taking bloody tablets, I'm against all tablets.' He said there were no after-effects and it wasn't illegal. If they were enhancement tablets that would have been different, but these were designed to have the opposite effect! They said to give it a go and on the Saturday I scored two goals. Then the next week I missed a couple of chances and told him what he could do with his pills!

It was in Australia at the end of the 1964/65 season that Docherty discovered he had a potential scoring genius in Peter Osgood, who took his chance with five goals against Tasmania in a 12–0 massacre.

We went to Australia for six weeks – I was initially with England on tour and joined after a couple of weeks. It was a time Docherty could have healed the wounds and got us together, and we could have got a relationship back with him. It didn't happen and within 12 months three or four of us had left.

Barry broke into the England side in 1965 with his first cap against Scotland at Wembley. It was his most noteworthy international, as England played the entire second half with only nine men and still drew 2–2. Barry invited an honest appraisal of his qualities, omitting to mention that England caps have never been easy to earn.

> I've always been modest about my abilities, maybe because of the advice I had from Roy and Alf. I knew my touch wasn't the best and don't think I would have lived today, as there wouldn't be the space to use my pace. I was a grafter who worked my socks off and got my goals in the box using my pace. When I was picked for England I had scored 27 goals that season [1964/65] so deserved my chance, but I was one of those players who didn't have enough class to step up to international play. It's a massive step and with another three or four games I might have made it.
>
> I scored one goal for England, against Yugoslavia, a near-post header – that was special. It all happened the year before the World Cup in 1966 and, if I'd scored all those goals the next season, who knows what might have been. I've no regrets whatsoever though. Terry and Bobby both won three caps for England, but we all played in different games. Maybe if the three of us had played together we may have got 25 caps each, but I'm happy with my four. Terry made us – he and Johnny Haynes were the best passers of the ball I've seen. You made a run and the ball was there – it wasn't coached, it was instinctive. I was not in the same class as Bobby as a finisher, who was also a very brave player and straight as a die, on and off the pitch. I lacked a certain amount of self-belief in the early part of my career but, given a bit more time and experience, I might have made it on the international stage.
>
> What I respect for myself is that I worked so hard to get my four caps – maybe other players would not have got them as they didn't have the right attitude or application. Years later, Terry said when he was coaching Crystal Palace that he used me as an example of someone making the most of their abilities. I think Ossie and Rodney Marsh, both fabulous players I played with, wasted their ability.

The League Cup final in 1965 and subsequent European ties gave the young side the perfect arena to assert their rapidly growing reputation.

> The best goal I ever saw was by Eddie McCreadie against Leicester in the Final. I had to sit out the first leg and Eddie played as an emergency centre-forward. It was on a very heavy ground and he took the ball

from the halfway line, beat five men, then rounded Gordon Banks before putting it in.

The best goal I scored for Chelsea was against Blackburn in a 5–1 win at the Bridge [October 1964]. I was in the old inside-left position and shot from about 35 yards with my left foot, which was unusual. It curled into the top corner and I scored a hat trick that day. I never really scored too many great goals, mine were little flicks and touches, Lineker style.

Other notable games were the European Cup ties against AC Milan in 1966. They were classic encounters, the feathery touch of the Italians against the high mobility of the young Chelsea pretenders.

We lost 2–1 in the San Siro, won 2–1 at home, then lost the toss to see where the replay was and went back to Milan. I scored one of my most important goals for Chelsea, we drew 1–1 and battled away into extra-time. We were down to nine men with Johnny Hollins hardly being able to walk because of an ankle injury and Eddie McCreadie carrying a pulled muscle. So at the end we were absolutely gone, and I remember we went down the tunnel to the dressing-room, which seemed like miles away. Docherty and Ronnie Harris were in the centre-circle with the press around for the toss of the coin to see who would go into the next round. I couldn't just sit there in the dressing-room and as I walked up the steps I saw Ron leap in the air. I don't know where I got the energy from, but I ran back to the dressing-room and told the boys – that was a great moment. They were so much better than us but our spirit saw us through.

Leeds were the hardest team I ever faced, early on they were vicious, but eventually they turned into a great footballing side. We played them in the fourth round of the FA Cup in February 1966 and were winning 1–0 with about three minutes to go, when we put the ball in the corner and wasted time. They kicked lumps out of us and in the last minute Allan Clarke went through and McCreadie cut him to pieces. About six of their players got hold of him and I thought they were going to kill him! About six weeks later we were due to play them again in the League. As we walked off the pitch at the end they said to him his leg was broken before he started the next game. Eddie was a brave lad, but on the Wednesday before the League game he told us he didn't want to play – we said, 'You're not a bad judge!' He had been worrying about it all week and Docherty called him into the office on theThursday and said, 'You're not going on Saturday.' Eddie said why and Docherty said they would break his leg, which was a sensible decision. Dave Mackay was the hardest defender I faced, but he could also play. You also lined up at Liverpool and had big Ron Yeats, six feet seven inches, and snarling Tommy Smith with no teeth waiting behind him. Ron wasn't very mobile but it didn't make any difference as if you chipped it over him Smithy was waiting for you!

I played for England against Austria on the Wednesday in October 1965 and, when Ossie was told by Docherty he would have ten clear games, he dropped me on the following Saturday against Leicester without having the decency to tell me. I know I wasn't playing particularly well at the time and was lucky to be in the England side, but the first I knew about it was when I read it in the paper. Then Eddie McCreadie was injured during the match and I came on, but it was the worst thing that could have happened as I had a bad game and we lost 2–0. I asked for a transfer during the season and played at Sheffield United (the game after Leicester), when I was told the club had arranged a move for me. Driving to United's ground Joe Mears said to me, 'Son, read that and maybe you'll stay with us,' and gave me a petition with 3,500 signatures addressed to the chairman. We won 2–1, I think I had a fair game and the reception I got from the Chelsea supporters was absolutely fantastic. We came back in our own carriage on the same train as the fans. I got back to London and about 500 supporters were at the station asking me to stay, which I did until the end of the season.

To accommodate Ossie during the 1965/66 season, for a while Barry played wide on the right, where he turned in some of his best performances. Nonetheless beneath the surface lay rancour and dismay, and Barry was criticised by Tommy Docherty after a disappointing second semi-final defeat in the FA Cup towards the end of the season.

Four days before we played Barcelona in the semi-final of the Fairs Cup, we lost 2–0 to Sheffield Wednesday. We just had a bad day – it was rubbish when Docherty accused Terry and I of not trying, as if anyone would do that in a semi-final. Then two days before the Fairs Cup game we played West Brom at home, which was of no importance whatsoever. As usual all 18 players reported to the ground at six o'clock, and Docherty didn't come into the dressing-room until seven, so nobody knew who was playing. He walked in, put the team sheet on the board and walked out. The only person who was dropped from the semi-final side was myself and I went spare. I tried to find him, but he disappeared and didn't even come in for the team talk, which Dave Sexton did.

He wasn't at the airport for the flight to Barcelona the next morning, as he was signing Charlie Cooke, which was the beginning of the end for Terry. He eventually walked into the bar and I asked to speak to him. He said he didn't have time and I just flipped. We had a terrible row and I said, 'If I'm not playing, I'm not going,' which was maybe a bit harsh. He said I was not playing so I got my bags off the plane and walked out. The press saw the whole thing and the next day the papers were full of it, but I don't regret it. The first three months were great, he could pick you up, then when you got to know him he was a horrible man, I didn't like him. We knew Dave Sexton, who was a lovely guy, was the man making the decisions and carried him.

Docherty gave me a lot of hassle in my life, but I was once watching a game in the 'crow's nest' at the top of the stand where he would sit and bawl from above. Upfront was dead with no movement whatsoever, Docherty looked at me and said, 'The only time I appreciate you is when you're not playing!' As a back-handed compliment, I think that's the only praise I ever got from him.

The increasing enmity between the turbulent manager and several of his finest players proved irreconcilable. The Sheffield Wednesday semi-final was Barry's last game for Chelsea and he moved to Birmingham City in May 1966 for £55,000.

At the end of the season I had a choice of Birmingham, who were in the Second Division, Leicester, who needed a striker to play off Derek Dougan and would probably have been the best move with hindsight, and Coventry, up and rising under Jimmy Hill. Stan Cullis, the Birmingham manager, was a lovely man and I was persuaded by Clifford Coombs, the chairman, one of the nicest men I ever met in my life. He had a lot of money with ambitious plans to take the club forward and wanted a big signing. Bert Murray also came with Fred Pickering from Everton and we had a couple of good years, but it didn't take off in the way I thought it would. I was in partnership with my first wife's in-laws in a hotel business at Eastbourne, when my father-in-law died and I needed to get back south, otherwise I would have stayed there, as they were a lovely club – I have no regrets though. The best goal I ever scored was an overhead kick for Birmingham against Arsenal in a fifth-round replay of the FA Cup [March 1968]. It was a ball that came in from 25 yards – I did a complete somersault, hit it and turned at the same time. It went in like a rocket and was one of those dream goals. What was strange was that I never did any overhead kicks for Chelsea and never practised, it just developed at Birmingham. The Birmingham supporters still talk about it today.

Barry was desperately unlucky to be in a losing FA Cup semi-final side three times, 2–0 to Liverpool in 1964/65, the Sheffield Wednesday tie, then for Birmingham in 1967/68 to West Bromwich Albion, again 2–0.

We should have won the first semi-final, as John Mortimore scored a perfectly good goal. He went up with Tommy Lawrence, got his head to the ball and it went into the back of the net. Then he hit the keeper, they gave a free kick against us and we conceded a goal within five minutes. I also lost in the League Cup semi-final with Birmingham against QPR, which was heartbreaking. Chelsea won the League Cup just before the final started at Wembley, so I never went there for my club side.

An injury to Rodney Marsh prompted a move for Barry to Queens Park Rangers in a £50,000 deal early in the 1968/69 season. Although he scored on his debut in the home game against Manchester City, Barry initially found goals elusive.

It was hard playing with Rodney early on, as I never knew what he was going to do next! Then eventually I hit it off with him – I realised I would never get an early ball, so you let him have time on the ball to do his tricks and then made your run. He was one of the best touch players for a big man I ever saw and never understood how I scored so many goals. He would say, 'With all my skill, you get more goals than me!' I had two good years there, the second year I scored 27 goals, we finished fourth in the League and it worked like a dream.

Early in the 1970/71 season Millwall made an offer of £35,000, which was subsequently upped to £40,000. Barry was settled at Rangers and surprised at their willingness to release him, but the move gave him an unexpected boost.

The time at Millwall was two of the most exciting years of my life. I signed after about seven games into the season and they were bottom of the League and struggling. Benny Fenton became defensive-minded and played a 4—4—2 system, saying to the four in midfield, 'If you get forward, you must get back,' so in the end they wouldn't go forward! Derek Possee and I had the whole of the width of the pitch to work on and we caused havoc in that division. The big centre-halves didn't know what to do and we scored over 40 goals between us – we were the highest scorers in the League. I liked and respected Benny, he had one unbelievable asset as a manager, a wonderful way of making you feel ten foot tall, which was handy as far as myself and Derek Possee, who was five foot nothing, were concerned!

The second season was the most disappointing in my career, as we were one point from promotion to Division One for the first time if we had beaten Preston and Birmingham lost to Sheffield Wednesday. With 26,000 at the Den and people on the roof of the stands, we were winning 2–0 with ten minutes to go when there was a buzz of excitement. Everybody was cheering and news came to us that Birmingham were losing 1–0. The crowd came onto the pitch and we played the last five minutes with them standing on the touchline. With about two minutes to go I saw Benny walk from the touchline towards the dressing-room and could sense his pride in the way he walked, that he felt he was a First Division manager for the first time. When the final whistle went thousands came onto the pitch, and Possee and I were lifted high by the dockers, salt of the earth they were, and they took our shirts off. Then we heard Birmingham had won 1–0 and the dockers dropped me, and I fell straight on my back and nearly killed myself! Harry Cripps, who was Millwall through and through, cried like a baby in the dressing-room. On reflection I don't have any regrets about the moves I made, although I do regret spending the last years of my career outside the First Division.

August 1972 saw Barry sign a two-year contract at Brighton, where he experienced the managerial nuances of Brian Clough.

In my second season Cloughie kicked me out of the side. It all happened around the break-up of my marriage, I was drinking too much and feeling sorry for myself. I didn't even realise he knew my personal problems, which summed him up, as I had great respect for him in lots of ways. He made me train with the youth team in the park and barred me from the ground. On New Year's Day I decided to take stock of the situation, as I felt I still had a couple of years left in me. I played for the reserves shortly after, really had a go for the first time in six to eight weeks, and scored a couple of goals. Cloughie, who was watching, came into the dressing-room afterwards and asked to see me the following morning. I thought he was going to transfer me somewhere, but he said I was in the first team on the Saturday. I was shocked – he could see that and told me, 'I've been waiting seven weeks for you to pull yourself together. I know about your divorce and everything, but I know you had the courage to come through it.' I scored six goals in 13 games after that.

Going back all those years, Jimmy Thompson was also scouting for Highland Park, the best club in South Africa. In 1974 their manager was over from South Africa and saw me play, when I had a good game. He approached me and it was a big decision to make. There were about eight games to go until the end of the season, so I asked Clough if I had a future at Brighton. He said, 'The way you're playing, son, you'll be here for another four years.' Then he gave me a free transfer at the end of the season without even telling me. Jimmy told me the offer was still open, so I went there. I had a fantastic two years, played in a good side alongside Chris Chilton from Hull and we won three trophies out of four one year. I also met my second wife Megan there, so it was the best thing Cloughie could have done for me.

When I returned I guested for St Patrick's in the Southern Irish League. Within about three games they offered me the manager's job until the end of the season. We avoided relegation in the last game, then they offered me a two-year contract. I had a fabulous working relationship with the chairman, who was in his eighties. The club had a bingo hall in Dublin, which was making a fortune, although the footballing side wasn't. I brought Terry Venables over for four games to guest for us, and also Gordon Banks and Allan Harris. We got some of the best players in Ireland as the money was always there, and in my first full season finished third in the League and lost two semis. Every minute of my life was devoted to St Patrick's and I was getting a bit of a name for myself, as I was successful. Then Megan, who was travelling around Europe and knew I was in Dublin, came to stay. We were just friends at the time but hit it off and after that my life and priorities changed. At the end of that second season the chairman died and the bingo hall was sold. Within six weeks of the new season I knew we had no chance and resigned before it damaged my reputation.

I came back to England with Megan and played for Dereham Town, which was a good standard in local Norfolk football. I was about 40, but still felt reasonably fit and they asked me to take over as player-manager. I got the side fit for the first time in their lives, but it didn't happen. I was playing poorly, the team was mid-table and it was disappointing. We played a game before Christmas and I had ten yards' start on the centre-half and he beat me to the ball over 20. I came in at half-time and said to the lads I was never going to play football again. We won 15 games on the trot after that and they said to me, 'Why the bloody hell did you start in the first place!' I then managed King's Lynn, which was a step up, but terribly hard. If I had been successful I could have used it as a stepping stone in management, but I had bought the milk business from my mother and was up early, and all hours of the day. It was a round trip of 80 miles to King's Lynn and I decided it was not for me. That was the end of my management career. I came back to my local side Horsford, where we had a Sunday morning team, which I enjoyed.

We sold the milk round in the mid-eighties and bought a newsagent's just outside Norwich, which I am still doing. I love the business, it's hard work but I enjoy it.

I have no direct contact with football, although I would be happy, given the time, to coach youngsters – maybe when I retire.

Kate and Emma are my two daughters from my marriage to Megan. I have a boy, Andrew, from my first marriage and two grandchildren, Albert and George. Sadly I lost my other boy, Mark, from my first marriage.

PETER OSGOOD – *150 goals in 379 appearances*

When romanticism thrived in the swinging sixties the ball was heart-shaped, and Peter Osgood converted the difficult nuances of the game into a pageant, a celebration of entertainment. With the comfortable stride of a natural athlete, Ossie's fluid movement enabled him to play as an out-and-out striker or in a deep-lying position. Such mobility, aided by a ball control delicate for a tall man, rapidly made him the King of Stamford Bridge, the idol of the Shed. 'Osgood is Good,' they chanted in delicious understatement to the melody of Big Ben. The instinctive crowd-pleaser, Ossie would glide past defenders with contemptuous ease before smashing or stroking the ball home. Born at Windsor in 1947, Ossie was undoubtedly one of the most talented and exciting players of his generation, but was almost lost to the game before his career started.

> I played for Windsor schoolboys, then was captain of Berkshire but the scouts were never interested in me. I went for a trial at Reading and they didn't fancy me. Then I was offered a trial for the Arsenal, which I ripped up, as I thought if I can't get in at Reading, what hope was there for me at Arsenal! I used to play with my mum's brother, Uncle Bob, and my other uncle in the Windsor Corinthian side on a Sunday. It was a family thing and we had a good team, we got to cup finals and won the Leagues. Uncle Bob wrote off to Chelsea and one day said to me, 'I've got this trial for you at Chelsea. I'm taking you up with Micky [my brother] on Saturday morning.' I said, 'You must be joking, we've got a big cup game with Spital in the afternoon.' Bob said, 'No, we've arranged for you to play in the first half of the trial.' We got there and I said to Fossie, 'Mr Foss, can I play in the first half?' He said, 'Yes, certainly, son.' I said, 'For how long?' Fossie said, 'We'll see,' [then] took me off after half an hour and asked me to sign a form. I thought it was my expenses and I was not good enough. He said, 'I've pulled you off as there are about eight scouts here wanting to sign you.' It was an incredible start, then we won the cup game 3–2 in the afternoon and I scored two goals!
>
> Dickie Foss was special, you only have to look at his record, and a superb guy to work for. He said Greavsie was his jewel and I was next to him. That's quite a compliment bearing in mind all the great players to come to the club, as I don't mind being second to Greavsie.
>
> My first cup game for Chelsea was when I replaced Eric Whittington in the second leg of the 1964 South-East Counties Junior Floodlit Final. I scored two goals against West Ham, who included Johnny Sissons and Martin Britt, and we won 3–1. Then I scored a goal in the Challenge Cup final for Chelsea reserves against Brentford, but we got beaten 2–1. In every Cup final I scored for Chelsea, which is a lovely record – the big occasion was my scene.

Ossie's first-team debut in a League Cup replay against Workington at the Bridge in December 1964 had the press singing his praises. He had been substitute for the first match, a 2–2 draw, but remained on the bench. Chelsea won 2–0 and Ossie scored both goals, described in his autobiography, *Ossie the Wizard*.

For 81 minutes I did nothing. Then George Graham moved through and found me with a clever ball on the edge of the area. I slipped through, veered right as the goalkeeper came out to open up the angle, and clipped the ball across him. Four minutes later I did it again. Tommy Knox streaked through, hammered a shot against a post, and I was there to turn it firmly into the net.

It wasn't long before the delicate artistry and goalscoring power of Chelsea's gentle giant stamped him as a regular. Tommy Docherty let him know that, barring injury, he was in the team for a run of at least ten matches. It gave Ossie a great confidence boost.

I still call Tommy Doc 'Boss' today. I was a strong personality but The Doc gave me my chance. He dropped Barry, an England international, and the Chelsea fans booed me in my first game. The Doc stood by me, it paid off for him and I appreciate what he did for me. But it was different for the other players – they brought this outsider in and resented him. It was their club and he broke up their niche as it was 'cliquey' at the time. It wasn't just three's or four's, it was all eleven or twelve, a big bunch of boys there who grew up together.

It was an inspired move on the part of Docherty and Ossie became a regular fixture in the team for the remainder of the season. In January 1966 he scored an exceptional individual goal at Burnley, which he recalled in *Ossie the Wizard*.

The ball was cleared out to me and I took it and strode off. The pitch was sticky yet I seemed to be skimming over the top of it. Big John Talbut came at me, and I left him slithering with a change of pace and direction. Then I turned inside Dave Merrington and dribbled round him again, as he moved in at me from the other side. Next I took on John Angus. I body-swerved him. There was nobody to pass to, none of the lads were up supporting me, I had to go on alone. By this time Talbut had recovered and was racing back to cut me off. I turned him inside out as I gathered speed and, as goalkeeper Adam Blacklaw came out, I finished the 50-yard run with a blistering shot that bulged the net. The Turf Moor crowd applauded me all the way back to the middle. I can remember spectators in the stands rising to clap me and Alex Elder the Irish left back said, 'Great goal son'.

On several occasions Ossie was referred to as another Hidegkuti, playing a similar style to Roy Bentley over a decade earlier. He could operate in a deep, fluid position and Tommy Docherty encouraged Ossie to learn from the continental style of two other Hungarians.

> Tommy took us to Wembley to watch Ferenc Bene and Florian Albert play on the right and the middle – we watched their movement and near-post runs. The deep-lying role was a nice position for me as the two central defenders didn't know whether to come or not and it was hard to mark me.

Just when it seemed a glittering career was gathering momentum fate struck a cruel blow in another League Cup tie, this time at Blackpool in October 1966. After 30 minutes Ossie went for a 50–50 ball with Blackpool's left-back Emlyn Hughes in the centre circle. They accidentally collided and Ossie was carried off with a fractured leg. Fortunately it was a clean break of the tibia just above the ankle and no complications sent in. Nevertheless at the age of 20 it was not easy to accept such enforced absence from the game, during which time he missed the 1967 Cup final. Ossie overcame the lack of confidence that can arise when a player suffers a serious injury, and remarkably was an ever-present in the 1967/68 season. He sought inspiration from Dave Mackay, who stormed back from similar injuries. Tommy Docherty felt he fully recovered, a view not shared by Ossie.

> When I came back I didn't go past people as quickly as I used to. I come from a big family, was still growing as a lad and put on one or two stone in weight as well, which is a lot. You'll never know how different a player I became.

Ossie's form was irrepressible and he won his first England cap against Belgium at Brussels in March 1970.

> I was in the England Youth team, then the Under-23s and coming through the ranks. I got into the squad of 40 for the 1966 World Cup, but not the final 22. I got a phone call from Dave Sexton on the Sunday, who said, 'Ossie, would you go out to Belgium?' I said, 'Dave, you've got to be joking, Martin Chivers and Rodney Marsh are already out there.' 'Bobby Charlton can't play.' 'Yes, Dave, I'm not being funny but I'll only be carrying the bags out there.' 'If you do you're definitely playing.' I went out on the Monday, played my first international and we won 3–1. I made the 22 for the Mexico World Cup in 1970 and got

two caps against Czechoslovakia and Romania out there. Then Alf Ramsay never picked me for four years after the World Cup – he picked me in 1974 against Italy. Although I got all my four full international caps under Alf, if you look through the record books you will see he never liked flair players. That's why people today say why did Tony Currie, Frank Worthington, Rodney Marsh, Alan Hudson and myself only get 20 caps between us? When you look through the squad he played Martin Peters, Geoff Hurst and had one jewel, Bobby Charlton. Everybody knew what they were doing and the job they had to do. You can't say to me, 'Do this, do that,' cos my mind would go wandering. I would be looking to see where the ball was looking for somebody to go and get that ball quick so that I could play with it.

In 1970 Ossie became the first player to score in every round of the FA Cup, a record that still stands. He was Leeds' nemesis in the final replay at Old Trafford, with his spectacular diving header, which is safe in the mental store. Ossie understandably ranks it alongside the Burnley goal in 1966 as his greatest ever.

> The Leeds goal was completely different from the Burnley one. There was a breakaway from Ian Hutchinson, who gave it to Charlie Cooke. There was a big cross-over ball in midfield, I went on the blind side and Charlie knocked it in for me. When I got in there I thought I was offside, as I had so much space and there was no-one near me. I was very lucky because Dave Harvey was in goal instead of Gary Sprake, who I think would have come and clattered me. Dave was on the line and hesitated, which gave me the time to have a little look at him and see which way to put it. It was a great build-up and team goal – all I had to do was make the run. Dave Sexton taught me about running off the ball. I think the 1966 Chelsea team was marginally stronger than the 1970 side, as they were still blossoming and had lots of football in them. But if you look at the players they had, when they left they didn't do very well, so I wouldn't like to say who would have been the winner between the two sides.

The emergence of Ian Hutchinson added a further dimension to Ossie's game, a striking partnership that flourished when Hutch was able to steer clear of injuries. With Ossie's inspiration and Hutch's perspiration, they cemented a relationship on and off the pitch, which contributed to their telepathy.

My partnership with Hutch was the most effective I had at Chelsea. If he could have stayed fit, there's no end to what we could have done together. 1969/70 was our peak season when we scored 59 goals between us, 31 and 28, and could have played blindfolded. I will always remember a game at Ipswich when Hutch went in at the near post and got too far, but he just flicked it the other way. Hutch knew I'd be there waiting for him and I knew it was coming. I just stood back when everybody went to the goal-line and had a little tap-in, thank you very much. The only time he let me down was when we played Manchester United at home. I hung back on the six-yard box when the ball came across and went to volley it, but just laid it off to Hutch. It hit him on the shin and went past Alec Stepney into the net. The annoying thing about that was he ran away and started waving to the crowd – I thought thanks very much!

He was a big, honest, typical centre-forward who could have played in the forties and fifties. Defenders would be frightened to death of him nowadays, he would slaughter them. He would go through a brick wall, people couldn't hurt him, and he never went down unless he was badly injured. He was a nonentity as far as skill was concerned, but once he got into his stride had a good left and right-foot shot on him, was superb in the air, and of course he had the armoury of a long throw, which helped tremendously. He was terrific to play with, very brave, too brave, as he was always injured, which was a shame as we hit it off so well. He's my best mate and we've been best men at our respective weddings.

The Chelsea side of 1970/71 was magnetically successful and European glory was consummated with a 2–1 replay victory in May 1971 over Real Madrid at Athens in the final of the Cup Winners' Cup.

It wasn't a great Real Madrid side we played. They were rebuilding a bit, but were still a force to be reckoned with. We fancied ourselves against them, as we knew we had plenty of grit and the flair as well. In the replay John Dempsey scored a goal early on and the second came from a dummy from Tommy Baldwin. We worked well together, he was screaming at me, and two players went with him and gave me the chance. I curled it in the corner with my left foot, it was a terrific goal. Again it was a team goal, but a great goal to score in the final, that was the main thing. I had the knack of doing that.

Ossie reflected on some of the memorable goals he scored, including the fourth-round Cup tie at Anfield in January 1966, where he silenced the Kop with his first FA Cup goal.

> The Liverpool goal was a little brave header from a corner. I didn't know Tommy Smith at the time – if I had I definitely wouldn't have gone for it, you will see him next to me, he did an overhead kick! We went 1–0 down early on from Roger Hunt and, after I equalised, Bobby Tambling scored the winner with a header. It was a joy to play in that game and a great education and privilege for me to come into a fantastic side. I never really scored that many times at Anfield, but I just liked playing there. They were always a good side to play against and when Ian St John had his testimonial [in April 1973] he invited Chelsea up. It was usually Liverpool v Everton in those testimonials, but we had 30,000 there, so I think they must have liked the way we played football. Apparently Bill Shankly offered £100,000 for me once but Tommy Doc turned him down. A few years ago I spoke to Peter Robinson, who used to be the chief executive at Liverpool, and he said, 'I've still got the letter from Bill saying go and get three players, Gordon Banks, Mike England and Peter Osgood.' Real Madrid came in as well but again Tommy Doc said they couldn't buy me and that was it.
>
> Another goal I will always remember was against AC Milan at Stamford Bridge [February 1966 in the Fairs Cup], a terrific left-foot half-volley outside the box that went into the top corner and the keeper never moved. When we played Arsenal [2–2 draw in the sixth round of the FA Cup in March 1973], it was a left-foot volley again. Years later they showed it when I did a programme with Bob Wilson and I started laughing. Bob said, 'What are you laughing at, Ossie?' I said, 'That was 27 years ago, you still dive for it and don't get any closer!'
>
> I played against some hard Italians and Germans, but remember Mike England more than anyone, as he was a big, hard boy who gave me a lot of stick. He was one of the few I could say overall probably got the better of me. The best defender I played against was 'Mooro', a different class. Dave Sexton used to say, 'Get in close to him one against one.' When I came in at half-time Dave would say to me, 'What happened?' I would say, 'Every time I get near him he takes the ball off me!' Roy McFarland was also a good footballing centre-half, strong, but not dirty.
>
> Eddie McCreadie was a bubbly fun guy, a typical Jock, full of

himself. He didn't want a normal family car, it had to be a Sunny Alpine when it first came out. That was why he got the push in the end when he managed Chelsea, as he wanted a Mercedes, but they offered him a brand new Rover. He was a smashing lad and I've got to admit you were brought up not to like the Jocks, but they all became my best mates and I'm glad to say still are.

Alan Birchenall was like a breath of fresh air when he came to the club. He was a superb player and it's a shame he didn't stay longer, as he was a pleasure to play with. Birch made out to be shy at first but he certainly wasn't, as he was a bubbly character and the most outgoing guy I think I've ever met in football.

Everybody says I was a flair player but I was a team player. I should have been more greedy, as I made lots of goals – as many as I scored. I wasn't a goalstriker like Mick Channon and told him one day, 'For God's sake, Mick, you've got to pass to me there.' He said, 'Ossie, when I see the whites of those posts you've got no chance!' That's a typical striker. I could play with both feet – although my left peg wasn't brilliant I scored a few nice goals. My pace was all right over five or six yards, which is all you need. I would back myself against anybody with my control which was second to none, and I wasn't bad in the air.

At the start of the 1971/72 campaign Ossie captured the headlines when Dave Sexton transfer-listed him for allegedly not trying in Chelsea's opening games. Despite all the speculation, Ossie was eventually taken off the list.

Dave and I are older and wiser now – I'm great friends with him now. I ring him up, that's the way it should be, but I was very hot to handle. He saw some good things, but picked more the bad things than the good things. I think he would probably say, 'Hang on then, I should have buttered Ossie up a bit more,' instead of going the other way with me. He would have got more out of me as I would have worked harder for him. At the end of the day I always tried to give 100 per cent, but I was never a stamina player, I don't think most skilful players are.

When Lawrie McMenemy splashed out a record £275,000 to bring Ossie to Southampton in March 1974, it coincided with the club's unsuccessful battle against relegation, although his arrival galvanised the city and put thousands on the gate. Ossie's skills were ultimately wasted in the Second Division, although he showed powers of commitment and concentration that, had they been displayed earlier in his career, would surely have led to more England caps. He accumulated 28 League goals in 126 appearances and helped Southampton win the 1976 FA Cup final, a 1–0 victory against all the odds over Manchester United, managed by his mentor Tommy Docherty.

I went to Southampton because I was impressed with Lawrie, who I also call The Boss today as I respect him. He said it was an old club that needed rebuilding and he had plans for it. I was to be the jewel to start us off and thought that was good enough for me. He respected me as a player for what I was and wouldn't try and change me. I knew it would take a while to win things, longer than it did, but I was prepared to work at it, finish my football down there at the age of 32–33 and say I helped get Southampton on the map. I had already won the FA Cup and played in the World Cup and, while I never thought we would win the League at Southampton, I got as much satisfaction helping rebuild them and had a superb time. Lawrie got rid of all the old boys, which people resented, including Mick Channon, who walked off the pitch in practice games. But Lawrie had his sights on what he wanted to do and, whilst we went down the year he bought me, we won the FA Cup, went back up in 1978 and have been there ever since. It was a friendly club and I'm still welcomed back – Ted Bates would always have a chat with you.

I went on loan to Norwich for a month, which I enjoyed, but was disappointed with John Bond. We went up to Everton, which was snowed off, and they just left me and said I had to go back to Southampton the following Monday. They didn't even say cheerio and, although I admired Bond as a brilliant coach, I was very disappointed with that. Kevin Keelan the goalkeeper made me feel very welcome and they had a nice little set-up. Duncan Forbes still kicked me in training, I tried to explain I was playing with him now.

Lawrie offered me a new contract but I had a lot of problems off the pitch. Really I should have stayed, he tried to help but these things happen, you look back and regret it, but you have just got to get on with your life. I went out to the States with Philadelphia Fury [in December 1977], and it was completely and utterly what I didn't want. I was there for six months and didn't like the razzamatazz at all. At least John Dempsey, Alan Ball and Colin Waldron joined me there, which made it a bit easier.'

After more than four years, in December 1978 the prodigal son was parachuted back to Chelsea for £25,000. It was a gamble by manager Ken Shellito, but at the age of 31 Ossie was unable to retain a first-team place.

Ken brought me back to the Bridge, I never wanted to leave in the first place. Blue has always been my colour and always will be – I love the Saints but it will never be like Chelsea. In my first game at Middlesbrough I scored a great near-post header after five minutes, and we got beat 7–2. Everywhere we went we got murdered and after three weeks Ken got the elbow. Then Danny Blanchflower came in and it was ridiculous, as he was trying to play this one-touch football like Spurs in the old days, but we didn't have the players to do it. He was a lovely man but he should never have come back into football.

I've got my principles in life and when Danny Blanchflower got the sack [in September 1979], Geoff Hurst became manager. He got the squad together with Bobby Gould, called out the names and said to me, 'You're number 16.' I said, 'Why am I last in the squad then, Geoff?' 'Cos you're not fit son.' I said, 'How long have you been coaching here?' 'Three months.' I replied, 'How long does it take you to get a player fit then? You've just stabbed Danny Blanchflower, a great man, in the back, he's left because of you. You've never helped him coach one bit. You used to sit on the ball on the side-line. I'll play for the reserves tomorrow at Oxford for the kids, but I'll walk away after that.' Hurst said, 'I've heard that all before.' I said, 'I'll pick my cards up on Thursday, get them ready for me.' I played with Chopper and a few of the boys at Oxford and we drew 1–1. I went in on the Thursday, picked my cards up and walked away. But I should have stayed as I enjoyed playing in the reserves, the kids appreciated me. I would never criticise them, they were learning the game – you get more effort, respect and response by encouraging.

In our days it was much easier to get away from the spotlight but now it is such high profile, they are like film stars. I saw the world and met lots of wonderful people, I've been into the dressing-room at Chelsea and Steve McQueen has been sitting there. When Raquel Welch was over promoting a film she said she wanted to meet me and Dickie Attenborough arranged it. When we played against Leicester, Raquel waved goodbye to me as she left just before the end of the game (and a massive cheer went around the stadium), and I got the biggest bollocking of my life from Dave Sexton! She was a lovely lady and enjoyed her soccer. It was a nice moment – how many people can say they have met Raquel Welch?

I met Michael Crawford and Denis Waterman and great sportsmen like Ian Botham and Viv Richards, lovely men. There's also a special guy called Jim Pearson, a Scot who was a centre-forward with

Newcastle and Everton, with a lovely family. I would have missed all that. I was very lucky I only had two clubs, whereas when these guys move around all the time, I couldn't have handled that. I think I had a bit of ability otherwise I don't think I would have stayed in football all that time.

I have only one or two regrets – I wish I could have got more caps, but basically it was too easy for me. I didn't think you had to work at it but you do. When I look back I think I should have put a bit more effort into training, but my sort of style was like the foreign style. I should have played for Brazil or in Spain as it was all playing and training with the football, not so much the hard slog – that just wasn't me. When we got the ball out in training, I'd be out there for two or three hours, no problem at all. I remember one foggy day when we went on a cross-country on Epsom Downs and Marvin Hinton and I saw Ron Suart standing at the back. We went about 20 yards away and sat waiting for the rest of the players to come back, then we jumped in behind them. They thought we had done ever so well, but we hadn't – we'd been sitting there for about 25 minutes – Marvin and I were always last!

After retirement in September 1979, Ossie embarked on a nomadic coaching career in such diverse locations as the Far East and Butlins.

I took a year off when I packed up football, and tried to analyse what I had done with my life and where I went from there. I bought the freehouse pub 'The Old Union' in Windsor and got Hutch involved, as he was leaving Chelsea and I thought it was an ideal opportunity. We got out of the pub after about five years, as we had a bit of a row over women as usual. When Alan Ball became coach at Portsmouth he offered me his job at Butlins. For five days a week I was driving round the country coaching at these holiday camps, keeping myself fit and loved it. I did that for about three years and had a great time. Then I got a phone call in the summer of 1986 from 'Ballie' offering me the youth team coaching job in place of Dave Thomas. I think there was uproar initially with the playboy image, but in the first year we went up to the First Division with super kids like Darren Anderton, Darryl Powell, Kit Symons, Andy Awford and Paul Musselwhite, a lovely lad who was our goalkeeper. I used to do everything for them, drive the minibus and get the kit ready, and we were like mates. They didn't call me 'Boss', they called me 'Ossie'. I was there two years and loved every minute of it. I enjoyed the coaching side and am proud of being able to get the best out of young players.

Then I moved to Dubai in the Far East to do some coaching. I also did TV and radio work when they wanted me, but that sort of thing was too regimental. Training was all right as you knew it was only going to be for an hour and a half, but the media work week in, week out was not for me. I don't do hunting, ferreting or fishing any more, although I still like being outdoors. The ferrets were just an outlet for me. When I was playing my mate and I used to relax with them and basically it was just an excuse to get away from my missus and get into the pub by 12 o'clock! It's just golf and horse-racing nowadays. I have three boys, Anthony, Mark and Darren, and three grandchildren.

My life now is lovely – I have a golfing business organising weekend breaks in Hampshire which is run mostly by my wife Lyn. I do the PR job and get the people, and Lyn takes over from there. Towards the end of 2000 we had 84 people down one weekend and 78 the next. We have been doing that for about ten years now and built up a nice business. I have been down to eight but play off a handicap of 16 nowadays, because of the problems with my legs, that's my handicap. When I lived at Tadworth, Hutch, Chopper, Tommy Baldwin and I used to play all the time at Walton Heath – we still do golf days now. I also love my after-dinner speaking, as you are expressing yourself, telling gags, which is superb, but the best job I've got is hosting the sponsors on matchdays with Chelsea.

IAN HUTCHINSON – *57 goals in 143 appearances*

It wasn't often the legendary Scottish manager handed out plaudits to the opposition. When describing him as, 'A very brave man, very brave,' Ian Hutchinson was one of the few non-Liverpool players to be paid a compliment by Bill Shankly. Hutch was a throwback to the old-style forward, with a bustling technique and bucketfuls of courage. A deadly marksman who became a fine header of the ball, there weren't too many frills in his game, but Hutch provided excitement for the fans and headaches for defenders. He was never afraid to venture where the boots were flying, but a potentially sparkling career was marred by a succession of injuries, forcing him to retire with the peak of his powers still obscured by the clouds of time.

Jimmy Greaves felt that, but for his terrible run of injuries, he could have established himself as an international. Born at Codnor, Derbyshire, in 1948, Hutch was a multi-talented youngster.

> My love of football started at school in Littleover – I was captain in the third and fourth year for the cricket and football teams. When I left school I went to work in a factory and joined the works side, International Combustion. They played in the Derby District Senior League sub-section 'B', which was a good standard.
>
> I also played schoolboy cricket for Derbyshire – I smashed the ball all over the place, a bit like my mate Ian Botham! When I was 17 Donald Carr, the old Derbyshire captain, offered me a position on the groundstaff. Around the same time Nottingham Forest sent a scout to watch me at International Combustion and invited me for a trial. I was offered £15 a week to play cricket and £25 from Forest, so chose football.
>
> I played right-back in the Forest youth and 'A' side for over a year, mainly on Thursday afternoons and had to ask permission from the factory for time off. Johnny Carey was the Forest manager but he gave me the elbow. I struggled when I came back to the Combustion side, as they had two very good right-backs, so they put me upfront and that's how it started. I scored 75 goals in my first year and 80 in the second.
>
> I was spotted by Burton Albion, who signed me in 1967 as a part-time pro in the old Southern League. I was on £10 per week compared with about £5.70 for a 44-hour week as an apprentice at the factory. Then Cambridge United, who were the top club in the Southern League, bought me for £2,500 and I had a year with them. Bill Leivers the manager was a lovely man, although I found out he got a £400 bung out of the transfer fee. Mind you I got a £400 signing-on fee.
>
> Frank Blunstone and Ron Suart came to one of the matches to look at our goalkeeper Chris Barker and bought me in July 1968 for £2,500 [doubled after a dozen games]. I was still only 19 and signed a one-year contract as a part-time pro so as to complete my engineering apprenticeship, which took five years, until I was 21, much to the dismay of Dave Sexton, who couldn't get insurance for me.

During the early days Hutch developed a secret weapon which became a significant tool in Chelsea's armoury.

> Even when I played cricket I never realised I had the ability to throw

the ball a long way. I had only taken an occasional throw-in before, so Ron Suart had us all lined up on the touchline at Mitcham, where we used to train, and said, 'I want you to throw it as far as you can.' They were training pitches at Mitcham, not full-size and the first few players went and got it near the six-yard line. I took the ball, followed through and it went past the goalkeeper over to the other side of the pitch! Suart said, 'Do that again,' which I did, just as far. Suart had this thing about throwing the ball to the near-post and flicking it on for someone to come in at the far-post and, when I played in the reserves shortly after, I used it a few times.

In October 1968 Hutch made his first-team debut at Derby, familiar territory to him, in a League Cup replay. Although beaten 3–1, there was an early sign of promise from Hutch, as he swept past a couple of defenders and saw his angled shot blocked on the line by a despairing lunge from a Derby defender. Hutch was still combining football with his apprenticeship when his home debut came three days later against Ipswich. He was soon able to experiment with his throw-ins (once measured at 112 feet) on an unsuspecting opposition.

Ron Suart came down during the game and said, 'Throw-in, launch the throw-in.' Alan Birchenall went up with Bill Baxter at the far-post from my throw and Baxter scored an own goal, which inspired the newspaper headlines, 'Hurl 'em Hutch'.

My dad told me to get my apprenticeship in case the football didn't work out so, sharing a house with Tommy Hughes, I got up at six o'clock in the morning, caught a train to Byfleet, then I had a bike outside the station to get me to the factory. I worked for George Thomson at Byfleet Machine & Tool Co. and the lads were brilliant there – they even got me playing football in the forecourt. After one night game, when I was battered and bruised, I wondered more than once what I was doing in the factory! The headlines this time said, 'Part-time pro proves it's no joke'.

I scored six League goals in the last 12 games that season, and one of my best was at Everton in March 1969 when we beat them 2–1. I always remember the early goals and it was Grand National day, so we played in the evening. I beat Brian Labone and Tommy Wright for a near-post header. It came from a through ball from John Hollins, who made so many goals for us.

The following season (1969/70) Hutch was virtually an ever-present, scoring 22 times. Within a year he was playing Leeds macho-men at Wembley, 'wondering what I was doing there!' As the mercury, always sensitive between the sides, rose, it was Hutch's goal in the Cup final which forced the replay. John Hollins chipped a free kick from the left and Hutch planted a flying header past Sprake's right hand to level the score at 2–2.

> 'Holly' clipped it to the near-post for me. He was a great player, a great 'pinger' of the ball and never stopped running. We took the credit but couldn't have done it without players like him. The Cup final was so disappointing, as from a kid it was a dream of mine to play at Wembley. When we turned up it was covered in about 500 tons of sand, because it had been over-used. The pitch was like a pudding and, with extra-time as well, I was absolutely knackered. Peter Lorenzo was interviewing the players as we went down the tunnel after the game and said to me, 'Hutch, you've just scored the equaliser, can I have your comments?' I didn't realise it was a live interview, but I was battered and bruised and uttered an expletive. He said, 'What were your first impressions when you scored the goal?' I said, 'Oh, no, extra-time!' He said, 'You don't mean that, do you?' but I was knackered as the pitch spoilt it. Leeds were the top 'Johnnies' and we were the entertainers, and on a decent pitch I would have fancied our chances even more. But the pitch was so terrible it didn't allow players with a lot of skill like Charlie Cooke to run with the ball.

While the match was not endowed with strong enough themes to survive longer in the memory than other finals, the replay was different. Seconds before the end of the extra-time interval Hutch's windmill throw from the left again wreaked havoc. Jack Charlton, challenged by Ossie, misdirected his header across goal, where David Webb headed the ball firmly and decisively into the net.

> We went to Old Trafford, were 1–0 down at half-time, then stuffed them 2–1. It was a decent pitch and we knew the ball was going to come up at the same height. One momento from the final is that I swopped shirts with Norman Hunter, which I have framed. It all happened very quickly – I remember when we played Santos in May 1970 in Venezuela and Pele was in their side, I asked to kiss his hand! Likewise when I played a friendly against Holland Ajax in July 1970

and Cruyff was playing – I was totally in awe of being on the same pitch as them.

Hutch's potential was rewarded with two Under-23 international caps, but during the second half of the 1970/71 season injury problems started to bite. He had a cartilage removed from his right knee in April 1971, and frustratingly missed the European Cup run. Hutch was testing his right knee in a Combination fixture at Swindon in August 1971 when, after scoring, he tragically broke the left leg, which kept him out for the remainder of the season. The next comeback was triumphant, but short-lived.

> The best goals for me personally came after I had been out injured for 22 months. I scored twice against Norwich at the Bridge in December 1972, we won 3–1 and they were very special.

Hutch only appeared twice more that season but bravely played through the pain barrier for a further three seasons, scoring 17 goals in 55 appearances. He even managed his only senior hat trick on a Chelsea tour of Australia in June 1974.

> We beat Illawarra 4–1 in Wollongong and the Man of the Match, would you believe, was the goalkeeper! I scored twice loads of times and Dave Sexton, who was a lovely fella, would say, 'Get another one.'

Hutch increasingly suffered from severe physical handicap, and a succession of knee injuries brought his career to an end. It was February 1976, the eve of the quarter-final FA Cup tie against Crystal Palace, with Eddie McCreadie in charge.

> I had played right up to then but my knee was swollen and I had to have cortisone injections to get me out on the pitch. I went up to his office and said, 'Eddie, I'm still in pain – these injections aren't making any difference.' He didn't coax me by saying, 'Don't worry,' he said, 'If you can't play on Saturday, you can't play at all.' The next thing I knew was, when driving home on the radio, I heard, 'Hutchinson has retired.' I was very surprised and disappointed with Eddie, he was my soul-mate and lived with me for six months when he was unwell.
>
> Among the best defenders I played against were Spurs' Mike England and Phil Beal. Mike England would look after Ossie, who would say to me, 'You've got an easy afternoon, you've got Beal.' But

he wasn't a bad player either! Then there was Roy McFarland and Colin Todd from Derby. McFarland picked me up and Todd tried to look after Ossie. The biggest problem I had, in addition to hard defenders like Norman Hunter and Tommy Smith, was Forest's Sammy Chapman. I was still only 20 when we played them in a League game at Forest in my first year. Alan Birchenall, who also got the elbow from Forest, was playing, so he was keen to make an impression. We came in 2–0 up at half-time, Birch got one and I got the other. At the start of the second half Chapman knocked my front two teeth out, then elbowed me in the nose, and it broke and I went down. Ossie said, 'The next corner go in and give him a whack back.' I said, 'All right, bruv.' The ball came over, I went for Chapman and, crack, gave it all I'd got with my elbow. Ossie looked at me and I said, 'I've broken my ****ing arm!' It was so painful and I've still got the scar to prove it. But Chapman was off and out for six weeks!

Ossie was majestic, peerless and a privilege to play alongside. We made many goals for each other and combined so well. He had so much skill and would say I couldn't control a sack of cement and, 'Who's this guy from Derby I'm having to play upfront with?' but I proved them all wrong. We've been great friends now for over 30 years and I was best man at his second wedding and vice-versa. He is also godfather to my son.

I went to Dartford in August 1976 as a favour to Elton John, as his cousin Roy Dwight, who played for Forest, was manager. The summer of 1976 was really hot and I remember he came to my house in Horsham when I was sitting by the swimming pool and said, 'I want you to play for me at Dartford.' I said, 'Where?' 'I'll give you £2,000 cash signing-on fee and pay you £75 a game.' I said, 'How do I get there?' They put me in at centre-half and I played five games before one day I trod on a glass beside the swimming pool. I had five stitches in my foot and told them I couldn't play that night. They insisted I played so I got a friend to drive me to Dartford. I went into the boardroom and showed the doctor the stitches and he confirmed I couldn't play. Ten days later I played centre-half and the knee started playing up again. I went into hospital and they took out some bits and pieces from my knee. Unbelievably Dwight and the chairman turned up at the hospital and gave me a form to sign. When I asked them what it was, they told me I had to repay the signing-on fee. I told them to go away in the strongest possible terms.

Chelsea benefited from the insurance monies when I retired, so they granted me a testimonial. I had a match in 1976 against an International XI, but it was on a cold, wet night and didn't reach the £25,000 they guaranteed me. So I had a second testimonial in 1978 against QPR which Ossie, Alan Hudson and Bobby Tambling played in.

I stayed on the Chelsea staff as commercial manager for two years, which I enjoyed. I knew the people in the office and it was nice that the fans recognised me. Then I took over the pub at Windsor with Ossie and we had a great time. After that I took a pub in Taunton where I got to know Ian Botham and Viv Richards, as the Somerset cricketers often went there. Don't those West Indians know how to party – I would hand over the key and tell them to lock up when they'd finished.

I have one child, Benjamin, who is in his twenties, and am now with Elaine, my partner of seven years, who was an actress, and we live in her flat in North London. I love my golf and play off a handicap of eight. I support a number of charity functions, like Sparks. I have collected coins for a long time and I'm still involved a little. I also enjoy cooking and am a qualified cordon bleu chef – Dave Sexton encouraged me to take it up when I was injured.

My main regret is having so many cortisone injections and painkillers, but at 21 I wanted to play all the time. They would say, 'You'll be all right for Saturday,' and you don't think about the long-term effects – now you'll never see a knee like mine! When the club doctors came into the treatment room with their little sachets it seemed to be always Ossie or I who would get the jabs. Now because of our injuries a group of us are taking legal action against the Football Association. Geoff Strong is leading the action – he has two metal knees.

KERRY DIXON – *193 goals in 420 appearances*

A tall, natural athlete, Kerry remains the only forward to threaten Bobby Tambling's goalscoring record. He possessed the template qualities of a striker – power and pace, allied to potency in the air and, above all, was a clinical finisher. Born at Luton in 1961, Kerry's happy knack of scoring was already taking shape at school, even if he did not find the rich pickings of professional football easy to secure. Rejection came early when, despite scoring a hatful for Luton Town Youth, he was unable to secure a contract with his local League side.

My father Mick was a professional footballer with Coventry and Luton, and we come from a sporting family. My sister Jane ran for the county and my niece does now, so we've all been quite quick. I was always a striker and scored a lot of goals at Beechwood Junior School. When David Pleat turned me down at Luton he decided at the time it wasn't right. He said he might have done me a favour as he felt my attitude wasn't right, which was fair enough. Maybe it spurred me on to a higher level of play. When he bought me years later for Luton he acknowledged he made a mistake.

When Luton didn't offer me a contract I went to Chesham United in the Isthmian League. Their manager was Brendan McNally, who played full-back at Luton with my dad and is my godfather. He was involved in the tackle that broke Roy Dwight's leg in the 1959 FA Cup final. He did ever so well for me and introduced me to senior football. I was 16 at the time and took a lot of blows from the experienced players. But it was a good education, I played well and had a successful trial at Spurs.

Kerry scored in a 3–1 win, then two goals in a 4–0 Cup final victory against Oxford led to the offer of a one-year full-time contract. He turned part-time professional in order to keep his engineering job.

I trained two evenings a week with the kids and played on Saturday mornings. I top-scored with 32 goals in the South-East Counties League that season, but was again told I wouldn't be taken on. A committee of Keith Burkinshaw, Pat Welton, Bill Nicholson, Peter Shreeves and Ron Henry decided on the future of each player and I lost out 3–2. The two people who were with me for most of the season, Shreeves and Henry, both voted in my favour and those who hadn't seen me play much decided against. Peter told me later that they had Mark Falco, Terry Gibson, Colin Lee and Ian Moores, who had to play at some level, so there wouldn't have been enough games for me as well. This time it was political and I was the one who lost out. Peter was very good to me and says it was a mistake.

When Spurs let me go Brendan McNally, who had moved to Dunstable in the Southern League, was only too pleased to have me back. Although Orient and Brentford offered me trials I had been kicked back twice, so was content at the time [1979] to go back into non-League football. When I left school I started a toolmaker's apprenticeship at Cardale Engineering – it was a four-year apprenticeship with five years at college, so it was much easier bearing in mind I was still working in the factory. With Stuart Atkins we scored 89 goals that season and I got 52 of them, which was a non-League record at the time. Then Maurice Evans, Reading's manager, paid £20,000 for me [July 1980], which was the second-highest fee for a player transferred from a non-League to a League club. He saw my potential and was obviously a reasonable judge – I had a lot of respect for him.

When I went to Reading I started as a part-time pro so as to complete my apprenticeship. Within eight weeks of finishing I had a major fall-out with the new charge-hand at Cardale. It would have been stupid of me to risk it all within weeks of completing, but I have always been an impulsive sort of person and react to certain situations. However this was not my character on the field, I was quite cool and didn't give referees much bother – I was booked no more than five times in my career.

In his first season Kerry top-scored, despite not always being first choice. Having completed his apprenticeship, he signed as a full-time professional at the start of the 1981/82 season. He was second highest goalscorer after Neil Webb, with 12 in 44 games, but acknowledged it was not an easy start to his League career.

My first two years weren't spectacular, it was tough and a steep learning curve for me. I was only training three days a week and learning the way of life as a pro without the benefit of an apprenticeship as a footballer. In my third year it started to take off when I scored 28 goals in the 1982/83 season and won the 'Bronze Boot' goalscoring award for the Third Division. One of my most memorable matches was in September 1982 when Doncaster beat us 7–5. I scored four and one of the Snodin brothers scored a hat trick for them – it was a great game apart from the result!

Despite his best endeavours, Kerry couldn't prevent Reading from avoiding relegation to the Fourth Division, which inevitably heightened the interest of other clubs. A transfer to Chelsea in August 1983 for £175,000 was fast looming on the horizon.

I scored goals regularly during my last season at Reading and was linked with a number of clubs including Ipswich, Coventry and Sheffield Wednesday, and picked up Brian Roach, an agent, during the summer. He arranged for me to speak to them once the fee Reading wanted, which was unknown to me at the time, had been reached. I was due to speak to Bobby Gould at Coventry when Chelsea came in for me. Their manager John Neal was a friend of Maurice and had watched me a couple of times. Ken Bates picked me up in his Roller and took me down to Aberystwyth, where Chelsea were doing their pre-season training. I trained for the day, then met Ken, John Neal and Ian McNeill at the hotel in the evening. Ken is not a man who is beaten easily and they were very persuasive. They decided there was no way I was going to leave the hotel to speak to anyone else and made it quite clear that negotiations would continue all night if necessary. However Ken had already sold the club to me and I just wanted the opportunity to prove myself at a higher level, even though Chelsea were in the old Second Division at the time.

David Speedie had already been with the Blues for a season and their partnership upfront was not an instant success. Kerry played his first ten games alongside Colin Lee, the established number-one striker. It was a situation Speedo was unhappy about and, even when he was restored to the team, the two did not always see eye to eye. Animosity simmered until they came to blows in the dressing-room after a 1–0 home defeat by Manchester City in December 1983.

I think you should always be able to air your views with your friends. If it came to blows so be it, but you should be big enough to put it behind you and get on with your life. I've always been like that and we haven't looked back since. Everyone knew Speedo had a short fuse, but people were all too quick to talk about that side of his game rather than the rest. He was superb at holding the ball up, was very aggressive and always let the centre-halves know he was about. He would stick an elbow in or leave a foot in, which wasn't really my style. I liked to play it fair, but if a centre-half mixed it I would too. I was pacier than him and could get on the end of his flicks, so we complemented each other. You would think that normally the big man would knock it on, and the little fella would be on to it but, even though I could head a ball, he was fantastic in the air for his height. He had a great leap and could win a flick against a six foot centre-half, and I'd be on to it.

That season [1983/84] must have been very exciting for Chelsea fans, as since Ossie's days they hadn't really seen a team capable of doing anything. Then John Neal put this team together, signing unknowns Joe McLaughlin and Pat Nevin plus Nigel Spackman from Bournemouth. In addition Eddie Niedzwiecki in my opinion turned out to be one of the best goalkeepers I ever saw. However we weren't even considered promotion candidates and nobody expected it to happen the way it did. Under Peter Taylor, Derby were expected to be the side to beat, but we thrashed them 5–0 in the opening game and I got two.

As Chelsea surged to the top of the table, Kerry won a Silver award for heading the Second Division scoring list. The formidable partnership was cemented, with Kerry notching 34 goals for the season and Speedo weighing in with 13. Victory over Leeds at the Bridge in front of 33,447 confirmed promotion to the First Division. Kerry's goal in the final fixture at Grimsby was the catalyst for unrestrained celebrations among the 10,000 travelling fans, as the title was clinched.

We beat Leeds 5–0 and I scored a hat trick to spark off a massive party that day. The atmosphere at Grimsby was incredible and without doubt the most memorable game of a fantastic season. We were level on points with Sheffield Wednesday but ahead on goal difference, so we knew as long as we beat Grimsby we would secure the Championship. Grimsby supporters had one end and Chelsea fans were packed into the rest of the ground. I saw a Pat Nevin cross come over and headed the only goal of the game. People talk about Cup finals, but it felt like the whole ground erupted and that was my magic moment.

Kerry's big test came with the return of top-flight football to Stamford Bridge. He was off the mark in the opening game and his first Division One hat trick was secured in a 6–2 victory over Coventry at the Bridge in November 1984. He collected another match ball with four goals at Wigan in a FA Cup replay in January 1985. There was no stopping the inspired partnership as Kerry and Speedo accumulated 52 goals in the season. Chelsea finished sixth and Kerry completed a unique quartet of awards with 24 League goals.

I scored in the first game of the season, a 1–1 draw against Arsenal, which was arguably my best goal in terms of what it meant to me personally. It was against Pat Jennings, a world-class goalkeeper, and our London rivals too. It proved I was capable of scoring at the highest level and was another stepping-stone. Goalscoring is something you can or cannot do and I think you find your level as you progress. It was also a great start for the team and proved we were capable of holding our own in the First Division.

I then went through a barren spell of six games when I didn't score. John Hollins had taken over temporarily when John Neal had heart surgery. It was a difficult period as there were some people who doubted me and said I had found my level. Then I scored twice against Leicester at the end of September, and Gary Lineker and I finished joint top-scorers of the First Division – another 'Golden Boot' award. On the back of that I made my England debut in the summer of 1985 on a pre-World Cup tour and was conscious the 1986 World Cup was on the horizon.

The next season [1985/86] I was flying, with 21 goals by Christmas and again on top of the scoring charts. Then in the early part of January I had my worst-ever injury in the FA Cup tie against Liverpool, when I went to head a ball, twisted and tore my stomach. We had played on QPR's artificial surface in the fifth round of the Milk Cup the match before and I'm sure the effects of that plastic pitch jarred me up. It kept me out for over a month and even when I came back I struggled. People were starting to doubt whether I had the mobility and was the player I was. However in April at Old Trafford I scored two excellent goals and we beat them, although no-one gave us any chance. Bobby Robson's right-hand man Don Howe was watching and I believe that game clinched my place in the World Cup squad.

The injury seemed to mark a watershed in the partnership. While Speedo also had an excellent year with 22 goals to his name, the majority came in the first half of the season. Kerry, credited with 23 goals, also had the disappointment of missing out on the Full Members' Cup final due to a groin injury sustained the previous game at Southampton. The partnership never fired in the same way and changes in personnel were afoot.

The 1986/87 season didn't go right for John Hollins, the team was struggling and I think he prematurely broke up a successful side. That was one of the disappointments of my career. For whatever reasons he sold Speedie and Spackman and the team fell apart. John might acknowledge he made mistakes now, but he was sacked and Bobby Campbell was brought in. My form deserted me though I knew Manchester United were interested. I never got to speak to them as Chelsea turned it down and Ken Bates said he wanted £5 million, which is equivalent to about £40 million now – I only found out about it months later. I actually met Ron Atkinson on holiday during the summer and we had a chat on the beach, not anything improper. There was also a rumour that Real Madrid were interested in me. Raddy Antic, who used to play at Luton, was the manager at the time, so knew all about me. I told my agent I wasn't interested in going abroad, as I loved the club and felt comfortable with my family around me.

The goals continued, although not quite in the same volume as previously enjoyed, and Chelsea slipped into the Second Division at the end of the 1987/88 season. However, they bounced back at the first attempt and Kerry found the net 25 times in the League. He then scored 20 goals in the 1989/90 season and played at Wembley in the Zenith Data Cup final, when Tony Dorigo scored the only goal against Middlesbrough. On Boxing Day 1991 Kerry became only the seventh player to make 400 appearances for the club, and felt one of his finest Chelsea goals was the very last, the only goal at Norwich in March 1992. He took it with his back to the play, controlled it with his right foot and turned Ian Butterworth. From the edge of the box he curled a left-footer round keeper Mark Walton – it was world class and a fitting way to sign off. Kerry reflected on his other favourite Chelsea goals and some of the personalities at the Bridge.

I remember two excellent goals against Fulham at Craven Cottage [October 1983]. I cut in from the left-hand side to score one and the other I bent into the top corner. Gordon Davies scored a hat trick for them and we won 5–3. Against Charlton [also in October 1983] I beat three players and chipped Bob Bolder, which was a great goal. I remember a left-foot curler against Barnsley [April 1989], when I scored four goals – we beat them 5–3 and it was one of my best hat tricks. Then we won 3–1 at Millwall at the end of the 1989/90 season and I scored a hat trick which was every bit as good. One was a right-footer I bent in, then I drove past someone and slid in a left-foot, and the third was a header from a Graeme Le Saux cross. That nearly got me into the 1990 World Cup squad.

Eddie Niedzwiecki and Nigel Spackman, who roomed together,

were two of the main characters from the side. They were the instigators of trouble and used to lark around all the time – Nigel was as much a nuisance as anything else. You'd find your mattress tipped out of your room at the training camp and lying on the ground four storeys below. Or shaving foam all over the place. Or the top would be off the salt pot and you would tip it all over the dinner! It was a nightmare and you knew it would be either of those two.

Pat Nevin was part of a front three, which for one year was supplemented on the left by Mickey Thomas, a very good footballer. Pat was sensational and gave the Chelsea fans something to marvel at. I admired what he did and remember him showboating in the 4–0 defeat of Newcastle. He beat five or six men from the half-way line, but the infuriating thing for me was that he didn't cross it, he went back and beat them again, then crossed it! He did like a dribble and was amazing to watch when he got on one-to-one, as you just couldn't get the ball off him. I played with him recently in the Masters and he's still got it – it was impossible to get the ball off him!

Kerry carved out a special relationship with the crowd, which assured him a place in Chelsea's history as one of its most popular players. He reluctantly left the Bridge for Southampton in July 1992 for £575,000, ostensibly as replacement for Alan Shearer.

I always treated the Chelsea fans with respect and remember the hours I spent at open days signing autographs etc. I don't think they ever forgot that, plus the fact that I stayed loyal for nine years. There were some wonderful shared memories during the peak years of my career when I was rarely injured. When I look back the events that prevented me from breaking Bobby Tambling's goalscoring record were the biggest disappointment of my career. I had three and a half years left of my contract and could have waited for my opportunity to get the ten goals I needed. But Ian Porterfield said Tony Cascarino would get a run and he was signing a new forward line. It turned out they signed Mick Harford and Robert Fleck and, at the age of 31, I wasn't prepared to take a back seat and stagnate in the reserves, which is what Chelsea were saying to me. Porterfield said he had an offer from Southampton which was too good to turn down and I was free to talk to them. It was my decision and, as much as I wanted to break that record, Southampton were offering me a chance to stay in the top flight. The club that I loved told me I was not in their future plans and rightly or wrongly, I moved on. If I'd stayed I feel sure I would have broken that record, which will never happen now, as people don't stay at one club long enough.

Kerry made his Southampton debut in August 1992, teaming up again with Speedo. Neither player was happy at the club, and it was impossible to re-create the chemistry. Kerry was plagued by injury problems and played just nine games, scoring twice, his final match being in January 1993 against Leeds. His career was rescued by his home-town team the following month.

I got one injury after another which was unusual for me. I had a back injury in particular, which was my most embarrassing moment in football. I was in the middle of the training field and just bent down and my back felt a bit stiff. I thought I would be able to run it off but I couldn't get up! I had to be carried off the training pitch by the players doubled up. It wasn't a great time and after four months I knew it wasn't right for me.

I was really excited when I heard that David Pleat was interested in signing me for Luton. It was like a dream and when I was called in by Ian Branfoot it didn't take any time to agree. I was quite prepared to sit on a two-year deal at Southampton but I knew I didn't figure in his plans and he just wanted me out the way. When he was looking to offload me Luton didn't have the money, so initially I went on loan. I realised as I got older I might have to drop down to achieve my best but I really enjoyed it. I was on loan for three months, then had to go back to pre-season training with Southampton, which I was dreading. They were not dropping the asking price for me, so I went back on loan for two months before they let me go for a nominal fee. John Hartson later emerged to push me for a place towards the end of my two and a half years. David Pleat shared the role in the side and I modified my game to provide chances, as well as score goals. I was happy at the club with my friends and family just down the road, even if I was to be a bit-part player.

Kerry revelled in his new role, where his experience helped steer Luton clear of relegation worries and guided them to the 1994 semi-final of the FA Cup, before a 2–0 defeat inflicted by his old team-mates.

The Cup run was fantastic and we played in some great games. I was injured from the Newcastle game when we played Cardiff, and David brought me back for the quarter-final against West Ham, when Scott Oakes scored a hat trick. I made two of them in front of a full house and it was a wonderful night. We knew the semi-final was at Wembley and I was so excited. It was a great day, although of course it was sad we lost, but Chelsea were the better team and some of the stars of our Cup run didn't quite perform – maybe they were a bit overawed with the venue. The Chelsea fans gave me a wonderful reception and to actually have them singing my name after the game was very moving. It was probably the most emotional day of my life, apart from scoring for England on my debut. Whilst there was dejection in the Luton camp, when I got off the field Dennis Wise, who was my room partner for three years, commiserated with me.

After 20 goals in 88 appearances for Luton, in March 1995 a further transfer was effected.

David Pleat called me in and said he was moving me to Millwall. He had bought John Taylor that morning and it was clear he was looking for a younger player. I talked to Mick McCarthy, who thought I could do a good job for them, which I believe I did. Millwall fans were wary of me at first – they chanted 'Chelsea Reject', but they had Uwe Fuchs in the side, who was bought from Kaiserslauten for £750,000 and he was a flop. They paid £5,000 for me and when I scored on my debut the fans really took to me. I was only there for about a year but I loved it. I left when they were near the top of the Second Division and we had a very good side, with Ben Thatcher and Keith Stevens in defence, and Andy Roberts and Ricky Newman in midfield. However they bought two Russians, who just came to England to take the money, and sadly got relegated.

Towards the end of my Millwall days I was playing in the reserves when Kenny Sansom, who was Glenn Roeder's assistant at Watford, saw me. He felt I could do a job for them and, travelling to Millwall, the thought of going to Watford, even though they were Luton's deadly rivals, was quite appealing. However even some of the Luton fans wondered what I was doing. I was rumoured to be Watford's worst ever signing from the fans' point of view and after two games Glenn was sacked. The fans actually booed me before I kicked a ball for them and I only stayed nine games, as Graham Taylor came in and decided to do things his own way.

Kerry had long expressed an interest in coaching and was given the opportunity to stay in football by Third Division Doncaster Rovers, albeit a club deep in trauma and controversy.

When I was at Chelsea a Luton boys' team called Bramingham Spitfires asked if I could coach them. I coached, then managed, one of the sides (with ages of 12 to 16) for four years. I am proud to say that three of them, Jamie Campbell, Martin Williams and Mark McGonagel, made the grade as pros. I was always interested in coaching and in the summer of 1996 Doncaster approached me, initially as player-coach. I met Mark Weaver and was introduced to Ken Richardson, who wasn't the chairman, but known as the benefactor. I said I was only prepared to join them as manager in view of the distance from home. Mark Weaver said they were looking to change Sammy Chung, their manager, so I talked to them on that basis. When I accepted the job a few days before the start of the season the tricks really started as they hadn't informed Sammy. I was due to be introduced to the crowd as the new manager before the first game, and when I got there Sammy was in one office and I was in another! They made out they had not been able to get hold of Sammy, so the way it happened was very sad and embarrassing. But I got on with the job and loved Doncaster – the people of South Yorkshire were great to me.

It was a steep learning curve in management, and perhaps I was taught a harsh lesson early on in terms of relationships with a board of directors and the politics of football behind the scenes. I wasn't always getting what I was led to believe and the 'chairman' wanted a say in the side – I wasn't prepared to have that. It was never discussed with me and apparently had been going on for years. I told the fans midway through the season that my position had become untenable, but I was on a player's contract and wasn't going to walk out, and the club weren't prepared to agree a settlement. With the financial problems it was absolute pandemonium as the PFA were in daily with the players, and it was certainly not how a football club should be run. I got on very well with the players but in the end the receivers negotiated a settlement pay-off on my contract, as it was in the best interests of the creditors. I now believe a football person shouldn't necessarily be in charge of the buying and selling of players, you can't have a manager without any financial experience spending other people's money. Likewise vice-versa, as Ken Richardson took over the running of the team when I left and Doncaster went out of the League.

Kerry performed miracles to prevent the club from being relegated, and a League position of 19th was in itself an achievement. His departure came at the start of the 1997/98 season, but Kerry was keen to return to football.

> I only had a couple of weeks out of football when Phil Wallace, the Boreham Wood chairman, offered me the job of player-coach. Bob Makin, who was the manager, put together an excellent team – I took the training and the partnership with Alan Carington, the assistant manager, really worked well. It was the year Kingstonian won the Ryman Premier League but we beat them 5–0 at their place. We were the best footballing side in the League and the coaching was a joy. We were looking to go into the Conference but there were doubts expressed as to whether Boreham Wood could become a big club and, after finishing in the top six in both seasons, Phil decided to move on to Stevenage with Bob. Without Phil to bankroll the club, the budget was reduced. When I went back pre-season for the third year and saw the quality of players, without being disrespectful to them, I knew it would be a struggle and decided to look elsewhere.
>
> The managerial position was sold to me at Letchworth and in fact Boreham Wood were relegated that season, which was a shame. I felt Letchworth, who are in the Spartan South Midlands League, was a club with great aspirations and excellent facilities and they wanted to reach the Ryman Premier. I took over when we were third from bottom after about nine games of the 1999/2000 season and we finished fifth. We won our first trophy in 11 years and have done well this [2000/01] season. I have a very open mind as to whether Letchworth is a step up back into League football management for me. I now just play in the reserves at Letchworth and keep myself reasonably fit to play in exhibition and Masters games.
>
> I have two girls, Gemma and Kelly, who are not interested in sport, and a boy, Joseph, who is showing certain football abilities. I can see what perhaps my mum and dad saw in me when I started. As you get older you realise there's a lot to be said about natural ability being in the genes. I have a long-term girlfriend Michele and we live in Luton, near my parents. I have no desire ever to return to a factory and am concentrating on my media work with Sky. I also work for Chelsea on Saturdays, commentating at their home games.

The exceptional form of Kerry and Speedo in the mid-1980s had their international managers scribbling in their notepads and both made their full debuts in 1985. The first of Kerry's eight caps came on the pre-World Cup tour of Mexico, but it was his full debut where he made a stunning impact.

> I was so elated to be picked for England. Although Bobby Robson didn't specify which games I would play, he did confirm I would make my debut on the tour. I didn't play in the first two as Mark Hateley started alongside Gary Lineker. Although I came on as sub for the Mexico game, I made my full debut against West Germany in the Aztec Stadium, scored two goals and set up the third, which I chested down for Bryan Robson. We won 3–1 and it was a wonderful day for me. To hear the National Anthem, play well and score for England was a dream and the highlight of my England career. I then went on to the Los Angeles Colosseum and repeated it against the USA. I was in good form at the time, we won 5–0 and Lineker scored two as well.

The Lineker–Beardsley duet, which functioned so effectively in the 1986 World Cup, was to limit Kerry's appearances for his country. Although he won a further four caps in 1986, two were as substitute, and his last appearance was in 1987, when, by his own admission, his form had dipped.

> If I have an England regret, it was that perhaps I didn't get more games when I was playing well. When Bobby Robson decided to pick me in 1987 Chelsea were getting relegated and I had injury problems. I didn't play well in Sweden, we lost 1–0 and I was left out after that game. My biggest disappointment was not even being on the bench for the Argentina game. I scored more goals than any other striker in the pre-World Cup warm-up games, but he plumped for Peter Beardsley and Gary Lineker, which proved to be the right decision.

Kerry looked back on some of his contemporaries in the game.

> I respected Ian Rush, Gary Lineker and Clive Allen, who matched me pretty well throughout my career. They were all of similar age to me and people of great goalscoring ability. Tony Adams was one of the most difficult defenders I faced and is the best centre-half this country's produced in years. I played against him quite a few times, it was always difficult but I still scored against him. I scored the winner when they won the title in 1990/91 and we were the only team to beat them [2–1 at the Bridge]. QPR's Alan McDonald was always difficult as far as commitment was concerned. You knew you would get a

smack and I didn't particularly like playing against him. He used to snarl and was quite a handful. I also scored against him but would come off with a split ear, sore neck and cut ankles! Gary Pallister and Steve Bruce were two other excellent defenders as were Mark Lawrenson and Alan Hansen, wonderful pairings, but I got goals against them all. There wasn't anyone who prevented me from scoring.

DAVID SPEEDIE – *64 goals in 205 appearances*

The similarities were remarkable. He was an immensely talented Scottish forward who worked in the local colliery, comfortably outjumped taller defenders, but was prone to falling foul of officialdom with his combative nature. No, not a clone of Hughie Gallacher, but his own man in David Speedie. Born at Glenrothes, Fife, in 1960, like Gallacher, success did not happen overnight.

My dad was a semi-professional footballer with a non-League club and a Glasgow Rangers supporter with the rest of the family, so it was natural for me to support them as a kid. My uncle Jim was also a very good footballer and was invited to Manchester City for a trial, but he was more interested in wine, women and song! When we moved to Doncaster in 1964 the big club in the area was Leeds United, so I supported them. While I was a great admirer of George Best, my football heroes were Scottish – Denis Law and Billy Bremner, together with the Leeds team of the late sixties/early seventies including Allan Clarke, who managed me at Barnsley.

When I was playing junior football people felt I had a future as a professional, and I had trials with Doncaster Boys and Everton, but they felt I was too small. So it didn't happen straight away and when I left school I went to work as a miner at Brodsworth Colliery before I was spotted by Jim Iley, the Barnsley scout, playing in midfield for the local side. We were invited to play against Barnsley's youth team and held our own. Three or four of us were invited back, Graham Reid and Ian Banks were signed as apprentices and as I was 17 I signed as a professional in 1977. Martin Wilkinson, who was the youth team coach, persuaded Barnsley to give me a contract, so I owe a lot to him for getting me into professional football. Gerry Young also helped me a lot at Barnsley. It was there that supporters started calling me my nickname 'Speedo'.

Although we got promoted to the old Third Division, I only made about 22 appearances in my second and third seasons, which I wasn't happy with. Whilst it was an honour for me to play under Allan Clarke, we didn't always see eye to eye and he was actually the reason I left, as I felt I should have been in the team regularly.

In June 1980 Darlington manager Billy Elliott spotted the undoubted potential of Speedo.

Billy signed me on the strength of a reserve game against Sunderland. I was in the reserves a lot and, while Barnsley were in the lower leagues, we used to play Sunderland and Middlesbrough reserves off the park. It was a great side and we won the Northern Intermediate League, the Cup and Reserve team League. Billy said publicly in the press and on TV that within a season of me being at Darlington I would play for Scotland, but he didn't give me a pay rise! It wasn't till I went there that Billy saw something in me that no-one else did. He converted me to a striker half-way through my second season and I scored 18 goals. George Herd, the Darlington coach, helped me as a striker and all-round player with his wealth of experience.

In 1982 John Neal was convinced that an investment of £80,000 would produce a handsome return.

A lot of clubs had been to watch me, including Coventry, Liverpool and Chelsea, and I was tapped up by a few clubs including Harry Redknapp, who asked if I fancied a move to the south coast to play for him at Bournemouth. I said my contract was up at the end of the season, but I was looking to better myself. At the end of the 1981/82 season we played Southampton in a fund-raising game for Darlington. Lawrie McMenemy was friendly with Billy Elliott – they played Leeds the previous Saturday and stayed over. We beat them 4–2 in front of a full house of about 11,000 and I scored a good hat trick. John Neal, who had watched me a few times, was standing on the terraces. It was my final game for Darlington and I signed for Chelsea in the summer of 1982. John was a class manager and said, 'Once we get rid of the dead wood we'll be OK.'

Speedo's spat with Kerry in December 1983 after the Manchester City game has been documented, but the way John Neal rinsed the incident away with the water of soothing words made a deep impression on him.

> When Kerry and I had 'handbags at forty paces' in the changing-room, the gaffer said, 'That's Kerry and that's you. This is what you're good at, this is what Kerry's good at. You've got to learn that everybody has not got the same temperament or does the same things as you.' I sat back and thought he was right, and Kerry and I are friends now. You played in a partnership and if I felt my partner was not pulling his weight, I wasn't one to hold back. I used to call him a lazy so-and-so and sometimes I think I was a bit over the top. When I was younger and a bit immature I used to think everybody was the same as me and should be doing the same. John Neal taught me that everybody is different in character and I realise that now.

The partnership blossomed as the mutual respect developed into a genuine friendship, an essential ingredient in their telepathic understanding. Speedo's alert footballing brain and exceptional skill on the ball often created chances, and dovetailed perfectly with Kerry's predatory skills. Speedo also became attuned to Pat Nevin's idiosyncrasies – the two diverse characters took time to work each other out.

> There were no other striking partnerships during my career where I hit it off in the same way that Kerry and I did. You've got to be friends first and foremost on and off the field, appreciate each other's strengths and weaknesses, and try to help each other make a successful partnership. Kerry knew I would win balls in the air and he would get on the end of flicks and vice-versa. We just seemed to read everything we were doing and that applied for the whole partnership upfront. We also linked up well with Pat and would tear defences to shreds. Pat's a great lad, a very intelligent guy, but different, an odd-ball. He always thought I'd got something against him as he dressed differently and listened to weird music, but that wasn't the case. I just liked taking the p**s out of him!
>
> We went into the First Division campaign with a fantastic group of lads including Doug Rougvie, a great character on the field. I used to call him a gentle giant and he was a great presence to have in your side. We played Arsenal off the park in the first game. I remember Tony Adams saying to me when I beat him in the air, 'How can you jump

that high?' I was 5 ft 6½ in., I'm probably 5 ft 6 in. now with the bones starting to creak! It was just practice and timing because of my height, and when I was a kid at Barnsley I would go back in the afternoons with Mick McCarthy, Gary Mallender, Graham Reid and Ian Banks. We grew up together and used to practise crossing and finishing for hours on end. It paid off as we all became pros.

Speedo's relentless determination and aggression were part of his make-up – he was a persistent nuisance to the opposition and would not have been the same player if that level of intensity had been removed from his game. It created problems for him on and off the pitch.

I was brought up in a mining community, a working-class background and had to scrap for everything I got. You had to learn to look after yourself, as if you didn't you got your arse kicked, so it toughened you up. I'm a perfectionist and when I played got frustrated and people used to misinterpret me. I'd curse and swear, not at other players, but at myself. I wanted to achieve perfection in myself and that frustration sometimes boiled over. I still have problems now because of my so-called hard man reputation, but I'm not like that really. I like to go out and have a good time, but I have two children, Charlotte and David, and am a quiet family man. I don't go about abusing people and calling them names, but I get problems with people abusing me, thinking they can take liberties. The media portray you as something and people read it, and see how you play on TV. Jimmy Greaves summed it up once on a 'Saint & Greavsie' interview with Martin Tyler. Jimmy said, 'Well I would never have believed that was David Speedie. I expected this mad Jock who was going to stick one on Martin!'

Chelsea enjoyed a successful first season back in Division One, the only disappointment being the semi-final defeat in the Milk Cup to Sunderland in March 1985.

The semi-final was one of the most disappointing games of my career. The first leg at Roker Park should have been postponed, as it was like playing on concrete and we lost 2–0 to two dubious penalties. We brought them back to our place and I scored in the first five minutes to get us back into the game. Then the heavens opened and in the muddy conditions we were pressing and had loads of chances, but couldn't score. They broke away, Clive Walker scored a couple of goals and killed us off. I got booked in the second half sliding in on a defender who was trying to keep the ball in play. Then I got booked for another challenge and was sent off – it was a great disappointment.

Speedo's consistency prompted his international debut in May 1985 against England, and he was a regular member of Scotland's senior squad the following season. Four further caps followed in 1986 (he won ten in all), but a place in the World Cup party to Mexico proved elusive.

I felt I had a chance of playing for Scotland, which was one of my ambitions, as soon as I got into professional football. My debut was the highlight as we beat England 1–0 at Hampden Park in front of a full house, and I had a good night out! I played against Butch Wilkins, who said to me, 'Brilliant, wee man, great debut, well done.' The low point was when I missed out on the 1986 World Cup. After Jock Stein died I was told I was playing by Alex Ferguson. I had my inoculations, got my kit bag sent to me, sorted out my visa and passport, then the day before the squad was announced he changed his mind. I heard it was because Sir Alf Ramsey said that I might cause him problems if I wasn't playing, and he was right. I would have been moaning, but one of the highlights of Mexico '86 was that Brian Clough and Mick Channon said on TV that Scotland had left their best player at home. It was a great honour for someone like Clough and a fantastic ex-pro to be saying that. It made me proud and helped me get over the disappointment.

Another factor leading to international recognition was Speedo's superb hat trick in the Full Members' Cup final at Wembley, when Manchester City were defeated 5–4. Not entirely unconnected was his award as the Blues Player of the Year at the end of the season.

My two other ambitions were to play in the top division and in the FA Cup final. I never played in the FA Cup final but played in a final at Wembley, so that was good enough for me. The hat trick I scored always sticks in my mind – I can visualise every goal and it was an amazing day. Of the 70,000 crowd, there were probably 45,000 Chelsea supporters and it was fantastic just to play there. It might have been a 'Mickey Mouse' competition, but some good teams entered it and you still have to perform on the day.

After finishing sixth for the second year running, the 1986/87 season was an anti-climax. The partnership didn't quite fire in the same way, and when Coventry offered £750,000 for Speedo in July 1987, arguably the most potent striking partnership Chelsea had ever fielded was at an end. For three seasons the deadly duo started 145 games together, scoring 126 goals. They both shared a passion for success, which will long live in the memory of Blues supporters.

> I was sorry to leave but fell out with Ernie Walley, who did things wrong in my opinion, but I don't bear grudges. John Hollins was trying to change things and bring a sergeant-major into a club that was more disciplined with its players than any other club I played at. Nobody had to tell us to roll our sleeves up and fight on a Saturday. We all did it for each other, and sending players off in training for swearing was crazy – it's a man's game and we all do it. I looked positively at it, as I was getting a move back north nearer to my roots. I have a lot of good friends in and around Doncaster and when you don't see them that often, you miss them.
>
> My best Chelsea goal was in a night game against Blackburn at the Bridge in March 1984, which we won 2–1. The ball was played through to me just inside the Blackburn half and I spotted the keeper off his line as it bounced. I hit it on the volley, it looped over Terry Gennoe the keeper, just skimmed the underside of the bar and went into the net from 45 yards out.

Speedo's eclectic career moved on from Coventry to Liverpool in February 1991, followed by spells at Blackburn (August 1991), Southampton (July 1992), on loan to three clubs between October 1992 and March 1993, before a final move to Leicester City in July 1993, albeit just for a season.

> My game improved after I left Chelsea as I became more experienced, with an old head. I felt I played the best football of my career from 1987 until when I finished, apart from when I went to Southampton. I was transferred for financial reasons alone and was forced to go there in the Shearer deal. I wasn't comfortable about going, which was a negative attitude. I didn't enjoy it and couldn't get on with some of the players. I don't agree with back-biting and snidy remarks, and taking the p**s in a detrimental way about somebody's performance. I got Glenn Cockerill by the throat once after we played Leeds at home and threatened to sort him out if he carried on like that. I also ended up

having a fight with his chum Terry Hurlock. Supporters recognise what you are about and have been great to me. I've only been back to one football club where I've been booed by the supporters and that was Southampton.

I went on loan to Birmingham first, then West Brom under Ossie Ardiles. I felt it an honour and privilege for a World Cup star like Ossie to see something in me. I finished the season at West Ham, scored in the final game against Cambridge and helped them get promoted. I actually retired with a bad knee injury when I was at Leicester, but had three promotion years on the trot at Blackburn, West Ham, then Leicester.

I was out of the game for about 18 months and started playing in charity and testimonial games. I played in Gordon Banks' testimonial, scored a hat trick against opponents still playing and got the Man of the Match award. I had a strapping on the knee as it was weak, but felt I could still do a job for someone. Then Colin Pates asked me to play for him at Crawley, which I enjoyed for a while, then I felt victimised, as referees were booking me for nothing. I'd get poleaxed and nothing would happen, then I'd make an innocuous tackle and end up in the book. I finished playing a few games at Crook Town for my mate Kevin Smith, who was assistant manager at Hull. I played for Liverpool in the 2000 Masters tournament – there's about half a dozen teams I could play for!

Meanwhile Speedo had become a football agent and enjoys other activities associated with the game whenever, seemingly in common with most ex-pros, he can be dragged off the golf course.

I first got involved as an agent with Iwan Roberts and Richard Smith at Leicester. Their contracts were up and they asked for my advice. I had just finished with my injury and thought I could do it, so negotiated Iwan's loan to Wolves. I spoke several times to manager Martin O'Neill about a new contract, but Wolves were offering him more in a lower league. So financially he went there for the sake of his family and I took Richard to Grimsby. I had to get my licence and it went from there, although it has reduced over the last couple of years.

I also do question and answer evenings from time to time, mainly appearing with a comedian. I have a good rapport with people and have done evenings at Leicester, Chelsea and Blackburn. I'm not an after-dinner speaker, but I can stand up in front of a group of people and make them smile.

The most difficult opponents I faced technically were Des Walker and Terry Butcher. The hardest player I came across was Jimmy Case when he was at Southampton. He was the only person who hurt me, apart from being knocked out once by a cowardly challenge by Gary Briggs of Oxford when I was at Chelsea. I'd just scored for Coventry and was taking the p**s when Jimmy hit me so hard both my sock and shinguard disintegrated. I had the biggest stud marks from just over my knee to my ankle and that really hurt – it shook the whole of my body. We are great mates though and to me it was part of the game.

MARK HUGHES – *39 goals in 123 appearances*

For over a decade Mark Hughes was arguably the most effective target man in football. With a powerful physique and fiercely competitive instincts, he skilfully shielded the ball and brought others into the game with a wonderful first touch. Modest of his achievements, Mark has accumulated an astonishing collection of medals in an illustrious career, and will always be associated with his spectacular finishing, typically converting a trademark volley with stunning effect. Born in 1963, young Mark was an early convert to the Blues.

> I was about seven and just getting interested in football. Like most kids I supported what was perceived to be the most successful side of the time and obviously 1970/71 was a great period for Chelsea. I was a goalie for a while until I got fed up with it, and had a Peter Bonetti kit and gloves, which I kept for a long time. I also used to like imitating Ian Hutchinson's long throws.

Mark signed as an apprentice for Manchester United in November 1980, initially as a midfield player. 'I'd been there for about a year when in desperation the youth team pushed me up front.' He scored on his first full League appearance in November 1983 and never looked back. Within two years he was voted PFA Young Player of the Year, which he followed with the senior honour in 1989 and 1991. Over a period of almost 12 years, punctuated by a spell abroad with Barcelona and Bayern Munich, Mark was an integral figure of the side that won the Premiership twice, the FA Cup three times, the League Cup once and the European Cup Winners' cup once. In the final of the latter tournament Mark scored one of his finest goals at Rotterdam against Barcelona. He scored twice, but the second was a classic.

> Everyone thought I'd taken it too wide when I went round the goalkeeper and found myself faced with an acute angle. I hit it perfectly and was delighted to see it squeeze between the posts. Although I used to play for Barcelona, I didn't feel as if I was trying to make a point.

Mark moved to the Bridge on a three-year contract in July 1995 for £1.5 million, and, despite doubts in some quarters, it was a shrewd acquisition by Glenn Hoddle. While he was delighted to join the club he supported as a boy, it was not a factor in his decision to move south.

> I joined Chelsea as I felt it was the right time to move from Manchester United. I had the opportunity to join Bryan Robson at Middlesbrough, but wanted a clean break from United. It was a big decision for me, but I felt Chelsea were going places, and had three great years there.

In his first campaign Mark demonstrated the quality of his general hold-up play, spending most of the year as the lone striker, with two inside-forwards feeding off him. He managed his first hat trick for five years against Leeds in April 1996 and, with 12 goals, was second top-scorer behind John Spencer.

When Ruud Gullit succeeded Hoddle in May 1996, he saw Mark as an integral part of his team plans. Mark repaid that show of faith as the Blues stormed to the FA Cup final. In the tie against Liverpool at the Bridge in January 1997, Fowler and Colleymore had given the opposition a 2–0 lead in a one-sided first half. Gullit realised he needed to change things swiftly, and Mark replaced Scott Minto at the start of the second half. He obliged within a minute to set up a dramatic revival, and two goals from Gianluca Vialli and one from Gianfranco Zola completed a remarkable comeback.

> I always seemed to do reasonably well against Liverpool from my United days, probably because they were big games, which I have always enjoyed playing. It just seemed to continue at Chelsea and in the fourth round of the Cup I was probably a bit angry, as I wasn't playing from the start, and took it out on the pitch.

In the semi-final at Highbury, Wimbledon were overwhelmed 3–0 with a timely double from Mark, to set up the 2–0 defeat of Middlesbrough at Wembley. Mark's worth to the side that season was best gauged by his award as Chelsea's Player of the Year.

> One of my Chelsea highlights was the semi-final, when I scored a couple of goals and played really well. It was my fourth FA Cup winners' medal and, as no-one had ever done that in the 20th century, is something I am really proud of.

Mark carried his form through to the 1997/98 season and demonstrated his adaptability by playing upfront with Gianfranco, Gianluca and Tore Andre Flo, as Gullit rotated the striker positions. He also appeared occasionally in midfield, and Gullit encouraged Mark to adapt his play, which further enhanced his reputation.

> I used to waste energy flying around the pitch getting into personal battles with centre-halves, rather than making my presence felt physically. Ruud told me to save my energy, he didn't want me chasing full-backs, he'd rather have me running towards the ball, which no-one to that point had really highlighted to me.

The year was climaxed with an MBE in the New Year's Honours List for Mark's services to football: 'I am proud of my MBE and the recognition is nice, although it was more for my family than me – it was great to be able to take them to the Palace.'

Early in 1998 Mark came off the bench to head a precious goal against Arsenal in the first leg of the Coca-Cola Cup semi-final at Highbury. In the return leg Mark gave Gianluca a dream start to his managerial career, with a powerful low drive from the edge of the box in the ninth minute to level the scores. The Blues worked hard to secure a 4–3 aggregate victory and another meeting with Middlesbrough at Wembley. Mark started the final and, although he didn't score, played his part to the full in a 2–0 victory.

A dramatic season was heading for glory in Europe. Mark's contribution was again telling in the second leg of the semi-final of the European Cup Winners' cup against Vicenza at the Bridge. With the scoreline finely poised at 2–2 on that tense April evening, Mark was summoned from the bench with just 20 minutes to go. The force of the crowd pulsed through the ground as, inside five minutes, he unleashed a terrific volley to win the tie. Although Mark was restricted to a non-playing substitute, the 1–0 defeat over Stuttgart at Stockholm proved a fitting end to his Chelsea career.

> My best Chelsea goal was in the semi-final against Vicenza. I came off
> the bench when we needed to win 3–1 and were running out of time,
> so I was pleased to make a difference.

While Mark played alongside Gianluca Vialli and Tore Andre Flo in the
rotational system, it was his successful alliance with Gianfranco that set the
pulses racing.

> Franco is a great player and I was very lucky to play with him. He's a
> great professional with a wonderful natural ability and humble with
> it. He's a great man and it was a delight to play with him. You need
> respect for your fellow player to make a successful partnership, an
> understanding of the way they play, their strengths and weaknesses
> and you hope something clicks.

Signed by Southampton in July 1998, Mark moved in the knowledge that he
had more chance of playing regular first-team football at the Dell. A spell with
Everton was followed by a move into Division One with Blackburn, where, in
the sunset of his career, he had the satisfaction of picking up yet another medal
when Rovers headed the division at the end of the 2000/01 season.

Mark has latterly combined playing with the responsibility of Wales' team
manager. One of his proudest moments was in 1984, when he scored the only
goal on his full international debut against England. What made it special for
Mark was that it was played at Wrexham, just a few miles from his home town
of Ruabon: 'The goal itself wasn't one of my best. A free kick was floated into
the box and I managed to get my head to the ball.'

In April 1985 he scored a spectacular goal in the 3–0 victory over Spain,
again at Wrexham, in a World Cup qualifier.

> The goal gave me a lot of recognition. We had to beat Spain to keep on
> course for the 1986 World Cup finals. When the ball came to me in the
> air I met it on the volley and it flew into the net from 25 yards. I've been
> more fortunate than most – I've had many great moments and goals,
> so it's very difficult to highlight one goal, but my first Wales goal still
> rates very highly.

Mark has always been a dichotomy. With a combative nature that earned him
the nickname of 'Sparky', he is quiet and unassuming off the pitch, a
contented individual in the company of his wife and three children, Alex,
Curtis and Xenna.

I don't really know where that competitive instinct comes from. I always felt football was a vehicle for the other side of my personality, which I was able to show and get away with. Other people don't have the means to do that – I was able to get rid of any frustrations I had on the football field and invariably I did. Although I always respected the ability of defenders I faced, there wasn't anybody I feared. I didn't really worry about what they could or couldn't do against me.

Mark has earned huge respect within the game, and the regard he is held in by his fellow pros is typified by Leeds' manager David O'Leary encouraging his young striker Alan Smith to channel his aggression as productively as Mark. Mark was relatively relaxed about being utilised as a role model by a younger generation: 'That's a consequence of getting old!'

GIANFRANCO ZOLA – *51 goals in 183 appearances*

A thoroughly pleasant, professional player with a superb attitude, Gianfranco Zola sets the best example possible to youngsters – invariably he has to be dragged off the training ground by a JCB. Franco is a man small in physique, but a giant in vision. He succeeded, first, because he is a very fine player and second, because he is a natural with genuine humility. He is an uncomplicated man who gives the appearance of enjoying what he does and smiles easily and often. From the moment he trotted onto the pitch for his Stamford Bridge debut in November 1996, Franco's personal appeal and charisma were instantly communicated to an expectant crowd. His control, change of pace and ability to beat defenders are of the highest standard. His runs are brilliantly timed and he has the ability of doing the totally unexpected. He also has the gift of almost perfect balance, which enables great players to evade tackles and keep possession of the ball. On top of this, he can score marvellously crafted goals and his free kicks are out of the top drawer. Franco is a man from humble origins in Sardinia, who has given a lesson in manners to every professional sportsman in the land. A genuine hero and candidate for Chelsea's greatest player ever.

I was born in a tiny village in Sardinia called Oliena in July 1966 and grew up there with my mother Giovanna, father Ignazio and sister

Silvia. My first experience with football was with the local boys' team called Corrasi, where my father was the chairman. I started at the age of 11 and played up to the age of 17. It was a good standard but we all played for enjoyment and I had some very good friends that I played with for many years.

When I was 18 I went to play for my first professional team, Nuorese, who were based in a town near my village. They were a Serie C2 team then, which is the equivalent of the Third Division, but they have had a lot of problems since then and are now out of the League. As a boy my favourite team was Cagliari, the biggest team in Sardinia. All my friends supported them and we dreamed of playing for them. Their greatest player was Gigi Riva, who is the all-time top goalscorer for the national team.

I had many friends as a child, and we all shared the same love of football. It is very important for me to stay close to my family and friends and I love going back to Oliena when I can. I went to a village school as a boy – it is not the same as in England. We didn't have a school team, I learned to play by myself and with my first team Corrasi. All in all, I had a very happy childhood. My family have always been very supportive of my career, especially my father Ignazio, who loves football as much as me. My mother and sister also like to watch me.

I'm married to Franca and we have two beautiful children, Andrea and Martina. I met my wife when I was very young. I was playing for Nuorese and met her at my cousin's house, who she went to college with. We married in a town near Oliena, where Franca lived. She wasn't a football fan then, but of course she is now. My children are the most important thing in the world to me and I was worried about them when we first moved to England. I never imagined how well we would settle into life in England.

I began my professional career with Nuorese after playing for Corrasi, and then moved to another lower-league team in Sardinia called Torres, where I played for three years. Then in 1989 I signed for Napoli. The coach at the time was Albertino Bigon and it was a very good time for me. It was my first time in Serie A and I was playing with Maradona, which was a dream. I was young and learned so much from him, it was just a joy to watch some of the things he did. I also made my debut for the Italian national side while at Napoli, in November 1991 against Norway in Genoa.

Then I moved to Parma in 1993 where I had another great three years. Nevio Scala was the boss and I enjoyed myself tremendously. The football was great and my only disappointment was that we didn't win the title while I was there. I was sad to leave Italy but I was looking forward to joining Chelsea and, after only a short while, I realised the massive difference between the two countries when it comes to football. The main difference is the media side of things. In Italy the press are asking questions when the final whistle is blown and they don't stop talking about the game until the next one comes around! In England you play the game, then forget about it and go home to relax. I know which approach I prefer and it is one of the reasons I love England.

The actual football is also different in both countries. The game in Italy is more tactical and defensive, whereas things are more attacking and faster in England. I am proud that I settled into the style of play in England so quickly and I have been able to perform well for Chelsea. I am as happy here as I was in Italy. I still have a lot of ambitions in football – the moment I don't have any ambition left will be the time to quit football. I've had a wonderful career and am very satisfied with what I have achieved and the fans at Chelsea are the best I have ever known.

When Glenn Hoddle had enquired about Franco earlier, Parma quoted a fee of £10 million. In November 1996 it was £4.5 million, a steal. After a quiet start Franco's confidence soared when scoring his opening goal in his third match, a 2–2 home draw against Everton. Typically, it was a 30-yard free kick. Another goal of fearsome velocity came against West Ham when he twisted and turned Julian Dicks inside out, and he celebrated Boxing Day with two in four minutes at Aston Villa.

After just 28 games in English football, Franco was Chelsea's first-ever player to win the Football Writers' Player of the Year award in 1997. It was one of Franco's proudest nights when he was presented with the trophy by Sir Stanley Matthews at the annual dinner in May. At the end of the presentation Franco went down the line of 16 past winners on the top table, shaking them by the hand. No winner had ever done that before, and it was typical of his humility.

The 1997 FA Cup final was not a classic Franco performance and he looked tense throughout. With a 2–0 victory secure, when he made way for Gianluca Vialli two minutes from time, Franco graciously smiled broadly. He had played his part to the full in the earlier rounds, particularly the semi-final against Wimbledon with the second goal. Franco's swift change of direction had been enough to open up the space for a whiplash shot into the corner.

Franco made a slow start to the 1997/98 season, with just two goals scored before November. He was finding it difficult to adapt to Ruud Gullit's rotational system, but his approach play was still of the highest order, even if the goals had dried up. The turning point for Franco came with a superb hat trick when Derby County were demolished 4–0. Chelsea played inspired football and Franco opened the scoring, with a second from Mark Hughes before half-time. Franco's hat trick goal was world class, when he linked up brilliantly with Roberto Di Matteo before placing the ball perfectly beyond Poom. Surprisingly it was Franco's first hat trick in senior football – maybe because he creates as many goals as he scores.

> The third one was the best, the action was perfect. Robbie's pass was magnificent. I made a good run from behind and flicked the ball to Robbie with my heel. It was a great day and the game I think should be sent to schools. I don't want to exaggerate, but it really was quality football.

In the New Year Franco hit a purple patch in the Cup-Winners' cup, with a glorious left-footer into the bottom corner against Real Betis in the last minute of the quarter-final second leg at the Bridge, as Chelsea ran out 5–2 winners on aggregate. The comprehensive defeat of Middlesbrough in the Coca-Cola Cup final was sandwiched in between the Real Betis game and the semi-final against Vicenza. Trailing to Vicenza, a leaping Franco met a cross from Gianluca to send a header flying past the keeper to level the scores, prior to Mark Hughes grabbing the winner. With Mark, Franco formed a deadly partnership – Franco compared it with his spell with Tore Andre Flo.

> I really enjoyed playing with Sparky and we played great together. We found ourselves playing very well together by chance. I came to play as a midfielder, but Luca got injured and I played in front with Sparky. We worked very hard for each other and it made it easy. It worked immediately because we didn't have to change our style. It was really natural and we linked very well. With Tore things went better than I expected. I had to work harder to see the ball because Sparky won the ball. You had to give us both balls to our feet, low balls, because both of us were skilful players who preferred the ball to our feet rather than the deep or high ball.

Despite sustaining a groin injury against Liverpool and looking certain to miss the final against VFB Stuttgart in May 1998, Franco returned to Italy for treatment and was passed fit to play. He spent 70 minutes on the bench, but, when called on to replace Tore, with his second touch fired the only goal of the game. From his first touch, the ball rebounded to Dennis Wise, whose lobbed half-volley was perfect as Franco raced into the gap. His first-time crashed half-volley into the goal was decisive.

> I thought this is the moment, Franco, take it, and fortunately everything went right because I hit the ball perfectly and it went where I wanted it to go. It was absolutely magnificent.

Franco felt much more attuned with pre-season training during the summer of 1998 – the previous year he found his first English pre-season failed to sharpen him sufficiently. This time the vital preparation was perfect and a key factor in a fabulous season, which climaxed when Franco was honoured with the Blues' Player of the Year award. At 32 he was carefully nurtured by Vialli, often substituted, which did cause some frustration. There were some breathtaking goals, including two volleyed lobs on the run at home to Middlesbrough and Leicester. There were also four directly struck free kicks and three headed goals, and he was top-scorer for the first time with 15 goals.

> Maybe in the first season I was able to play wonderful performances and score very good goals, but all the 1998/99 season I played more consistently and with more discipline. I think I played well. There was a moment in the season when I played really well, and there was a moment when I was struggling with my form, especially around February. But it was a year, considering everything, that I think I played a good season.

During 1999/2000, although the goals were not so easy to come by (it took until April to score in the League), Franco remained a regular in the side (44 appearances plus nine as sub). His contribution to the team effort remained unstinted, with the 1–0 FA Cup final victory over Aston Villa being the crowning glory. Franco constantly eluded the Villa defence in the second half and his wickedly-curled free kick into the near post led to Roberto Di Matteo's goal.

In 2000/01 the team remained stunningly effective at home, infuriatingly unpredictable away. The last day of the season was like a Las Vegas of frantic endeavour, but at least victory at Manchester City ensured a place in Europe for

2001/02. Franco also signed a fresh two-year contract, which delighted his following, as he reflected on the season: 'This year has been very difficult. The fans deserve more than we have offered them.'

Franco scored ten times for Italy in 35 matches and his international career was blighted by controversy. It was only when Cesare Maldini took over as coach that his form blossomed again. At the 1994 World Cup in the USA Franco endured a miserable 28th birthday when sent off in a bruising encounter against Nigeria, after coming on as substitute. He was back in the team for Euro '96, but again there was disappointment. After an exciting performance against Russia, he was rested with four other players for the second match against the Czech Republic. Manager Sacchi's decision to field a weakened side cost him dearly because it meant Italy had to beat Germany in the third round of group matches to survive. In the eighth minute of the game at Old Trafford the Italians were awarded a penalty, which Franco took, but his shot was turned round a post. The game ended 0–0 and Italy were out. His reincarnation as a top-flight international occurred at Wembley in February 1997, when he scored the only goal of the game and was voted Man of the Match. When Franco took Costacurta's pass wide of Sol Campbell and shot powerfully inside Ian Walker's post, it was the goal of a master. His first touch was perfect and the finish devastating.

> It was a very special goal for me. It was a big game both for me and Italy. To score against England at Wembley was a dream. You have to understand every player in the world would like to do it.

In his spare time Franco practises on the piano, loves listening to music and plays golf, more often than not with his alma mater Kevin Hitchcock. He spent the summer of 2000 running football classes in Sardinia, which he enjoyed immensely. It came as no surprise to see the master putting back into the game the benefit of his considerable expertise.

BIBLIOGRAPHY AND ACKNOWLEDGEMENTS

While every effort has been made to obtain permission, there may still be cases in which we have failed to trace a copyright holder. The publisher will be happy to correct any omissions in future reprintings.

Scott Cheshire, *Chelsea: An Illustrated History*, published by Breedon Books 1984.

Scott Cheshire, *Chelsea: A Complete Record*, published by Breedon Books 1991.

Scott Cheshire and Ron Hockings, *Chelsea: The Full Statistical Story 1905–1986*, published by Ron Hockings 1986.

Kerry Dixon, *Kerry: The Autobiography*, published by Queen Anne Press 1986.

Rick Glanvill, *Rhapsody in Blue*, published by Mainstream Publishing 1996.

Jimmy Greaves, *This One's On Me*, published by Arthur Barker Limited 1979.

Jimmy Greaves, *Goals*, published by Arthur Barker Ltd 1981.

Rob Greenwood, *Yours Sincerely*, published by Collins Willow 1984.

Paul Joannou, *The Hughie Gallacher Story*, published by Breedon Books 1989.

Tommy Lawton, *Football is my Business*, published by Sporting Handbooks 1948.

John Moynihan, *The Soccer Syndrome*, published by MacGibbon & Kee 1966.

John Moynihan, *The Chelsea Story*, published by Arthur Barker Ltd 1982.

Peter Osgood, *Ossie the Wizard*, published by Stanley Paul 1969.

Brian Scovell, *Chelsea Azzurri*, published by Collins Willow 1997.

Ian St John and Jimmy Greaves, *Football is a Funny Game*, published by Stanley Paul. Used with permission of the Random House Group Limited.

The Footballer journals, published by Sports Promotions Ltd.

Chelsea Football Club, incorporating *Onside*.

Hamilton Academical Football Club and Peter McLeish, Historian.

Independent Magazines (UK) Ltd.

John Vinicombe and *The Argus*.